THE CITY
SHARE PUSHERS

THE CITY
SHARE PUSHERS

First published in Great Britain in 1989 by:
Scope Books Ltd
62 Murray Road
Horndean
Hants PO8 9JL

Phototypeset by Barbara James, Rowlands Castle, Hants
Printed by Richard Clay, Bungay, Suffolk

British Cataloguing in Publication Data

Davidson, Alexander
The City Share Pushers: a dossier of coercion, insider
  dealing, sex, drugs and malpractice in and around
  the City.
  1. London. (City). Stockbrokers
  I. Title
  332.6′2′094212

  ISBN 0-906619-23-8

CONTENTS

ACKNOWLEDGEMENTS

I would like to take this opportunity to thank Nicholas Pine and his staff at Scope Books Ltd for their constant encouragement and support, without which this project would never have been completed.

My extreme gratitude too is due to David Hooper who has worked so carefully on the manuscript.

Thanks also to Tim Harland, Matthew Wingett and Barbara James for their diligent application and attention to detail.

For Countess Dent, who more than anyone else pushed me into becoming a writer and whose never sleeping mind has helped this book realise the light of day, I reserve a special thanks.

A secret thanks to my yuppie friend, best of sharedealers, in nostalgia for bygone days that will never come again.

I offer a final heartfelt thank you to ALL dealers great and small, who have over these long months inspired me to write . . . THE CITY SHARE PUSHERS.

*To those who have been so
painfully parted from their money.*

327   *CITY SHARE DEALINGS*

Mr D. N. Campbell-Savours

★ 4

That this House notes the well documented collapse of a number of licensed security dealers and futures brokers including Harvard Securities, Afcor Investments, Investors Discount Brokerage, Walter L. Jacob, Eyas Securities, Sheridan Securities, London and Norwich, DPR Futures and LHW (Burgon Hall); believes that the dubious, sometimes illegal activities of these operations have severely damaged the reputation of the City; expresses concern over the position of hundreds of thousands of investors who were deceived into investing tens of millions in often worthless shares and who have lost their money; blames the Department of Trade and Industry for failing to take early action under prevention of fraud legislation and for allowing sharp city practitioners to ramp stocks, produce false prospectuses and employ hard-sell tactics, including churning and price fixing, to maximise commissions; believes that clients were denied best advice and were victims of financial malpractice by those who were neither fit nor proper and who preyed on human weaknesses of ignorance greed and vulnerability; calls upon the SIB and SRO's to take early action for the protection of investors by instituting the widest possible inquires and investigations into persons who have been connected with market manipulation and to press for prosecutions wherever possible; calls upon brokers authorised under the Financial Services Act to make every effort to shed from their employment those whose professional conduct might jeopardize the development of London's international reputation as a properly regulated market; and congratulates all those who have risked their livelihood by exposing this scandal.

Early Day Motion laid before the House of Commons by Dale Campbell-Savours MP on 25th January 1989.

Dale Campbell-Savours MP

The author does not endorse all the
practices which he describes in the
following pages, and as a securities dealer
has always served his clients' interests in
a fit and proper way.

INTRODUCTION

THE CITY SHARE PUSHERS was conceived during lax hours in the offices of London & Norwich Investment Services Ltd (July 1987) where the author had been thinking to himself: 'What the hell am I doing sharedealing in this den of rogues?'

After working at the United Kingdom's largest market-maker in Over-The-Counter (OTC) stocks and shares, Harvard Securities, and elsewhere, the author had become somewhat disillusioned with the practices prevailing in what are called licensed dealers in securities.

Harvard Securities PLC, was the platform by which persons desirous of a career in stocks and shares could enter the profession without going through the hierarchical career structure of stock-broking. In the text you will see how powerful this company was in its heyday.

In the United Kingdom (unlike the United States and Japan) clients can buy and sell shares within a two week period called 'the Account'. Settlement of monies due is ten days after the end of the Account, and there are some twenty three account trading periods per annum.

UK clients have the unique privilege of partaking in what is known as account trading. This is where a client can buy and then sell the same share within the two week account, without settling for it. Any increase in value of the share when sold is paid to the client by the firm which has handled the transaction. The client is responsible where the share price has decreased. Unfortunately, many innocents are lured into this practice, but few emerge unscathed.

As you read on, you will see that this is not just a story of greed. What surfaces is an entire subculture, featuring investors, dealers, racy administration staff, and larger than life entrepreneurs.

Since the initiation of the Government's privatisation scheme i.e. selling of shares in Rolls Royce, British Steel, etc., the stock market, hitherto preserve of the wealthy elite, has infiltrated the home of the common man.

Now anyone and everyone can partake in the jamboree and can claim his slice of the cake. However, getting involved has its price, and unfortunately the price tag has often been manipulated.

THE CITY SHARE PUSHERS offers you, the reader, a passport into the world of High Finance, with an insight into the unscrupulous sales techniques of some sharedealers and financial futures dealers, as well as into the depraved state of the individuals who were up to their necks in it.

The Financial Services Act (1986) gave rise to the new regulatory body, the Securities and Investments Board (SIB), the watchdog organisation which operates in a similar manner to the Securities and Exchange Commission (SEC) in the United States.

Until the 29th of April 1988, known as "A-Day", the financial community had little or no regulation. Now a yoke has been thrown round the neck of stockbrokers, licensed dealers, fund managers, insurance brokers and even futures salesmen alike.

Prior to this yoke, what transpired? How did these firms operate? In what sense were the dealers qualified for the responsible tasks they undertook? What kind of men ran these companies?

As you read further, a web of intrigue stands revealed that has spread through the entire dealing community and beyond. The book relates the exodus of dealers from Harvard, carrying away in their heads the treasures of their trade, useful for selling not only shares but also more esoteric financial instruments, such as futures.

Why don't many dealers who have left the profession talk?

The reason is that they are scared, and want to earn their living without problems. Licensed dealers can play hard, and play dirty. Don't the dealers know it!

THE CITY SHARE PUSHERS is the only memoire of a bygone era in the history of High Finance, when regulations were lax, and salesmen were wild!

Who are these *licensed dealers?* It is a loaded question. Are they *stockbrokers?* The answer is emphatically "NO", despite the fact that some of their dealers are similarly qualified. Although providing parallel services to the stockbrokers, i.e. share recommendations, execution service, and portfolio evaluation, the licensed dealer differs in that he may be no adviser. The sole purpose of some is to retail the maximum amount of stock in the minimum possible time!

But not all licensed dealers and futures brokers are so grasping. Many, often long established firms are perectly respectable and honest, and rarely or never receive complaints from their clients.

Nonetheless, you will gradually come to understand how the over-the-counter market in the United Kingdom, and on the Continent, has faded into disreputable obscurity, unlike its namesake across the Atlantic which has developed a high profile amongst serious investors.

Before you read on, let me pose you these few questions. *Are you an investor? Better still, are you a gambler? Have you ever experienced the hard sell?* If your answer to any of these is yes, step inside these pages and find out how some of it was done from the other side of the fence.

Are you a salesman? Are you a company director? Have *you* ever smooth talked anyone? Have you even been a securities dealer yourself? If the answer to any of these is yes, step inside these pages too! You will doubtless recognise some of the character types and situations. You may even for a moment find yourself . . . .

Alexander Davidson
London
February 1989

Chapter One

ANOTHER WORLD

The question must again be asked, 'What exactly are licensed dealers?' In his book *Inside The Over-The-Counter Market*, Tom Wilmot, chairman of the best-known licensed dealer Harvard Securities, offers the following definition: 'Effectively companies other than stockbrokers or jobbers which are licensed . . . to carry on the business of dealing in securities'.

The author is for the purposes of this book broadening the definition to include all the cowboys in and out of the City of London, selling shares, futures, and occasionally other financial instruments.

Licensed dealers certainly advertise more widely, and seem more responsive to the small client than most stockbrokers. Why should you buy or sell shares and other financial instruments through them?

Most clients are compelled against their better nature by the voice of the devil on the end of the telephone. What is their dealer offering?

Many licensed dealers have specialised in pushing shares in small companies. These are high-risk investments, a fact often not made clear on the telephone, not always on the contract note. The market in question is the over-the-counter (OTC) market.

In the United Kingdom, as opposed to the United States, this remains a comparatively unregulated line of business, conducted through hectic but meticulously planned sales campaigns.

Commission-paid salesmen sit or stand at their telephones calling punters and reading aloud their sales pitch: a sheet of paper on which is scrawled details of their investment proposition.

Dealers at one licensed dealer would occasionally write ad hoc sales pitches, photocopy them, and hand them round to colleagues. These would be used without being properly vetted and were likely to contain inaccuracies. In the rough and tumble atmosphere of the dealing room, nobody seemed to care.

After all, even the official sales pitches were often too uninformative, or too ill-spelt and ungrammatical to be of much use. Facts were also likely to be outdated. The last year's figures cited might appertain to the year before that, and expansion prospects mooted may already have fallen through.

Sales campaigns in licensed dealers are vigorous, sometimes hysterical. Dealing managers and team leaders shout at, cajole and entice their dealers into selling large quantities of stock. It is not uncommon for a client on the telephone to hear swearing in the background.

The bustle enhances the impression of good business. All this has a snowball effect on the day's turnover, and on the individual dealers' commissions. Moral standards go by the board in an atmosphere that seems generated purely for the above purposes.

Dealing through licensed dealers can cost less than through stockbrokers, but usually costs more. Furthermore, your money is at risk, particularly when there is a thin market in shares, or where your shares are held under a nominee name for the convenience of your licensed dealer.

Punters get desperate when the firm they are dealing with is about to go bust. Clients of licensed dealer Prior Harwin, for instance, welched on deals they had agreed on the telephone when the Department of Trade and Industry (DTI) stopped the firm from trading at the end of 1986.

Tony Prior, Prior Harwin's chairman, then proposed a scheme to save both the company and investors' funds. Unsecured creditors should agree to accept a down payment of around 35p in the pound for money due to them, and to take the balance in redeemable convertible preference shares in Prior Harwin, to be paid off in four years' time.

The company was, however, wound up, and it was revealed that a larger number of stocks in its listings had rarely changed hands. Indeed, one property developer, Bexbuild Developments, had been listed by Prior Harwin a year after its market-making agreement with the licensed dealer had been terminated.

The business of selling shares at licensed dealers is often a gimmick which loses investors their hard-earned money. It could be argued that anyone who is idiot enough to send a cheque for thousands of pounds to a salesman of shares in unquoted companies he has never heard of deserves to lose it all. This is the way the young sharedealers feel as they put out the bait and hook in the mugs.

The author is not just saying this for sensation. He has seen it happen. Some sharedealing and futures dealing firms that are no longer in existence paid commission of over half all monies received from clients. The dealers thus earned thousands of pounds from one deal. Many cooperated with an uneasy feeling that the clients would never see their money again. As one top sharedealer put it, 'You're here to make yourselves money, not your clients.'

Yes, some dealers have an inkling which shares are dodgy. They misrepresent the prospects to clients. Afterwards, they blame the directors: 'We were led to believe it was a good stock', they excuse themselves. Who can prove they are lying?

The directors have their own more sophisticated excuses. If they don't wriggle free of blame, they don't in any case care. They have made so much money out of these operations anyway, they can afford to retire. Here are the big time smooth operators.

With all the press warnings, Jo Punter ought to *know* to avoid unquoted stocks, to avoid disreputable shares and futures dealing companies.

Once he has read this book, he will be put off careless speculation for life.

The hardest hit clients are frequently punters on the commodities and futures markets. Many are crazed gamblers who cannot bring themselves to walk away with winnings.

Again and again they must plunge until they have lost all. They will allow themselves to be stripped of savings by bucket shop practitioners who are not, strictly speaking, licensed dealers, but who operate on the same principles.

Futures punters know they are playing with fire which is why some ask not to be rung at home, and the name of the commodities firm is never to be given to anyone who answers the office phone. 'If my wife found out I'm playing with our capital, she would divorce me,' admitted one client.

The futures market is faster moving than the stock market. With a very small stake, vast losses and gains can be made. This is thanks to gearing. The investor buys a futures contract for around 10% of its value. He assumes whatever gain or loss the entire futures contract makes.

The time at which a futures contract gets sold is vitally significant. The investor, if he is going to make money this way, must have a broker who is committed to showing him a profit, as well as earning his commission off him. How many brokers are to be trusted?

Certainly the hard sell futures salesmen have, in the past at least, been in the game purely for their own commissions. They tended to be raw kids with a self imposed need to get rich quick.

They often wanted big money for private purposes, for example setting up a property company or buying a Ferrari. They were buccaneers, not careerists, and did not belong to the City proper. Some survive even now.

Licensed dealers proper are at their busiest when trading in government privatisations, perhaps the safest territory for the inexperienced private client. Their often heavily advertised, commission-free dealing proves irresistible.

Most firms will even trade before clients have received their allotment letters. Stockbrokers have refused to do this except for established private clients or institutions.

Licensed dealers trade on a scale that is only limited by their own resources. On the British Telecom privatisation issue for instance, Harvard Securities had planned to start dealing at 9.00 a.m. on the earliest allowable morning. The phones started ringing at 8.55 a.m. Within five minutes, they had received over one hundred enquiries. After three hours, two thousand inquiries had been made.

Harvard had dealt in 2 million shares by early afternoon, and the main problem became that of finding sellers to match buying orders from account traders, i.e. investors who were buying then selling the shares quickly in the hope of making an instant profit.

Harvard allowed no big orders over 25,000 shares, while it was willing to take up to 1 million shares on its books from sellers.

Some of Harvard's clients reneged on their agreements to sell when the price climbed, making ridiculous claims, like that the dog had chewed up the allotment letter, or that somebody had sold as a practical joke.

Harvard responded by installing tapes to record all telephone conversations. Clients as well as dealers are supposed to be protected by this, if the licensed dealer proves able to 'find' the relevant tape.

Some sellers of British Gas shares, prior to delivery of allotment letters, who had responded to press advertisements of the share-dealer Walter L Jacob & Co Ltd which has now been wound up, were told to send Jacob a cheque for half the proceeds. Salesmen claimed this would be refunded as soon as the seller's allotment letter arrived. The initiative as a whole was criticised both by clients and the national press.

Other sellers through this firm were encouraged to invest the proceeds in an unknown Las Vegas company, Electronic Speciality Products Inc.

Sadly Walter L Jacob & Co Ltd, described in this context by *The Observer* as perhaps the 'closest the UK has to an American-style boiler room operation', has not been the only licensed dealer to recruit clients in this way.

Tony Levens, former investment editor of *The Sunday Times*, offers sellers of government privatisations through licensed dealers generally the following warning: 'It may not be long before one of their sales people is on the phone to you with a very persuasive line, badgering you to buy high risk shares of a very doubtful quality.'

Also, licensed dealers send out often scrappily written investment newsletters, and sales promotion letters alike.

Newsletters are often issued on free trial to potential clients. Their recommendations may offer an idea of what stocks have the benefit of being promoted by the licensed dealer in question.

The editorial matter can be biased to presenting a favourable buying climate for speculative stocks. Typically *Market Maker*, the Harvard Securities newsletter, at a time when unemployment figures had

reached the 3½ million level, presented this rosy view of the City:
'The prospect of stronger cashflow has meant the reintroduction of
brandy and cigars after lunch; Beluga caviar is creeping back onto
the menu; pension fund managers . . . are starting to hail taxis again,
and the other afternoon in Throgmorton Street I actually heard a
Blue Button whistling.'

National newspapers and financial magazines present a more
detached view. Most attack licensed dealers mercilessly; hitting them
when they are down, they sow the seeds of their destruction.

Barbara Conway, the former *Daily Telegraph* journalist, who was
until recently publicity officer of the new watchdog over the financial
services industry, The Securities and Investment Board (SIB), has
criticised the practices of Harvard Securities over a period of years
in her reporting based on private investors' comments. Following
A-Day, Harvard Securities were unable to find authorisation. This
giant amongst licensed dealers was struggling as never before. No
longer were its hard sell tactics acceptable.

Part of the problem for clients is knowing what is really done with
their money.

Clients of McDonald Wheeler Fund Management, wound up by
the Department of Trade and Industry, had believed they were
putting their money into low risk projects. It turned out that they
had instead invested in an airline which never took off, a college
that had no students, and a luxury yacht.

It would have been of little comfort to investors to learn that
Chairman John Wheeler had, according to former business
colleagues, been living a luxury lifestyle, spending almost £70,000
on refitting his yacht, and thousands of pounds renovating his six-
bedroom house. He drove a chocolate-brown Rolls Royce. What a
far cry this must have been from his younger days in the priesthood.

The cost report from the Official Receiver read, as one investor
put it, like a 'financial horror comic'. Many blamed Financial
Intermediaries Managers and Brokers Regulatory Association
(FIMBRA), the overseeing regulatory body, for this fiasco.

John Grant, who ran FIMBRA, admitted: 'In the light of the
Wheeler affair, we've obviously got to review the whole system.' It
seems, however, that FIMBRA was financed sufficiently to check out
just one in five firms under its surveillance in any given year.

This was no compensation for the 2,000 odd investors who had
lost several million pounds in this. Amongst these was a retired
headmaster, who had his £70,000 life-savings in McDonald Wheeler,
and who you'd think would have known better.

Oonagh McDonald, the shadow treasury backbencher at the time,
said: 'Nobody should invest through FIMBRA until a compensation
scheme is set up.' This has thankfully now come about.

Unfortunately, just missing the introduction of formal compensation was the enormous Barlow Clowes collapse in 1988, in which investors lost tens of millions of pounds. They had thought their money had been safe in gilts (government backed securities). It transpired that it had been syphoned off into private businesses.

Who would compensate the investors here? As the DTI had failed to act when it had known of irregularities within the firm, did not the Government have a moral obligation towards the dupes? Of course, if it should offer compensation in this case, the Government would open up a Pandora's box of claims from other similar cases.

Also early in 1988 licensed dealers such as Eyas Securities and Afcor Investments were closed down. Futures firms such as Stox and DPR Futures, who used hard sales techniques in the mould of LHW, which did survive the onset of the Financial Services Act (1986), also bit the dust for various reasons.

Frightened DPR account executives, knowing their firm's appalling reputation, were asking themselves: 'Will we ever work in the City again?' Photographers hung around their offices at the Corn Exchange Buildings in the City of London. Executives told them to 'fuck off' and got on with dreaming how DPR might one day set up 'Down Under', where various bucket shops operated.

It seemed like the end of an era for licensed dealers. Others had been out of business for a while now. A few embittered investors would still remember defunct sharedealers such as: Buckingham Corporate, City Investment Centres and Ravendale Securities, Investors Discount Brokerage, Rayner Securities, Financial Management Services, Greenwood International, Hamilton Hogg, Strand House Securities, Sheridan Securities, London & Norwich Investment Services, Anderson Kimble . . . the list is growing all the time.

In fact some City professionals are saying that the licensed dealer should be a protected species, or it will shortly become extinct.

Even when certain licensed dealers have survived, the firms in which they were making markets have gone bust. Thousands of embittered clients of various licensed dealers, and of the bucket shops on the Continent on whom were foisted speculative shares bear testimony to this.

The question that haunts unlucky punters is, 'How much did their sharedealer know about impending catastrophe? Could he not have issued a warning?'

Funnily enough, many licensed dealers seem very keen to sell shares in companies which subsequently go bust. For instance, clients trying to sell back shares in Towerbell Records through Harvard Securities shortly before Towerbell went under, were urged to buy more. One client even received a letter from Harvard Securities saying of Towerbell: 'I expect the price to rise to higher levels and will advise further'.

Harvard Securities were paid to make a market in Towerbell Records, but as Tom Wilmot has pointed out, the dealer who sent that letter would not have known of the pending disaster, since dealers were forbidden access to the firm's corporate finance department by the so-called 'Chinese walls'. However, Wilmot has sometimes blamed his dealers for breaching dealing regulations.

'Chinese walls' too, apparently, prevented Harvard dealers from advising clients to sell out of Hilton Mining Shares, shortly before the share price virtually collapsed. Most dealers, however, anticipated something of the kind might happen once they were forbidden to sell clients out of the stock. 'If any clients want to sell out, let me have a word with them,' said director John Harris. Following this manoeuvre some clients changed their minds. What could he have said to them?

When bad news was finally announced, dealers were instructed to conceal it from their clients for as long as possible.

Although shareholders in Hilton Mining afterwards contemplated legal action because the prospectus had not revealed that Allan Hilton, the chairman, had been a director of Hilton (Products) which went into voluntary liquidation, their real grievance was against Harvard's selling techniques.

After the Towerbell Records fiasco, Tom Wilmot said: 'The OTC market is very very risky, as demonstrated by Towerbell. Of every ten new over-the-counter companies, at least two go bust.'

It is the client who bears the brunt of this risk. One punter refers to a typically fateful day:

1 August 1988 — " . . . the day I returned from a holiday abroad, Harvard telephoned me out of the blue (8th April 1986), and a chap who sounded like an enthusiastic young cockney told me how wonderful Towerbell was and that it was going places with top stars in tow."

" . . . My diary of 8th September that year notes: Towerbell shares have flopped."

Such risks have rarely been emphasised by telephone salesmen at Harvard and elsewhere, except through the compulsory wealth warnings stamped on all Harvard's contract notes.

The announcements on licensed dealing firms themselves prove often to be delayed and evasive. Rumours may circulate which present a licensed dealer in a too optimistic light. For instance, many firms have been perpetually on the brink of buying up a broker, but brokers are often quick to deny it. For example, the stockbroker AJ Bekhor refuted any suggestion that it might be merging with Harvard Securities.

Even the innocent bystander suspects that such claims contain more of wishful thinking than of substance, but he rarely realises how hard licensed dealers are. They will always be, superficially at least, a different animal from stockbrokers, and are proving unable to survive the implementation of The Financial Services Act (1986).

These beleaguered firms are still seen as what a national newspaper journalist has called the 'barrow boys' of the share industry, whereas stockbrokers are seen as more respectable. There are of course exceptions to the rules, and some of them well-known at that.

Dealers are sometimes told to sell stocks as a medium-term hold (i.e. wait six months for something to happen). In practice, under threat of dismissal or of heavy fines, or even of just not making so much money as they might, many dealers succumb to the temptation of exaggerating short-term prospects. Directors know this is going on and turn a blind eye. They know that it bumps up sales figures.

Inexperienced investors have often been known to put several thousand pounds into a little known company, on the strength of a five minute telephone conversation. Due to the large spread (i.e. difference between buying and selling prices), it usually takes a substantial rise to enable investors to sell out at a profit.

Dealers at one licensed dealer would habitually sell a stock whose price would rise for a couple of weeks or so — although not enough to cover the spread — before reverting. Clients were getting all excited about nothing.

Sometimes clients are advised to buy stocks, uncannily as it seems, just before the price drops. On occasions, they are advised to sell just before the price rises. Clients are often best advised to do the opposite to what their dealer recommends.

It was common for disasters about to strike stocks to be revealed as late as possible. Legendary at one licensed dealer was the 'announcement pending' on a company whose shares it was selling. A director would instruct dealers to tell their clients that an 'announcement was pending' in order to persuade them to buy more or to hold on to stock they wished to sell. Dealers would repeat this parrot fashion in the same optimistic note that the director had used on them. The more experienced dealers guessed it might paradoxically refer to a disaster on the horizon, but kept their thoughts from clients.

Clients often discovered disasters affecting share prices of stocks too late. The Corporate Finance Department of the licensed dealer pushing the stock, could arguably have alerted the dealing room earlier but it never did. Psychologically investors' money would be locked in, often until it had dwindled overall to less than half its original worth. Clients were ALWAYS complaining.

The few successes on the UK OTC market are always quoted as

if to make up for the failures. Their role is to thus quieten the critics. It is all part and parcel of the selling technique.

What a pity it is that clients trust their dealers. But if a firm is the only market-maker in a stock, where else can they go for specific information about the stock? It is rarely productive to approach the company in which shares are owned.

Clients frequently threaten licensed dealers with exposure to the Press, and this has proved a relatively efficacious way of getting bona fide complaints heeded. But not all clients complain.

It takes all sorts to make a clientele. The typical punter is a lot more naive than licensed dealers let on. Comparatively few sophisticated clients will touch licensed dealers with a bargepole.

What all clients have in common is a gnawing desire to make a quick profit, and a likely fatal gambling instinct. They pledge every deal to be their last one. But once they have committed themselves to an investment or two, the potential of a larger portfolio appeals, and they plunge beyond the point of easy return.

What sort of people are their dealers? The traditional dealer is spivvy and smart, but ill-educated. He is typically a former street trader or motorcycle messenger who wants to make a quick easy fortune. Dick Whittington has nothing on him. He may well run a car repair business or sell cheap jewellery on the side, in which case his dealing will lack single-mindedness.

One particularly spivvy dealer, during an official Harvard Securities party urinated all over the floor. Why didn't he just vomit in public like some of his colleagues? The answer is that he was wreaking a horrible revenge for having had his box of leads confiscated that morning, on suspicion that he was attending a job interview. After the party, he was sacked. The other dealers then had a tough time explaining his absence to his erstwhile clients, but one or two told the truth.

Generally, the streetwise dealers work in a separate camp from the more educated types, and never the twain shall meet. Self-evidently, each faction attracts its own sort of clients. Herein lies the secret of a successful licensed dealer's longevity: dealing relationships that span every class of society.

The educated dealers may, if they are lucky, later worm their way into stockbroking, and take their clients with them. In contrast, the streetwise dealers require quicker money, and may end up in a bucket shop on the Continent.

Most streetwise dealers will not make their home telephone numbers available to clients. They are constantly changing their numbers, or going ex-directory to stave off threatening calls.

Some dealers in either social camp will risk account-trading for themselves, often in tens of thousands of pounds, as a result of an

Harvard Securities PLC, 95 Southwark Street, London SE1 which has taken people off the streets and turned them into high earning dealers, sometimes within weeks.

inside tip. Not all will pay up their debts, however. One trainee dealer at Harvard Securities lost £20,000 from account-trading in several stocks. He then absconded to America without paying. He left no address. The dealer who had introduced him to his broker became understandably embittered.

Another trick is for the dealer to buy his stock through a friend, particularly when he has special knowledge that the price will go up, as did one dealer on Helical Bar, a well known property company in the UK whose share price then sky-rocketed from its post crash low.

However, the dealers who bought and sold for themselves in opportune moments while trading in new issues on behalf of clients have sometimes been found out and reprimanded, but not usually sacked, if they were good dealers.

Licensed dealers can be slow to deliver share certificates. One of the author's former clients is still awaiting certificates for American stocks he bought through the crashed Sheridan Securities over two years ago, a familiar story to clients of many licensed dealers (and many clients deal through several).

Without share certificates, a client can only sell his stocks (even if listed) through the dealer he bought them from, at that dealer's price, which may well not be competitive.

If the shares are held under a nominee name, the client will not get certificates at all. This means he may lose all his money if the sharedealer crashes.

Settlement on time, with the right monies, is another area in which licensed dealers let down the clients, but retain the advantage of having the use of the clients' money.

They guess at only the tip of the iceberg of what is going on in these firms. Clients' funds, against all regulations, are often mixed with company funds. Otherwise they are syphoned off into mysterious Liechtenstein trusts, or are invested in companies whose identities are kept secret. Where does it all end?

Clients of licensed dealers find a major problem in selling back their OTC stock. Until recently at Harvard Securities, dealers were penalised for taking back OTC stock if takebacks exceeded 10% of their total business. The dealers then resorted to extraordinary preventive measures, such as keeping sellers indefinitely 'on hold' until they rang off, or simply cutting them off immediately. If a seller had been ringing for fifteen or twenty minutes before the phone was even answered, he would naturally resent this ultimate insult.

One Harvard client is on record as saying: "I still hold 10,000 shares in the Harvard quoted company BURAD Holdings, and, since I have lost all confidence in the dealing room at Harvard, I am still puzzling over how to dispose of the shares without an inordinate amount of emotional effort."

A more skilful dealer manages to hold his clients into stocks through sales technique. One dealer of the author's acquaintance addressed sellers in this manner: 'Sell? You must be out of your mind. You should be picking up more!'

Indeed, most successful dealers deter sellers by bluffing, saying what the client wants to hear, like the Catholic priest who preaches only of heaven. Investors are so willing to believe in recovery around the corner that they will clutch at false hopes almost indefinitely. The inexperienced, particularly, cannot face selling out at a loss.

The highest earning dealers only take back OTC stock if their client needs the funds to pay for another stock; or if it is a stock that the directors want back, so allowing the dealers to retrieve in their names, and thus to evade a cut in their own commissions.

Excessive dealing to generate commission, known as churning, is commonplace. Top earning dealers sometimes coax their clients into massive account trades. The clients are taken in and out of the stock, then sometimes settle back in it before the account is over. It is a gamble that generates huge commission for the dealer, and usually even bigger losses for the client. Some dealers don't mind wiping out a client in this way if they have earned enough commission from the deal.

Dealers have usually been paid a higher commission for selling OTC than Stock Exchange listed, USM or Third Market stocks, so the more trusting clients may get sold a disproportionate quantity of OTC stock. Several top OTC dealers at one stage virtually ceased selling any stock but the riskiest and least promising. For their pains, they were paid more than almost any other dealers.

Technically, Harvard dealers should not have been selling stock to clients who had not dealt three times with the company, unless they had sent out written information about the stock. This rule was, however, often broken.

This poses no problem with experienced investors who understand what they are letting themselves in for. It is always the small naive investor who fusses, complains of breach in regulations, and cancels. Cancellations cost the dealers in fines, and can generate unwelcome publicity for the licensed dealer concerned.

The less scrupulous small investor will sometimes delay payment for his stock, then pay for it only if its price has gone up. He will, however, only get away with this once.

The rules against cold-calling have been widely publicised. Clients often make false claims of cold-calling; sometimes so they might avoid paying for the shares they bought.

If they have filled in a card, declaring willing for a dealer to approach them with urgent share recommendations, they are not being cold-called if subsequently telephoned.

A good dealer works hard. Greed has sometimes led him to trade for two licensed dealers at once. One top dealer used to take the odd afternoon off, and secretly work for another licensed dealer nearby, taking his commission payments there cash in hand.

It is not uncommon for one licensed dealer to send a spy to work in another. Secret agents of this ilk are at work all the time.

How are dealers best supervised? A dealer was sacked from one firm because he had leaked disloyal comments to the Press, and the tape was played back to him as evidence. At Harvard Securities, dealers were able to avoid having their telephone conversations recorded by dialling 9 on the brown internal phones and using that external line unrecorded.

A huge camera eyed the Harvard dealers from a corner of the ceiling, and its beady eye of a lens would swivel unexpectedly. As he watched his dealers from above, in the comfort of his own office, Tom Wilmot, the chairman, has been known to reprimand his staff via a loudspeaker. Once he ordered one of the directors to leave a female employee alone.

The only dealers who remain in their jobs are those who can sustain alertness during their long working hours. They must achieve social acceptability as well as regular business. According to one training officer, successful dealers tend to be 'all rogues'.

Bribery is rife in jockeying for good positions on the dealing floor of some firms. One dealer offered cocaine to his training manager which secured him some decent leads. Girls have got on through sleeping with a director, although usually they gain little more than temporary advantage.

Even the good dealers rarely stay long. How can a dealer spend his last few weeks in his present firm most productively? It is at this point that he starts selling his clients out of as much stock as possible, so as to release their capital for the investment propositions he will offer them in his next post. He must work unobtrusively, to prevent suspicion of his pending departure.

'Borrowing' leads or bargain books, so as to copy out clients' names and addresses at home, is another last minute activity considered profitable. The dealer can take these details with him, so he can approach other clients, as well as his own, from his new firm.

The most effective modus operandi is to raid the dealing room in pairs, early in the morning or evening while nobody is around. One will keep guard, while the other rifles through drawers. The spoils are stuffed into briefcases, smuggled out under the noses of security guards, and deposited somewhere like the left luggage at Waterloo Station (a dumping ground that has actually been used).

One Harvard dealer on his way to London & Norwich Investment Services Ltd left a carrier bag of leads at a nearby sweetshop, giving £10 to the silvery haired owner for hiding them behind the counter. He complied, his only concern being that it wasn't drugs.

Sometimes, of course, bags are searched, but the removal of company property from the premises of licensed dealers is rarely punished by anything more than instant dismissal, acceptable enough at the time to the culprits, as it coincides with their own plans. Work references from a licensed dealer are of dubious value, and rarely even asked for.

Another good time for one dealer to pinch leads from another was during the presentation of a visiting company chairman. Whilst dealers were firing difficult questions at the representative of an OTC-traded company on the floor of one licensed dealer, a couple of light fingered dealers were at work, helping themselves to their colleagues' leads.

The devil likewise found work for idle hands while the entire staff of Harvard Securities were gathered to gawp at Leslie Grantham, alias 'Dirty Den', the pub owner in the TV soap opera Eastenders, who was accepting a large cheque on behalf of the Spastics Society. Snapshots have captured him there forever, hugging giggling females of Harvard's administration department, while the other girls waved autograph books at him.

During the presentation, two briefcases were crammed full with used dealing books containing clients' names and addresses, and with leads that had been left carelessly lying around on desks.

Another objective for dealers in their last few weeks is to rake in all commissions due to them, and to avoid doing much work as further monies may not be paid. Dealers have talked their companies' financial administrators into giving them an advance, then have left. A good excuse, is the need to pay decorators in your flat; more than one dealer has used this one successfully. This is also, obviously, a good time to take a holiday.

Dealers are always relieved to see their monthly cheques, and, even more, to have them cleared. Some licensed dealers would stop their employees' cheques quite frequently. In other cases, issuing of cheques is sometimes delayed, or money due is retained in part, often on cosmetic excuses such as fines for overtrading etc. There may be promises that it will be paid back in three months, in direct proportion to clearance of outstanding client debts.

Once, a dealer at Harvard Securities admitted to a director that he had been paid twice, and the director sniggered. Word got about. One or two dealers thought that the dealer in question had spoken too hastily. Harvard Securities recalled the duplicate pay cheque, as well as truncating the value of the next one.

Dealers who threaten to take their old firm to court sometimes get money due, as well as their P45 tax forms. Alas though, not always. The number of former employees who have seriously contemplated legal action against a licensed dealer (or shareshop) is only matched by the number of clients in the same predicament. Indeed, action groups have been formed and petitions signed.

When good dealers move to another firm, this gives rise to extreme bitterness on either side. Solicitors establish rights, and money is at stake. It is too much like a divorce.

In November 1986, eight top dealers left Harvard Securities to start a new dealing floor that was, at the time, connected with the Tudorbury Group. Neil Miller, Harvard's dealing director, told his band of merry men: 'It'll never last. They've got no real backing.' His confidence proved, however, misplaced. The Tudorbury Group was a successful insurance fund that had some £100 million under management, and was headed by a founder member of Abbey Life, Clive Holmes. Major shareholders in Tudorbury included Royal Insurance, ▮▮, and Abbey Life. The securities dealing floor has lasted, albeit with much controversy. By mid 1988, many of its staff, and two of its directors, were ex-Harvard.

Harvard Securities organised a surprise raid on the premises of Tudorbury's new sharedealing floor, shortly after its inception. They obtained an Anton Pillar Order (a legally authorised raid) to recover their documents. Dealers' homes were raided at 5.00 a.m. one morning, and a number of Harvard's leads were discovered. For three months, Tudorbury's dealers were prevented from ringing clients with whom they had dealt before, but to whom Harvard Securities laid full claim. Agreement was subsequently reached out of court.

Tudorbury Securities was determined to offer a service in the interest of the clients. As one of their pioneers put it: 'Salesmen at licensed dealers get stick from clients who lose money. They can live with it for a few months, but not longer, which is why they have such a high turnover of staff. Here at Tudorbury, we will try to treat clients decently, get them good listed stocks at competitive prices.' Tudorbury's policy, had initially, and through the 1987 Bull Market, worked comparatively well; but by 1988, in the depressed market conditions, it had degenerated.

Another Harvard dealer moved to Sheppards, a Stock Exchange member firm, where he was telephoned and abused by a Harvard Securities director. The dealer left Sheppards of his own accord and against his manager's wishes, when he was offered a more lucrative position elsewhere. It was promptly announced to Harvard dealers that the rebel had been sacked from Sheppards. Afterwards, a Harvard director maintained: 'Whatever anyone says, he was sacked from Sheppards.'

When a group of top dealers walked out of Harvard Securities in May 1987, following ex-Harvard director Neil Miller, to start up a new broking firm Kingsley Paige, Harvard chairman, Tom Wilmot, hired a private detective to trail Neil Miller.

Early one morning, Miller noticed a car following his own Mercedes. He drew up next to it by a red traffic light. In the front seat sat a mystery man whose features were covered with an outspread newspaper. It was Tom Wilmot, Miller's previous boss. In the driver's seat was a hired private detective. Neil Miller grinned uneasily. 'Let's go and have a coffee Tom,' he suggested.

Intense negotiation followed, then shortly afterwards legal threats from Harvard, culminating in a bizarre series of scurrilous allegations and counter-allegations. Kingsley Paige dealers were saying to their old clients: 'Everything you've read, heard, or suspected about Harvard, I can assure you is only half the story. My advice to you is to sell your OTC stock immediately, while you still can. Send written instructions to Harvard by registered post, and they'll have to heed them.'

Harvard dealers were meanwhile telling their clients: 'Think twice about dealing with a new firm like Kingsley Paige. They're offering obscure American stocks; you may never see your money again.'

Dealers do not always move to UK companies. One dealer left Harvard to work for a Continental outfit called European Equity Research. He afterwards kept telephoning other Harvard dealers, pointing out that he could say what he wanted on the phone in his new place of employment as the calls were unrecorded. Furthermore, working hours were short, the dress informal, the commission exceptional, all income tax-free, and the weather beautiful. Why didn't they join him?

What he did not tell them was that European Equity Research was pushing shares in a little American advertising agency, 'Pilgrim Venture'.

The Securities & Exchange Committee (SEC) declared that 'Pilgrim has never engaged in any revenue-producing business'. Furthermore three of the company's directors, who had never met, had been paid for use of their names.

The SEC was proposing to take legal action against several Florida citizens over their alleged involvement with Pilgrim Venture.

In the UK as well as abroad, vendettas between dealers are rife. These sometimes take the form of physical violence, but are more frequently verbal.

A director of one licensed dealer rang up a former employee working for a stockbrokers, addressing him as follows: 'You took our clients with you, you little shit. The dealers have got to earn their livings too. You ran away from us like a silly little schoolboy, without saying where you were going. I was an East End boy myself; I was brought up the hard way. I'll get even with you for this, you see if I don't.' The dealer replied: 'Is that a threat?' The director said: 'You can take it any way you like.'

Another dealer, owed a few hundred pounds by the director of a firm he had just left, drove one night with some friends to his house, where they flung bricks through every window. He proceeded to ring that director on a regular basis from the continental share-dealer where he worked, saying: 'If you want your wife and children to keep their faces looking the same, you'd better pay your little debt.' Other dealers felt little sympathy for this director.

Generally speaking, as fast as one licensed dealer goes into liquidation, another starts up. Like it or not, licensed dealers, in one form or another, seem here to stay. So they are extending their repertoire of services to include unit trusts, PEPs plans and insurance schemes. Top dealers are inviting big clients into their offices, buttering them up with expense account lunches, putting them into new ways of investment, just as a good stockbroker might.

On a memo to Tudorbury Securities' dealing room, the dealing manager wrote: 'Remember, every day in every way, our clients' boots are getting fuller and fuller.'

The methodology and implications of this have not, to the author's knowledge, been revealed. Herein lies the purposes of this book.

Chapter Two

HIRE 'EM AND FIRE 'EM

The newspapers and media have invented the concept of the whizz-kid and highflier, the young hard-nosed businessman. In fact dealing in shares or futures is essentially a flair. Either you've got it or you haven't. Suitability for the profession is deep-rooted and genetic.

For the instinctive smooth operator, for whom attention-seeking, money and excitement are more important than morals, security and doing something worthwhile, it is an easy job. In fact it is the easiest way of earning big money he could possibly find. It has been said that working in advertising will give you the most possible fun you can have with your clothes on, and the same might be said of sharedealing.

'Good' dealers will derive motivation from the frowns of the establishment, the black looks of the wary and the total disinterest of 90% of the population. They will make themselves seen and heard like fireworks on a dark night, and their services will always find takers.

The route to becoming a Harvard dealer was not always straight-forward. Some just gained experience in a more menial capacity. Harvard Securities at its peak employed runners to act as go-betweens for dealers and market-makers. These were called Blue Buttons, just like the Stock Exchange juniors. Mostly teenagers, they were led to believe that if they worked hard they would become clerks or even dealers.

One Blue Button was originally scheduled for each dealing table. There were ten tables, so there should have been ten runners, but only three started. Boy, were they overworked. Neil Miller, dealing director, told all dealers to make frequent use of them, primarily for getting quotes on listed or USM stock from the market-makers' room adjacent, in which dealers were now forbidden to foray, but also for fetching new dealing books, notebooks, cups of coffee, etc. The runners' tasks proved humdrum alright, and to start with, the poor bastards were never allowed to pause for breath.

The dealers, under intense pressure to achieve sales targets, took their frustrations out on the youths. 'Richard', they would scream, or simply 'Thingummy', if they did not know his name, or still more commonly, 'Blue Button' or 'Button'. The first of Harvard's Blue

Buttons would be sweating and purple by lunchtime, like spent athletes.

Inevitably they settled in time into a more leisurely role. Whenever they passed into the market-making room they would linger to gossip and exchange banter with clerks and market-makers. Thus deliveries of quotes started getting held up, slowing the pace of the entire dealing room.

Dealers' rebukes got progressively more irascible. 'Hurry up, Button, you cretin.' 'You fucking moron,' was commonly shouted out. This level of abuse had a snowballing effect. The runners found themselves unfairly rebuked for the market-makers' errors, and for their whimsical misquotes or bid-only quotes that could ruin a deal.

Dissatisfaction amongst the Blue Buttons reared its ugly head. They started to lament their poor salaries and their dubious prospects. They were alarmed by the high turnover of dealers. Was it worth aiming for this position?

One of the runners rushed into work on Saturdays to help out with the vast backlog of administrative chores on the understanding this might help his promotion prospects. He was too trusting, like a willing dog. Another runner threw up his hands and walked out in the middle of one afternoon. He made no excuses or explanations and indeed these would have been unnecessary. He had been made to work ridiculously hard, and had suffered a constant stream of abuse when he failed to come up to scratch. The dealing-room rocked with laughter upon news of his flight.

Another runner, more intelligent than most, mingled exclusively with the dealers. This was a wise move. He was only 18 years old, but was making quite a market on the side in watches and jewellery that he would jokingly claim 'had fallen off the back of a lorry'. He seemed very streetwise for a kid who had just left school. He belonged there alright. His title 'Button' stuck even when Harvard shifted him into an administrative role; he was obviously too intelligent to remain a runner.

The turnover of runners was too high. A solution was found. The two dealers who achieved the least impressive sales figures by the end of the week would temporarily be made into runners.

They would don the new red blazers, standard uniform for runners that was cheap-looking and suspiciously school-like. There developed a scrabble amongst dealers to avoid going to the bottom of the heap.

These blazers were originally presented as a new uniform for all dealers. This proved a highly successful practical joke. One girl from Harvard's administration department insisted that one gullible dealer tried on an undersized blazer. While she measured him up for size, her fingers trailed the tape measure precariously into his crotch. This measurement was for his new uniform, she assured him, while his colleagues wolf-whistled and clapped.

Recruitment advertisements on behalf of one licensed dealer or another used to appear every few weeks in London or the national press. The style of advertisement was both low key, and up-market. There was no attempt to jump on the bandwagon of the more flamboyant recruitment advertisements for commission paid saleswork, for example: 'I'm Martin. I'm only 23. I earn a 5-figure salary and have three houses. If you've got the ambition, we will show you how. If you're young, enthusiastic, need to go places fast, and only live once, ring me on . . . ' . In licensed dealing, all the flamboyance was saved for the job.

Advertisements for Harvard dealers pointed out demurely that remuneration was no obstacle for the right person. Generally, it may be suggested that a financial background is useful. A training manager of London & Norwich Investment Services Ltd quipped that his firm might advertise in these terms: 'Apply to Mr Razor-Ready, Grab, Fuck It and Run Ltd, Box no . . . ' .

Nobody who sounded reasonable over the telephone was refused an interview at Harvard, and at the better established dealers. The recruitment managers were used to handling all sorts. Young hopefuls in dead-end jobs with a burning desire to make a quick buck were seen, along with unworldly yet ambitious and arrogant graduates. Many looked incongruously stiff in the casual-looking dealing room where they were interviewed. They soon relaxed though, and were encouraged to talk about their present jobs and their lives.

The recruitment managers searched for a curious combination, success in career or studies to date, coupled with frustration at its limited demands and prospects. Usually anyone who obviously wanted it was given a chance to try his/her hand at dealing — unless he appeared too pompous. If he had a dubious work record, or had been in any kind of trouble, it often didn't matter.

The training offered to potential dealers was generally informal — the opportunity to learn on the job, not by instruction.

Team spirit rarely mattered much since dealers were paid commission on their own business and preferred to develop their own methods of achieving this.

Various sales training techniques have been used which would seem extraordinary and perverse to clients — if only they knew.

The sales trainer of one licensed dealer introduced his aspiring trainees to a concept designed to inspire them, and to dispel the monotony of their task. This was telephone bingo.

Mid morning he would yell out to the trainees during lulls in activity: 'Everyone off the phone.' When all had complied, he instructed them each to write on a piece of paper ten numbers out of the 40 that corresponded with the internal telephone lines.

The trainer would then shout out a random number, for example, six. All dealers who had written six on their paper would scream 'Yeah' and would flick down the No. 6 switch on their phones, lighting up the panel. The person who got all his numbers called out would shout 'Bingo'.

The dealers, thus hyped up, would be in the mood for selling: 'Come on you wankers. Get on the phone and start shifting stock,' the trainer would shout. 'Get fucking working, you two arms and a heartbeat,' he'd admonish a slacker. Then to everyone again: 'Let's see a bargain, you fucking one arm hangers.'

Clients who rang in during telephone bingo would be kept hanging on indefinitely.

Once, a female dealer screamed 'Bingo' into a receiver, and a client got an earful of it. He said quietly: 'I say, is that . . . ?'

If a senior manager should come onto the trainee dealing floor, telephone bingo would instantly stop.

Still more frequently, this training officer would urge his dealers to ring the sex lines in New York, Los Angeles and Amsterdam. Once they had gotten through he would stride over panting, and would grab the receivers out of their hands. He would listen in, showing more powers of concentration than he ever did at work. His girlfriend, a dealer too, would give him a bored hard look, if she happened to be around.

'Fucking marvellous,' he would say. 'You guys listen to this stuff. Try it out on your clients.'

Some dealers, all sitting together, would be listening to these lines for hours on end.

'Stop wanking and get on the fucking phones,' the training officer would yell.

One of the most spectacular training methods at one licensed dealer was the floor contest. It was seen as an honour to partake in this. Three of the hardest selling dealers were elected, usually by vote.

Dealers would put down the phones, crowding in a circle round the contestants. They were like schoolboys urging on a fight. The purpose of it all was so they could watch how the real whizz-kids did it.

Each contestant took a fixed number of dross leads from a box. The dealing manager would tell them what stock they would be selling. It was usually something most found pretty uninspiring to sell.

All three would raise their telephone receivers at once. As they pitched one client after another, the dealers surrounding them would cheer, shouting 'Go. Go. Go . . . ' , calling out to individual contestants by their nicknames: 'Come on, Ripper!' 'Get 'em to mortgage their homes, Dupey.' 'Rip 'em up, Churney.'

Every dealer in the building helped with the encouragement. The hapless clients contacted would often buy, believing they were in contact with a hectic dealing room, thinking that they were presented with the investment opportunity of the decade.

One by one, the contestants would drop out of the marathon. The last one standing would be cheered on until he too dropped. Then the three would take the next lots of dross leads. They would get on the phones again, selling a different stock. The other dealers would shout, 'Rev it up. Go. Go. Go . . . ' , and the clients would again assume the shares were selling like hot cakes. This spontaneous buzz was more plausible than, for instance, the tape recordings contemporaneously played in the background at DPR Futures to give clients an impression of a busy dealing room.

Famous at one licensed dealer was the traditional 'one down, nine to shit' routine. This was initiated, so legend has it, when the lavatories were out of order. It may, for all the author knows, be practiced in some firms even now. This is how it worked.

The dealers — and not all trainees at that — stood at their desks, hands poised on their phones, knees bent. The posture was purposely uncomfortable, and had to be sustained only briefly.

The training manager would be standing with a privileged uprightness at the head of the table. He would start beating his fists frenziedly on the desk top. 'One . . . Two . . . Three . . . Go . . . , ' he would murmur. The other dealers would join in. Suddenly the entire dealing room used to explode into a harsh crescendo of directed shouting. The dealers become here as one. 'Ten . . . Nine . . . Eight . . . Seven . . . Six . . . Five . . . Four . . . Three . . . Two . . . One . . . Shit . . . ' The final 'shit' was pronounced like the pop of a bullet from a rifle.

The dealers would drop into their seats with a collective thump. Picking up their phones, they would thrust themselves on the punters, ramming stock, which was often of little value, down their throats.

Their enthusiasm started wearing thin after half an hour or so, but would nonetheless have generated an incredible upturn in business. All this is evidence that aggression more than market knowledge can sell shares. Hard sell specialists like Harvard have capitalised on this fact. Firms like Tudorbury Securities with a comparatively soft sell approach, consisted largely of dealers who have reacted against their original Harvard training.

Other aggressive sales training techniques lingered in some firms. To have one's hand fixed by an elastic band to the telephone receiver was the norm as it encouraged continuity of business — if it wasn't used too frequently.

Another technique consisted of the salesman standing on the table as he called a client. This meant that he was literally talking down to him, which worked wonders for his confidence. While this was going on at one firm, the table split and the trainee dealer slipped and sprained his ankle. He was made out to be a hero, and became a fully fledged dealer that day.

In fact, he dropped out later. Not being a born salesman, the pace of the dealing room proper proved too hectic and too competitive for his taste. His failure cannot have pleased the training officer, who was paid a bonus for every dealer who kept his place on the dealing floor. But training officers have learnt to be philosophical about such mishaps: 'Some stay, some don't,' they say.

Dealers who weren't going to make it left, often of their own accord, before getting sacked. They would start coming in late and drifting off early. Their excuses were plausible: 'I'm feeling ill' or 'An electrician's round at my flat,' etc. Why have so many trainee dealers failed . . . ?

Slothfulness has always been rife amongst trainees, many of whom it has to be said would feel qualms about putting clients into shares they hear through the grapevine are dubious. Many clients have suffered losses from poor recommendations in the past, for which they blamed the trainee dealer, who rang them up. 'I've dealt with your firm for several years. I've lost on every single share I've invested in,' was a typical moan. The record card for such a client was scribbled over with the comment of dealers: 'He's about to buy a house; has no funds; he'll see how the shares he already has do; he's going in for Rolls Royce, so has no money; he's still waiting for share certificates — once these have arrived he will think about further investment.' Then perhaps, 'Try again next year', or 'WOT (waste of time) or, more vehement, 'WOBT' (waste of bloody time).

Every so often, at one licensed dealer, a box was passed round the established dealers, and a collection was made of unwanted leads. This was fodder for the trainees, and they rarely got much else. These leads, rejected not without reason, proved almost impossible to crack, although the odd few good ones would always emerge like gold nuggets in the granite. The justification for this practice was that the dealer who could do business with such clients would thrive in the dealing room proper where he stood a chance of getting reasonable leads. The real reason for the practice was a genuine shortage of new leads. Despite this, many dealers earned staggering incomes by generating incredible turnovers. All that dealers needed was the ability to persist after the phone had been slammed down on them.

It could be argued that sharedealers were privileged. After all, many sales environments forced trainees to find their *own* leads.

At Harvard Securities, leads were distributed on a meritocratic basis, more to those who would get proportionately more business out of them.

Grubbing for business on dud leads was, at least, after a fashion dealing. Harvard trainees, while waiting for dealing licences to be sent from the Department of Trade and Industry (DTI), were given the job of establishing initial contact with persons whose names were perfectly properly provided by Dun and Bradstreet, the American business information service, which was not dealing at all. They would phone people all over the UK, and read to them verbatim from a script worded as follows: 'Hello. My name is John Smith. I work with Harvard Securities. We are sending you a free subscription to our newsletter on stocks and shares for three months. Is that OK?'

At this stage, the prospect would be anxious to establish that he was under no obligation. Once reassured, he often consented to receive the newsletter, perhaps to get his caller off the line. After all he had nothing to lose. It was just one more item of junk mail, and he wasn't paying for it. It might even interest him.

The prospect would receive, with an impressive newsletter, a little white card which he was asked to fill in and send back. He was asked to put on it his daytime phone number, and to tick a little box which indicated that he was willing to receive phone calls from dealers with urgent share recommendations. Beneath this box was another which he had to tick in order to receive the next three months' editions of the newsletter.

Once he had returned the white card, a client's name, address and phone number were processed into a lead, which would then be given out to a dealer. This system would be duplicated ad infinitum over the following months.

If one dealer failed to open a client, other dealers would attempt to do so, sometimes unknown to the first dealer, from duplicate lead cards.

All the trainees dealing with leads obtained from Dun and Bradstreet put their initials down on the white cards they sent out. The idea was that when the cards had been returned, each dealer would get the leads he had generated. Harvard trainees worked cheerfully on this understanding, whereas otherwise they would have slackened. Sadly, they had not grasped the situation. Distribution of leads was left in the hands of management, and they were allotted primarily on favouritism, next on sales figures.

Within months, some clients had in excess of 25 dealers contacting them from the same firm; many were also being contacted from other licensed dealers. It was clear that some clients would let their whole lives revolve around daily contact with their dealers. Middle-aged, semi-retired businessmen in provinces such as Manchester or Leicester seemed particularly susceptible to this. Why did share-dealing prove such a drawn-out business?

It could take a Harvard client up to half an hour to get through to his dealer on the telephone. If he was complaining about overdue money or share certificates, the dealer would probably refer him, or else promise to ring him back later. Thus a query and its settlement could easily drag on for hours. When he was pressured, the dealer might ring his client two or three times in the morning alone, selling shares and maybe taking some back to pay for it, a churning of stock that Harvard tacitly condoned.

Familiarity bred business so it seemed, as established dealers with a limited clientele continued to deal with the same few people day after day, generating sometimes fantastic commissions for themselves, as well as token fines for the overtrading habits that ironically were tacitly encouraged. Here was a treadmill on which trainees got launched, often too quickly. They were forced to start generating business, perhaps before they had learnt how to do it properly, and more importantly from their selfish point of view, before they had built a broad clientele.

Desperation and greed kept them going, so against the odds, they would achieve the prerequisite £4,000 or so worth of business a day, as well as somehow retaining much of their clientele, and in some mysterious way expanding it. To do all this, dealers needed to take an aggressive approach with clients, to wear them down.

The training officer of one licensed dealer always recommended to his trainees the cheeky approach: 'Call your clients by their Christian names. They love it,' he maintained. 'Be a bit cocky. They won't even realise that you're plucking them of their savings. They'll go down laughing . . . '

He once gave a demonstration to the trainees, picking on a virgin client whom a good trainee had been unable to open up. This was an Indian businessman, living in the industrial North, who for the purpose of this book shall be called Derek Patel.

The training officer lifted the phone, and the buzz in the room subsided in a split second. All trainees gazed admiringly at the man who was paid to teach them. 'Hallo, is that Derek Patel? One of my dealers has told you about these . . . . shares. Isn't that right, Derek? They're a fantastic chain of opticians. You're not interested? Why is that? (shocked) You can't afford it? But this is the way you could really make some money. Wouldn't you like to make a quick buck, Derek? What's your house like? (giggles from trainees) Do you need a new carpet? (more giggles.) You'd better have a go on these,

I think. Give 'em a few months, and you should see the share price double. How many? I think we should go in for 10,000 of *these* ones . . . '

He put down the receiver. 'Never let anyone say I can't deal. Mind you, Indians don't always pay, so don't blame me if he cancels.'

The trainees then tried to follow suit. The training officer distracted them with sneers at their tameness. He would give them the benefit of his theories that letting their hair down at pop concerts and football matches would be a therapeutic and profitable use of their leisure time. He yelled sporadically at them: 'Get on the fucking phone. Pitch them for 5,000 or 10,000 shares at a time. Don't let them go.'

He would put the better dealers on a table together. He wrote up the names of all trainees on the white board, and at the end of the day, he wrote up the sales scores of each one. It was as if marks for the day's work were being displayed in the school classroom, and they had a similar effect of inspiring competition.

The marks of one day were shown against those of the next, and so on. Later in the week, the training officer put asterisks against the names of trainees who'd achieved less than £2,000 worth of business through the whole week. 'The bottom three will be fired,' he warned.

The good trainees were thus encouraged. The useless ones were soon weeded out.

This training officer assumed responsibility for the sackings. The friendly manner in which he enacted these fooled nobody. At five O'clock in the afternoon, he would take aside some hapless individual. 'You're shit at this job, aren't you?' he'd say. 'Is there any point staying?' The individual concerned would pick up his P45 tax form from the accounts department and slink off. Everybody else would realise what had happened the next day, or the day after that.

Almost imperceptibly, 30 new recruits would dwindle to 20, 15, 10 . . . the final departures coinciding with promotion of the best onto the dealing floor proper.

Meanwhile, new trainees would drift in. The training officer would issue them due warnings at interview: 'This is a cut-throat business. If you sell, you'll make your fortune. If you don't sell, you'll be out. I make no bones about it.'

He would always teach trainees: 'If a client asks you a question you don't understand, say — "Hold on a minute sir, a call has just come through to me from the States" — put him on hold then, and ask me. I'll tell you what to say to him. Get back to him then. Say: "What was it you were asking?" The client will repeat the question. Then answer it, as if spontaneously.'

He demonstrated this technique successfully on clients in front of the trainees. It came into general use.

The dealers themselves started working variations on the theme. If one of their number was being kept on the phone by some whingeing client who had no intention of investing further, a colleague would rescue him, shouting: 'Smith (or whatever the dealer was called), Hong Kong, Line . . . '

Occasionally Harvard dealers would have colleagues shout out that only a limited line of stock was left. One dealer was telling a client that only 10,000 shares in a little known company remained on his books. 'Take them.'

A colleague in the background shouted out: '5,000.'

The client bought quickly, under the impression that the shares were almost gone. Actually, nothing could have been further from the truth.

A script was issued to trainees at one licensed dealer. It advised as follows: 'Listen to the client going apeshit about his experience of our investment recommendations, and agree with him . . . Then say this one should recover his losses, and that he owes it to himself to let us at least do that for him. He can give us this one last chance . . . ' This was recognised to be a masterpiece.

'So many clients have so much money to burn,' explained a manager of another dealing firm, as he handed round condoms to some six trainee dealers on his floor, 'blow them up big.' He said.

They complied, but he blew his up harder until it outswelled the rest.

'These are your clients' portfolios,' he explained. 'The harder you push, the bigger they will get. One day they will burst. You should aim to keep your client just below breaking point. Deal him and deal him, twice a day if you can. Once you let up, you will give him time to think, and he'll realise how much money you've lost him. Then . . . ' He picked a pin off his desk and applied it. The condom collapsed.

The best trainees and established dealers had little beyond brief academic demands made on them in the early days. There was the little British Institute of Dealers in Securities (BIDS) exam for which trainees attended evening classes. These would culminate in the sitting of a multiple choice paper. Always during this period the same paper was used, although a rumour that it would change at the next sitting was constantly promulgated by dealers who had once cheated, to discourage others from doing likewise.

The syllabus for this exam covered basic facts such as The Stock Exchange Account System, stamp duties, commissions payable by clients, how gearing works, etc. It seemed necessary to be able to do simple calculations. The story was that trainees had to pass the exam on the third attempt at the latest, or leave. The pass mark was 75%. Few turned up regularly for the lectures. Most trainee dealers were not the types to tolerate even a petty little examination like that.

Many trainees cheated for this exam, passing round a copy of the question paper beforehand. There was even a black market made in this paper. Consequently, most people who wanted to, passed, sometimes with very high marks indeed.

In practice, a number of dealers had not succeeded in passing the little BIDS exam, and obviously hadn't bothered to cheat their way through it either. They kept their jobs on the strength of the good business they did.

Dealers at Harvard Securities who gained high marks in the BIDS exam received a visit from Tom Wilmot in person. He would toss a coin on the desk before them. If they guessed on which side it fell, he handed over £100 cash. If they got it wrong, it was only £50.

It was not until towards the end of 1986 that the Stock Exchange Registered Representatives' and Traders' Exam was introduced. The better dealers, quite logically, fared best with this new thorn in the flesh, a qualification planned to be compulsory for giving investment advice under the Financial Services Act (1986). Here at last was an obstacle to the streetwise, although perhaps not an insurmountable one.

The exam is sat within the walls of the Stock Exchange building. Cameras are focussed on candidates, supervisors hover, and the taking of papers inside or outside the room is not permitted.

The means of studying for this course are various. One route is to buy the Henley Distance Learning course from the Stock Exchange. The training officer of one licensed dealer issued photocopied versions of the text to all dealers. Those who then sat the exam were instructed to put on their application forms that they had studied the course privately, so the fact that they had studied from but not paid for the Henley course would not be traced.

This training officer was teaching the course internally even before he had passed the examination himself, as did later one of the directors of his firm.

Both probably adhered more to the essential facts than did the lecturers on the City University evening course which the author attended.

Many lecturers here seemed unnecessarily thorough, too much in love with their subject. They were rewarded with frequently half-empty lecture halls, giggling, murmuring audiences that threw paper darts, etc. The rowdier element worked for licensed dealers, as opposed to stockbrokers.

One lecturer expressed his opinion that the new third tier market would wipe out the OTC. An OTC dealer loyally argued against him with a vigour that is rarely seen in a university environment. 'You speak of the OTC market as if it doesn't exist. Let me assure you it's alive and kicking,' he said, reeling off an impressive string of figures. The lecturer shook his head, smiling faintly.

That dealer is now a stockbroker. How he misses the good old days when he would punt out OTC stock, even though the punters had invested so often in vain.

Many Harvard dealers have failed the registered Representatives' and Traders' exam.

In keeping with their true natures, some look out for a dealer who has passed it, and beg him to sit it again, for them. 'Do it in the provinces this time,' they urge. 'You'll never get recognised.'

They offer several thousands of pounds. If the dealers who have passed it decline, they say: 'Don't say never. Think about it . . . '

Mysteriously some dealers who had appeared beaten by the exam, turn up in Stock Exchange member firms with a pass under their belt. 'How did they get it?' the author wonders.

Some dealers gain exemptions — sometimes dubiously — on the grounds that they have traded in the market for at least two years prior to a cut-off date.

Life is no bed of roses for the new dealer, least of all if female and of a gullible disposition. Here is the sad story of the initiation of a new dealer at Eyas Securities who for the purposes of this book shall be called Sandra.

Sandra was a dealer lacking in professional experience, who had a highly strung temperament. Being easily provoked, she was the sort of person who automatically attracted ridicule. Licensed dealers are the last places on earth to serve as sanctuaries from such treatment.

The other dealers at Eyas Securities slipped a faked client card into her box which bore the name Sir W Induppe (i.e. 'wind up'). There followed the address of a well known gentlemen's club in Victoria. A £250,000 portfolio was recorded. His bank was listed as Coutts, in the Strand. However, the telephone number would put her, unwittingly, through to the administration manager downstairs.

The dealers hinted to Sandra that she might do a massive deal with Sir Willie. Excited, she rang the given number. The voice on the other end of the line sounded charming. She liked the sound of Sir Willie.

She sweet-talked him down the line, worming her way into his heart, and talking money. The pounds, shillings and pence were dancing before her very eyes.

Egged on by her colleagues, she pitched Sir Willie on half a million shares in OTC traded Crane Holdings, at 28p. She knew that the commission accruing to dealers was 4p a share, and she was calculating her own gain even before she closed the sale.

Sir Willie seemed as excited as she was, and firmly sold to boot. He said that he would be visiting the Eyas offices within the hour to settle for these shares in person.

When she had put down the phone, Sandra leapt out of her seat. She tore across the dealing room, then up three flights of stairs, screaming that she had closed Sir Willie, and that she had made several thousand pounds in that one day.

Back on the dealing floor, Sandra rang her boyfriend. 'Our financial problems are over,' she said.

She started to pace the dealing room like a lioness in a cage. 'I'm not wearing a proper enough business suit to meet Sir Willie in,' she moaned.

'Go home and change,' ordered the dealing manager.

Without hesitation, she scurried from the building. She was back within three quarters of an hour in a suit that was, as one dealer pointed out, hardly more business-like than the previous one.

She practised what she'd say to Sir Willie on the other dealers. They all assured her that he was probably a multi-millionaire.

The great man's arrival was announced via the receptionist downstairs. Sir Willie strolled onto the administration floor where Sandra, and a consortium of dealers, had gathered to meet him.

He was clad in a long dark coat with a fur collar, and a scarf. His gloved hands fingered an old leather briefcase. She gazed into his dark sunglasses. He was puffing a fat cigar, the smoke concealing his facial features.

Sandra was feeling nervous. Would he back out at the last moment? All the other dealers were gawking at Sir Willie, gasping at the sight of him in all his glory. She tried to put him at ease: 'Why don't you take your coat off?' she said. Sir Willie shook his head: 'I never take my coat off. It would destroy my standing in the community.'

Pulling out a cheque book, he added solemnly: 'I sincerely hope these Crane Holdings will not fall in value . . . '

Upon hearing this comment, a dealer in the background shouted out: 'Crane Holdings have just this minute dropped back 10p a share. They're now only 18p.'

Sir Willie started. Easing his cheque book back into his coat pocket, he demanded: 'What's this I hear?'

'A temporary easing of the price,' choked Sandra. 'The value of these Crane Holdings, now they're only 18p, will probably double. You'd better settle for them quickly while they're still at this low price.'

She almost begged him to write out the cheque. Meanwhile Sir Willie was slowly dropping off his disguise. Bit by bit, hat, scarf, and gloves, dropped to the floor. Then his coat came off.

The Eyas Securities administration manager stood beaming before her, and said something in Sir Willie's accent. Everybody roared with laughter. Even then she didn't catch on. A dealer kindly explained.

Sandra prostrated herself. Sobbing and screaming, she thrashed about like a woman possessed. Getting on her knees, she explained her deplorable financial condition to the manager. She had mortgage commitments, huge expenses. She demanded a cash advance.

When the manager refused it, she got up and ran back upstairs to the dealing floor.

They all found her on the telephone to her boyfriend again. She was whining to him about how Eyas Securities had played this awful trick on her, how embarrassing it all was. He tried to calm her, but she slammed the phone down on him.

She turned to the dealers and complained this time about her heart condition. All this stress could have caused an aneurysm.

Her grumbling and the dealers' laughing were sustained all the day. Even the directors had known of the trick. This was Sandra's first day there.

Sir Willie Induppe had travelled to various dealing firms, including: Buckingham Securities, Tudorbury Securities, Fox Milton & Co, InstantRate, and Equity Share (now UK & General). The author understands that this venerable client is about to be introduced into a Stock Exchange member firm. Beware of Sir Willie lurking . . .

Sir Willie's success is due only to the dealers' greed. They will do and say as much as they dare, to get the client's money. Their level of professional knowledge might be negligible.

Once a brash young dealer arrived on the dealing floor of Tudorbury Securities. His goal was to make himself a fortune. He kept pestering the others about what is known as 'account trading' (where one can buy and sell the same stock within a two week period, hoping that the stock price will have risen). 'How do you do it?' he would ask.

One morning, the other dealers said to him: 'We've got a stock that will make you rich in a day. It's called Node Check.'

They punched up 'Node Check' on the SEAQ (Stock Exchange Automated Quotations) screen. This was basically a mock quote used to check that the system was functioning. It had a price indication, number of market-makers, etc. Everything to indicate a real stock quote. The new dealer assumed it was a genuine stock.

'I'll get you 10,000 of these on the account through my stockbroker,' said one of the dealers. 'You should make a bomb!'

When the transaction had been completed, the new dealer paced the room all day, dreaming of the profits to come. Every half hour or so, the other dealers would re-check a quotation on 'Node Check', only to confirm the price was rising rapidly.

That evening, the screen revealed that Node Check was up by 20 points.

'You're brilliant,' said one dealer. 'You got in just in time. I'm sorry I missed this one!'

The new dealer thought he had hit the jackpot. To celebrate his fortune to come, he invited the other dealers for a drink that night at the local pub.

In the pub, beer glass in hand, he waxed lyrical about how he would spend his earnings. A flashy car first. Then a new flat. The other dealers chipped in with suggestions. They treated him like one of them, complimenting him on his astuteness, until he began to genuinely believe that it was he who had selected Node Check, that he was an expert on account trading before he'd learned anything about the stock market in general. And he, just a teenager . . .

Little did he know that the experienced dealers were about to teach him a lesson.

The next morning, this young dealer arrived at Tudorbury half an hour early. He rushed over to the SEAQ screen. The opening price for 'Node Check' had already been set by the dealing manager, who had arrived a little earlier. It showed a 50 point drop.

'I'm ruined,' muttered the young dealer. He started pacing the dealing floor. As the others arrived, he told them: 'Node Check dropped right back.' They laughed in his face. 'What an idiot you are! Haven't you caught on yet?'

When the trick was explained to him, he spluttered with indignation. Filthy language rose to his lips.

The dealing manager was still laughing: 'Before you get on the market, you should know something about it yourself. I hope this teaches you a lesson. You don't want to get in debt. It doesn't reflect well on Tudorbury . . .'

A dealer at Harvard Securities was subject to frequent telephone calls from one elusive Mr Bottomley, who wanted to buy a stake in For Eyes, but who insisted he couldn't be contacted on the phone. He always seemed to be ringing from a callbox, on grounds that the walls in his office had ears.

Once a woman who called herself Mr Bottomley's secretary, rang 'on his behalf'. The tiresome twosome asked about shares in For Eyes: their PE ratio, dividend yield, and a host of other conversation-stoppers that all left the trainee dealer tongue-tied and credulous. Naturally he was eager to do business, and so turned to his training officer for assistance.

On one of these calls, the training officer answered the phone, making his voice sound posh and polite, like that of the trainee in question. He recognised Mr Bottomley's voice immediately. He and his 'secretary' were two senior dealers in the adjacent building, taking the mickey. He warned them not to waste his trainee's time.

With time-wasters amongst his trainees, he was somewhat sharper.

If somebody came back from lunch late without having informed him, he really berated the offender. 'No one messes me about, do you hear? If you're late without getting permission beforehand just once more, you're sacked.'

A training officer of one firm would write out his own sales pitches for the trainees. He was hot neither on spelling nor on grammar, but his style was flamboyant and persuasive. So were his oral extravaganzas. 'Everybody's going to the .... winebars, sir. The mark up on drinks is high, and they're doing high class food now as well. People like to be seen there . . . Everybody's booking up boating holidays, Sir . . . You haven't heard of ....? You must be the only one who hasn't, Sir.'

His pitches contained little, perhaps too little in the way of technical information, such as profit figures, PE ratios, etc. If a client asked one of the trainees about the balance sheet, etc, the ignoramus would turn to his training officer: 'What's the PE ratio of ....?' he might ask.

'How the fuck should I know?' the training officer would reply.

He accompanied his trainees on lunchtime booze-ups in the local pub where he regaled them with stories of his hectic social life. Every night, he seemed to go out to posh nightclubs, to restaurants and to major pop concerts. He boasted of the various women he would 'fuck'. At the root of his lifestyle was pots of money, treated almost entirely as disposable income, given that he still lived with his parents. The trainees aspired to his means and his ways.

Harvard dealers only rarely visited clients. Once, the Harvard training officer allowed a dealer to visit a wealthy businessman who had expressed an interest in picking up Hard Rock Cafe shares, (as he had contacts there) but only if they could meet up.

Neil Miller, the dealing manager, was critical of this manoeuvre, saying of the dealer: 'He could be doing four or five deals back in the office. He'd better pull off a biggie.'

The training officer coached the dealer in what to say: 'Tell him you've worked in the City for some time. The Hard Rock Cafe shares should go up to £1.60 in about four to six months. They're now 90p. While you're about it, get him in for some For Eyes.

'If he starts asking about figures, or asking questions you don't understand, tell him: "Listen — I earn my living by making people money. Don't worry about all that. Just do what I say." When he says, "What makes you so sure about these shares?" you must reply, "I can't divulge my sources." '

The dealer managed to sell 10,000 shares in Hard Rock Cafe which were in fact to rise in value as he intimated. Back at Harvard, he was warmly congratulated. He had been a share salesman for just a week and a half, and the deal put £200 in his pocket.

Clients of one firm who were pushed into the shares of a restaurant company were pulled out of them once the price started to rise. The dealing manager yelled at his dealers: 'We need .... shares back on our books for an American buyer. If you don't fucking get the clients out, I'll ring them up and do it myself!'

This way when the price was around quite low, dealers churned clients out of stock saying: 'It's reached a peak, we think.' The price shot up immediately afterwards.

The discrepancy between the facts and what one licensed dealer told its dealers to pass onto clients was sometimes revealed when a company's executives addressed the dealing floor.

The representatives of a printing company told dealers of one firm that their shares were a five year hold.

Shortly before, the dealing director had pressed a trainee dealer to offload 5,000 of these shares on a client, for a three to six month hold. If the dealer failed to do this, commissions he had already earned for selling shares in another company would have been withdrawn.

In panic the dealer had offloaded the stuff on to a willing client. Three to six months later, the client had lost half his money. His dealer had by then left the firm.

It is only the inexperienced dealers, who know nothing about the stock market and who are desperate for money that can be manipulated this way.

Trainees at Harvard Securities were not in practice made to send out details on stocks to clients they were pitching who hadn't dealt three times, as all dealers were supposed to.

After all, Harvard's own information sheets (Section 9s) and the more formal 'Extel' (information) cards were often not available. Supplies were low, and had often run out.

Cold-calling, at one licensed dealer, when the salesmen got desperate, was just not tolerated, it was actively encouraged. If clients complained, dealers would pretend they had sent something out. It was often a case of deal and be damned. This is exactly what everybody did.

The training officer, who endorsed all this had picked up his standards from his dealing director, who was later to claim of him: 'He was like a lost lamb when he started. I taught him everything.'

Another training officer at this firm was a married man, less extravagant and more self-disciplined than his counterpart, although lacking his flair. He was good at getting people to come to work on time and to work hard. He kept excellent written records, but his guidance on salesmanship was of less use than his colleague's.

Harvard trainees were sometimes penalised for underperformance with a dose of debt collecting. This was much detested. Clients too could be rude, and no commission was paid to debt collectors for the money they raked in. The unfortunates were sent over to the other building from which they would ring clients who owed money, and would demand of them immediate payment. The trainees were often not tactful enough. 'I'm not paying,' a typical debtor might retort. 'I never agreed to buy these shares at that price. You must be the fifth person I've explained it to this month. Please don't bother me again . . . . '

Other supposed debtors would claim they had sent in their cheques. People were often not contactable at the given telephone numbers. Nor indeed were telephone numbers always available.

Dealers, debt collecting in pairs, were often so frustrated with the task that they did other things instead. They rang the various commercial recorded lines which hinted they were offering sexual innuendo, which proved only to be glamour girls talking about dieting or holiday-making. Another favourite pastime was to chat up the girls from Directory Enquiries while they were getting phone numbers. Some called this 'Dial-a-swelling'. Most satisfyingly, of course, debt collectors made an enormous number of personal calls, sometimes international ones.

Trainee dealers put on debt collecting for more than a day or two at a stretch would often walk out of Harvard from sheer boredom and frustration. Everybody seemed to find this amusing.

Likewise, dealing in public issues such as Rolls Royce hardly proved inspiring for dealers at one firm. Anyone who opted to work full-time on British Gas for instance, was busy six days a week, thirteen hours a day at one stage.

Eventual payment was promised at the rate of 50p per deal, but this proved pie in the sky. Profits were divided amongst those who had helped out, and payment turned out to be at a substantially smaller rate. Naive trainees were often thus coaxed into doing hard, boring work for little remuneration. Some felt deceived, and so justified in pressuring their clients in turn.

Dealers who put the client first were bound to fail. They were trying to be advisers and salesmen at once. These roles naturally conflicted. The general attitude was that dealers were paid to sell specified stock, and only that stock — not to discuss the market generally.

Trainee dealers at some firms quickly developed a personal interest in stocks and shares, based on the new found possibilities of making quick money for themselves. Their methods of forecasting the way prices would go proved ad hoc and unconventional, unhampered by hard examination of figures and ratios, such as accountants might undertake.

Dealers used their clients as guinea-pigs for their untried techniques. One trainee of the author's acquaintance believed she could predict the movement of both specific shares and the market as a whole by the tapping of her fingers. She was widely regarded as a crank. Her colleagues, however, used methods which proved no more reliable, such as charting graphs for daily price movements and basing future patterns purely on the past. They applied such chartists' techniques after a simplified fashion, and were surprised, not sorry, when they tested them out on clients and got them wrong.

Clients often suffered from their trainee dealers' recommendations and advice, not dreaming how ignorant they were. Dealers would bluff even more audaciously than clients. The relationship between dealer and client would often become a fantasy world, based on speculation presented as logic.

Dealers were always out to make money on the side. A pyramid venture was started recently at one licensed dealer, every participant contributing £100, and bringing in more people. The rules of this game became progressively more complicated, but the outcome was predictable: sizeable losses for the unwary majority, and substantial gains for the smart few.

Less often admittedly, trainee and fully-fledged dealers at this firm indulged in games not for money. There was a popular guessing game called, 'Let's spot who's going to be sacked next'. This often took place in the pub and involved thinking aloud. There was a ghastly self-fulfilling prophecy about such sessions. Sometimes, the training officer joined in. In this way, he gained a lot of insight into the psychological make-up of different sheep in his flock.

Knowledge of the stock market was limited for most dealers. Academic basics can be drummed into a reasonably receptive dealer through the BIDS or Stock Exchange courses, but the practical market know-how that was most needed could be grasped only over a period. As soon as most dealers actually *knew* anything, they would get disgusted with what they had been doing, and wanted out.

There was initiated at Harvard a practice of dealers taking turns first thing in the morning, to deliver a little speech to the rest of the dealing room about the latest financial news. To prepare themselves for this, Neil Miller, the dealing director, told dealers to read a quality newspaper — preferably the *Financial Times*, but the *Daily Mail* at a pinch. He asked dealers at random to deliver the goods, and berated anyone who was obviously unprepared, particularly if he belonged to the streetwise contingent whose daily newspaper tended to be the *Daily Mirror* or *The Sun*. 'Those papers are alright to read when you're sitting on the toilet, but not for the financial news,' he once shouted.

At most firms, getting up to date with financial news was, like anything else, taken more seriously by the trainees than the dealers proper.

From time to time, shares which one licensed dealer was pushing got a wee mention in the national press. Sadly, this mention was not always favourable. Financial journalists knew how to turn on the sarcasm.

'It's been tipped in the Press,' the dealing manager of this firm would announce in a matter-of-fact tone of voice, as he paced the dealing room heavily, like a schoolmaster in his classroom: 'Ring all your clients and make 'em double up. The share price should go through the roof.'

Dealers would scream down the blower: 'Did you see The *Sunday Times* last week Sir?' knowing that he would probably have missed the relevant bit, just as they had. 'After the weekend tip, we've had a flurry of buying. Get in now while the price is still going up.'

The dealing manager would be hovering breathing down the dealers' necks like Big Brother, nodding approvingly if they sounded convincing, or else shouting: 'You need to be more fucking aggressive' (so the client could hear him in the background).

The client was almost invariably cajoled into further so-called investment. He would rarely bother to check the exact wording of the so-called share tip.

Dealers thus learned to regard every mention of a share in the newspapers as a tip. They frequently did not read what was written. It was no source of information, only an instrument for their smooth talking.

They later took all the techniques they had learned at their dealer into stockbrokers and other financial services outfits, where it was often too late to unlearn them. Their formative training had been in a class of its own.

The clients themselves have been known to become dealers. Such clients would be young, and living in London. They would become so hooked on their daily interaction with their licensed dealer that they would ring up and ask for job interviews, often with the connivance of their own dealers. They might well get taken on.

The author knows of a client who did this after he had lost a frightful lot of money. 'If you can't beat 'em, join 'em,' he had said. Indeed he proved far more successful a dealer than he had a client, despite the poverty of his company's share recommendations, and by proxy his own. He had the gift of the gab, which one training officer described as the main prerequisite. Others have described this particular quality as being a 'good bullshitter,' or a 'smooth operator.'

There was one legendary example of client recruitment at Harvard. One top Harvard dealer was taking a taxi ride into the City, and he fell into conversation with the driver. 'I'm looking for something better paid,' the driver said.

'Come and work for us,' the Harvard whizz-kid rejoindered. 'I'll get you an interview.'

The cabbie was taken on, did brilliantly, and was made a team leader, eventually taking brief responsibility for running the dealing floor. All this is history.

When dealers leave, they sometimes become clients of their old firm. At first, they may intend this as a joke, sometimes giving a false name. Often though they proceed to deal seriously enough, as blindly hooked as punters, and no less destined for disillusionment. The author has come to an overall conclusion that, perhaps, clients and dealers are very much the same sort of people.

Unlike the trainees, established dealers pick up market gossip with a lightning instinct. When Tom Wilmot at Harvard told dealers around the time of Big Bang: 'You should all understand thoroughly what's going on. You're living through history. This is something you'll be able to tell your grandchildren about,' the trainees were thrilled, the established professionals not greatly interested.

Disillusionment with the way they are treated by their firms has led many trainees, along with more experienced dealers to look for new jobs. After commissions were cut at Harvard, a vast number of Harvard dealers joined the search. All chased the same vacancies.

City employment agencies have been inundated with job hunting dealers who often confide: 'We're earning thirty or forty thousand a year, but we're working for a bucket shop. I'm looking for an opening with a stockbroker . . . . '

Many, perhaps most City employment agencies, rate employees of Harvard and of other licensed dealers cheaply, on the grounds that they are not sought after by many recruitment managers of Stock Exchange member firms. Share salesmen are regarded as on a level with hard sell futures salesmen. One ex-Harvard dealer who was recruited by a stockbroker found his new colleagues surprised that, with his Harvard background, he should be there, although doubtless his sales ability impressed them.

Salesmen from Harvard and other licensed dealers who have been interviewed for jobs at companies such as Barclays de Zoete Wedd, Greenwell Montague, and Kitcat & Aitken have sometimes felt an obligation to explain their present work position. Dealers have felt a need to deprecate their own firms' values, to disassociate themselves from them.

Getting a job at another licensed dealer was somewhat easier. Few could at this stage afford to be as choosey as Fox Milton & Co Ltd when they sacked a new dealer on the grounds that he was dealing with his old Chartwell clients, so enraging Chartwell Securities. 'We wouldn't want him to play the same trick on us, stealing our clients so he can deal them elsewhere,' said Fox Milton director Philip Raisey.

But theft of clients is the norm in the industry, and is rarely the reason for anyone being sacked.

On Wednesdays, firms advertising vacancies in the *Financial Times* have been inundated with phone calls from licensed dealers. Harvard salesmen would make inquiries at lunchtimes from the public telephone boxes just outside the building, despite the risk of getting spotted there.

More adventurous dealers have been known to go to New York. In this strange, go-ahead land, where the British accent is appreciated as much as enthusiasm for a sales career, quite mediocre dealers have landed choice jobs.

The training managers, dealing managers, compliance officers, and most of all directors of licensed dealers are seen as more tainted by prevalent sharp practice than the salesmen, due to their greater organisation and decision-making responsibilities.

These men are barred from Stock Exchange member firms. They are too egotistic and their work methods are too eccentric for transference.

When they quit licensed dealers or are shunted out at around the age of thirty upwards, just when they start to crave job security, they are forced into a hostile world. They will be constantly trying to get back into licensed dealers, or else will settle for a different sort of trickery.

The smartest managers set up their own firms. Thus one bright spark, ex-Harvard Corporate Finance, set up Gibraltar-based European Equity Research on a budget of £3,000.

His team started with a plank resting on two wooden packing cases, for a desk. Three portable telephones were available for contacting clients. He and his dealers made good money before selling out. He left, not alone, for Bailey McMahon.

Of course some managers drop out, giving reasons of personal ethics. Here is what one manager wrote to his directors:

'After some soul searching, I resign immediately as dealing director of Afcor . . . . I personally abhor high pressure sales tactics adopted by Afcor. I like to sleep at night, and applying "scorched earth" tactics in selling OTC stocks to some unsuspecting people makes me cringe . . . .'

By October 1987, a year after Big Bang, the inflated City salaries were slipping. Although a few analysts remained bullish about the market, most had serious reservations. Licensed dealers as well as stockbrokers were feeling the pinch of sudden market setbacks, and not altogether satisfactory trade figures. One recruitment manager put it like this: 'A year ago we were buying teams . . . now we're filling holes.'

What with their incapacity to move onto proper City jobs, even occasionally to jobs in their own industry, it is no wonder that employees of many licensed dealers, temperamental at the best of times, were often driven to drink.

Dealers crowded out exclusive wine bars as well as the pubs. They would drink side by side with City workers, but would never quite bridge the communication gap. There was an invisible, somehow natural, barrier.

It was of no health benefit for dealers to have delivered fresh orange juice and cordon bleu sandwiches midday if they drank themselves blind on champagne, quality wines and designer beers in the evenings.

Dealers threatened with the sack would agree to sell knowingly atrocious investments, or to perform other morally dubious tasks in an effort to make themselves indispensable. The training officer of one firm was temporarily made dealing manager. He kept the room's business on the move by constantly shouting: 'Anyone who doesn't work is going to be sacked. And that includes the team leaders.' He tried to wriggle out of his responsibilities however, but his boss said: 'If you want to keep your job, this is what you must do.'

The training officer of one licensed dealer taught the Stock Exchange Licensed Representatives' and Traders' Examination in the evenings to dealers who had to be pushed into attending his classes, like unwilling schoolboys. They vented their frustrations on him, and he would protest: 'I'm only doing my job.'

Dealers at this firm suffered the indignity of getting illegally fined for coming in late in the mornings, even if it was only five minutes after the starting time of 8.30 a.m.. Their dealing manager would sack anybody who refused to pay up.

In those days, dealers were seen running madly from the nearest underground station at 8.20 a.m., or else clambering into taxis. Even then, they didn't always make it on time.

A few dealers accepted the fines as a matter of course, especially as accumulated funds got spent on drinks for everybody in the local pub on Friday night. More resented them.

Once a very average 19 year old dealer was asked for £5 cash. He said, 'I don't think so.'

'Why not? What's so special about you?' said the dealing manager.

'The trains were bad this morning,' the dealer retorted.

'Give me your box of leads. And fuck off,' said the dealing manager.

The dealer didn't budge. 'I'll give you the cash later this morning when I get change.'

A team leader who had arrived two minutes late one morning, refused to pay his fiver. 'This is illegal,' he said. He declined to hand over the cash, no matter what was threatened, and he was too good a salesman to be sacked, so the dealing manager yelled over to the accounts clerk: 'Deduct £50 from his month's wages.' 'You know you're doing wrong,' said the team leader, who was like a bear with a sore head for the rest of the morning.

He was a powerfully built man, who had aroused resentment at the firm because he had constantly called the administration staff 'morons'. However, he did too much business to get sacked.

Shortly afterwards he left the licensed dealer, which then tried unsuccessfully to get him sacked from the stockbroker he had persuaded to give him a job.

If dealers were discovered looking for jobs from other licensed dealers, they would usually get fired on the spot. Sometimes, another dealer tipped off a director as to the identities of miscreants, so as to curry favour, for which he might reap a tangible reward like extra leads.

Poor dealers were sometimes kept on by firms by being shifted into administrative positions, e.g. a dealer at one licensed dealer was made manager in charge of Personal Equity Plans (PEPs). This shift in position marked a decline in status as well as income, but was preferable perhaps to being sacked.

This man was the firm's intellectual. He had an extraordinarily leisurely manner, and unlike most dealers had a genuine knowledge of the stock market.

After being virtually the first dealer at his firm to pass the Registered Representatives' and Traders' examination, he was applauded by his colleagues only to be shunted off the sales desk into the back office.

Once a top dealer rushed to his new desk, tapping him on the shoulder: 'I've got a client on the line,' he said. 'He'll buy ten grand's worth of ... (an electronics company), if I tell him the latest profit figures. What the hell are they?'

The intellectual raised his eyebrows. He tapped new tobacco into the bowl of his pipe. 'Why should I help you stuff another client, just so you can make yourself rich?' He then looked the dealer up and down. 'You're earning £60,000 a year, and you can't even buy yourself a decent suit.'

This ex-dealer was shunted next through various clerical jobs, ending up as a training officer. His predecessor in the position commented: 'He's been dragged all over the company. What a way to fucking humiliate someone. What next? The dustbin?'

Other poor dealers were kept on in dealing jobs, because they were good at answering telephone inquiries, or at dealing on government privatisations.

At this stage, Neil Miller was saying to all Harvard dealers: 'Some of you lot think you're better than what you are, just because you're earning big money here. If you leave after only a few months' experience here, believe me, you will find it hard to get a good job elsewhere. After a couple of years experience at Harvard, maybe you'll be worth something.'

Consultants in the specialist employment agencies, however, argued otherwise.

One Harvard dealer had registered with an employment agency which stupidly sent his curriculum vitae to Harvard. Neil Miller sacked the dealer on the spot.

The dealer contemplated suing the recruitment agency until he found a better job. For several months hence, Harvard dealers were reluctant to use employment agencies.

Harvard Securities had always had a high staff turnover. Harvard dealers who had left knew better than to say where to, since the walk-out of its top dealers to London & Norwich Investment Services Ltd in May 1987.

It was alleged that at one licensed dealer, directors traced dealers who had left them, whether of their own accord or not, via their bank accounts.

More than one ex-dealer has claimed that their old firm would still have an employee's banking details, and would ring the bank to check whether the ex-dealer was currently receiving a direct debit, and if so, from what firm. If it was from another sharedealing outfit, the old firm would know where to find him.

A network of ex-dealers discovered what they were up to. From then on, many changed banks, with the sole purpose of giving their previous firm a run for its money.

Directors of licensed dealers rarely have secure jobs. Some would read significance into an incident in which the best educated director of one licensed dealer suddenly became history.

One Friday afternoon, after a heavy lunch, the director in question telephoned a co-director. 'I'm quitting the company,' he announced.

It was the third time he had proposed this. On the two previous occasions he had retracted his resignation. This time, as if aware of that, he added: 'And I'm never coming back.'

'Are you sure?' asked his colleague.

'Yes, this is it,' the director reassured him.

At 5.30 p.m. the resigning director appeared on the dealing floor. No dealers believed he was quitting. Nor would they have wished it.

That evening, a consortium of dealers led the slightly worse for wear director to a riverside wine bar in an attempt to convince him that it was worth staying with the company.

At this stage the director revealed news of a letter he had submitted that afternoon to his colleague, verifying that he was serious about resigning. Nonetheless, the dealers who were gathered with him at the wine bar, succeeded in changing his mind.

On the morning of the next Monday, he was found gracing the licensed dealer's premises. At 11.30 a.m. his fellow director summoned him, and reminded him of his resignation.

The poor man frantically tried to bargain for his reinstatement, admitting that he had been not altogether sober, and apologising for making a resignation he did not want. His pleas were to no avail. His colleague insisted that he leave the premises.

For the next six months or so, this former director was often seen by dealers in various winebars. He reminisced how loyal he had been to his firm and how cruel he felt was his reward.

Early in 1987, a memo was circulated to all Harvard staff assuring them that Harvard would still be in business that time the following year, and that appeal options would be taken up, should the Stock Exchange turn down their application for membership.

In order to fall in with Stock Exchange requirements, Harvard introduced a wretched task for dealers, viz. the filling in of client profile cards. A dealer was supposed to ring all his clients and ask them questions as to age, tax position, investment objectives, etc. If a client refused to answer, the dealer wasn't blamed provided he time-stamped the client profile card, and recorded appropriate comments.

Dealers were expected to get these cards filled in at the same time as fulfilling their quotas of business, but nobody had time. Threats were levelled that if cards weren't filled in by deadlines, good leads would be taken from dealers. These threats were not idle, although they were usually only directed at those who didn't do much business.

At one licensed dealer that used client profile cards, the dealers scribbled fake answers on their cards, time-stamping them at any old time, despite weak threats from their dealing director that he would be checking on the tapes to see that everything was being done properly.

Trainees, or inexperienced dealers alone took the task seriously, and had the most burdensome time of it.

Later, Stock Exchange officials paid a visit of inspection to the firm. All desks had been tidied, and leads without client profile cards attached were locked or hidden away. Top dealers with plummy accents who had passed the registered Representatives' and Traders' examination were primed to speak with the inspectors. Few were surprised that the whole exercise did not win over the Stock Exchange.

The firm reacted to their failure to get membership by hard selling in its most ruthless way. The licensed dealer showed itself in its true colours, as one of the roughest, toughest sales teams in or around the City.

A dealer will occasionally work against the system, making his clients money against the odds. One top dealer and team leader invited his four team members out to a wine bar one evening.

Here at a private table before a crackling log fire, he passed round the claret and addressed his minions as follows:

'You'll find pressure on you here to sell these bloody OTC. It's the way to ruin your clients. You might make quick money, but you won't survive as a sharedealer. Do what I do. Sell some OTC, and a lot of main market stocks. I'll make sure you don't get sacked for it.'

His team members proved intolerant of what they termed 'his hypocrisy', for he sold a fair quantity of OTC stocks himself, in accordance with their dealing director's instructions: 'The stock must go, just get it off my books.'

Another of his team resorted to all the tricks of the trade: discretionary dealing, roll-on account trades, etc. He even off-loaded tens of thousands of pounds worth of stock on to a client committed to a mental asylum (for which he was sacked). All three were hard selling in accordance with instructions, and were happy with the big money they were making.

Subsequently, two members of this team complained about their leader to a director: 'He's slowing us down,' they moaned. 'We must go to work on another table.'

While they shifted their things, the fourth member of the team stayed in his old place, cackling with laughter. He alone stood by his team leader. However, the cry was raised all over the floor: 'They've removed their team leader.' Some thirty young dealers applauded the courage of these two.

The team leader and his fourth dealer went on to be stockbrokers. The remaining two graduated to FIMBRA authorised share-pushers. Even at this early stage in their careers, fundamental distinctions in approach were emerging. But this firm was a training ground for these diverse types. What direction they moved in next was up to them.

Harvard dealers know more than their counterparts at newer bucket shops, and so have more choice of career direction. Trainees at the hard sell futures firms, for instance, have been encouraged to learn still less about the markets. They learn little more than how to sell, and to sell wide.

New recruits of one futures selling bucket shop were made to listen to a tape recording of a 'model' sales presentation. They were not told that the client on that occasion had cancelled the deal. The few who discovered this later, naturally felt that this part of their training was not helpful.

One new salesman at DPR Futures proved so ineffectual and lethargic that his colleagues found it comical to teach him wide techniques. However, he went extra wide, and ended up getting in more business than any of them.

This aroused their resentment, and consequently their respect. Successful salesmen in bucket shops scorn weak or moralising colleagues, just as they do all the clients. Nonetheless, although jealous as wildcats, they respect their own kind.

The professional exams for futures dealers are hogwash as far as the directors of some firms are concerned. They are only suffered in such places in order to appear respectable in the eyes of the Association of Futures Brokers and Dealers (AFBD).

Very few Account Executives (AEs) at DPR Futures knew *anything* beyond the most basic facts about futures. This was compensated for by their self-laudatory claims such as: 'We have our own team of analysts, and a good research department, etc.'

The DPR directors had worked at LHW and set up DPR along the same principles. They had even initially used somewhat similar stationery, although with an altered logo.

DPR salesmen followed a traditional training course lasting a week. The programme, subject to minor fluctuation, was as follows:

DAY 1
Technical training and homework assignments.

Prospective AEs are given a gigantic calculator. This is a free perk and endears some to DPR.

A few will leave during the day. News may later leak out that they were "spies."

DAY 2
Further technical training and homework assignments.

The history of DPR is told. Any prospective AEs who imagine that their starting at DPR is a serious career move are asked to leave.

DAY 3
An explanation of options.

Trainees are told that they are *salesmen* and not investment advisers or analysts.

One or two top senior Account Executives (SAEs) boast to the AEs about how much they are earning, making them all feel they are onto something really good. They also talk about the perks of the job, such as Porsches.

DAY 4
Review for an exam on the following day. Also, the signing of work contracts. Meeting with other DPR directors. A few more trainees will meanwhile have departed.

DAY 5
The Day of Reckoning, in the form of a three hour written exam.

The Corn Exchange, 52-57 Mark Lane, London EC3. The very aptly named offices of DPR Futures Ltd, which was known by its staff as ''Deller, Page and Rip-off''.

This takes place in the morning. Predictably, several trainees have not shown up.

After lunch, AEs are given a sales motivational talk, then are whisked onto the dealing floor. They are given a desk, a box, and a telephone. They are assigned to a team and introduced (if that's the word) to their team leader.

Stacks of old recycled client coupons are shoved their way, and the sales manager screams in their ears: 'Rock, roll and rev it up.'

This is their signal to hit the clients. If they slacken, they are told to 'bull up' so loudly that their eardrums quiver. They are standing for the rest of the afternoon.

Many are discouraged. Some are unable to work. They feel thrust from DPR's list straight into hellfire. This seems to them more like a building site than a City office.

By this stage a few will have decided that this is not for them. They proceed not to turn up on Monday, the next working day.

A FORTNIGHT LATER:
The exam results are posted up. Trainees who have passed are told: 'Well done' and are considered professionals. But here in this field, still more than in sharedealing, they must have a flair for bludgeoning money out of punters if they are to survive.

Trainees who flunked the examination must be seen to be rebuked. They get summoned into the conference room. Here their superiors criticise them for failing after they have been given such brilliant training. Next they deliver this ultimatum: 'Unless you get at least X clients in and on the market over the next week, you're history.'

So long as they can sell, AEs will never *have* to pass the exam. Some of those who failed choose at this stage nonetheless to drop out. This seems ironic as they will usually have boasted that they were the top sales people at their previous firms.

Nobody who leaves a firm like DPR actually gives notice. There is an art in quitting a bucket shop. One sort of fades away.

Some AEs cheat on the internal exam, and the author knows of one SAE working at DPR whose girlfriend, an AE there, obtained the question papers for him in advance. No wonder he then passed with very high marks.

Early on, a deceptive, but strangely effective form of sales training would take place at DPR. The trainees would tackle what appeared to be virgin client coupons. They were unwittingly put through to an SAE in the dealing room next door.

The SAE would pretend to be a client, with money to burn. The AE would pitch him, convinced that this was the real thing. The more ignorant the AE was, the easier he found it to be enthusiastic.

Afterwards, the SAE would disclose his identity, then pick holes in the AE's sales techniques. One SAE applauded an AE who had come out with this line about futures: 'This stuff is granny bonds, it's so simple.'

The burn-out rate of DPR's AEs was tremendous. Even the good ones might remain for only a matter of months. The smart trainees started secretly copying down client details from their second week, to take with them should they suddenly leave or be sacked.

The DPR sales manager once introduced a game some might find offensive, to a dealing force, amongst which were three women.

'We're playing a game today,' he shouted, 'called "Cunts off the Chairs".

'You may ask me why "Cunts off the Chairs"? For the women, this is because you have cunts. For the men, it's because you are cunts.'

All AEs immediately turned to stare at one of their number, a poker-faced young man, who described any client who wouldn't buy from him as a 'cunt', even scribbling comments to that effect on the client record cards. This prime focus of attention had not even the grace to blush.

The game was played like this. No AE was permitted to sit down until he had given the manager a form for a bike (so a courier could collect the client's cheque), or for a TT (telegraphic transfer from the client's bank to DPR's), or for Red Star (British Rail delivery: this was a comparatively slow method of payment. The client's cheque would take a few hours to arrive).

One AE almost immediately handed in a form for a telegraphic transfer, and within 15 minutes the client's funds were being transferred to the company's bank. The AE then sat down triumphantly.

The game was sustained until mid-afternoon. By this stage, enough business had been generated, and everybody was allowed to sit down.

The salesman who brings insufficient business into DPR usually gets sacked. This fate might be waived if he is considered a good influence on the other dealers.

One such person was an African who started working at DPR. His skin was so dark that he caused another black AE at DPR to comment: 'I'm from Jamaica, but I've never seen anyone that black.'

This new AE was not, however, self-conscious about his colour, and he socialised easily with his new colleagues. Because clients might not have accepted his African name, he worked under the pseudonym of Peter Mackenzie.

At about the time he started, DPR was working to get its AEs more 'revved up'. Peter Mackenzie proved unusually bullish and his deep voice would reverberate throughout the dealing floor with the force of a thousand rapids: 'Hallo, sir. Peter Mackenzie here. Deller, Page and Rycott in the City of London. I want you to come into the market. We are going short on cocoa. Cocoa prices are falling. You stand to make a lot of money. The minimum investment is £1,500 sterling. You can get onto the market by cheque, or do a telegraphic transfer from your bank to ours, or I can send round a bike . . . '

At this stage, the prospective client might reply: 'I'm skint.'

Peter Mackenzie tried not to take 'No' for an answer: 'Might I suggest selling your shares? We have brokers here who will sell them at best. We take the capital and put you directly on the market. How very clever. It's very smart . . . '

Usually failing to close, Peter Mackenzie would gently hang up. Seconds later he was on the phone again, bulling into the next prospect.

He never sat down throughout the day. He was even known

occasionally to sprint on the spot. His colleagues perpetually shouted at him: 'Can't you lower your voice? We can't make ourselves heard,' but he only laughed.

Here was an example of an AE who was perfectly 'revved up'. This is why he was never sacked, even though his bullishness didn't make for enough sales. He just was not able to bring in business the way DPR would have liked him to do. Making an excuse of illness in the family, he quit DPR, and returned to his hometown in Nigeria.

Two AEs of DPR, while travelling one night on the London tube, openly discussed the 'Rock, roll and rev it up' tactics used in their dealing room, in front of a carriage full of commuters.

One person (allegedly a DPR client) was appalled at what he overheard, and later complained to the DPR's directors. The AEs who had so offended were instantly sacked. The directors determined that no AEs should be allowed to so transgress again, which led to a clause in the work contract forbidding employees at any stage to divulge trade secrets to the outside world.

Despite their high staff turnover, DPR had little to fear from former employees. Most would find their next jobs in similar bucket shops. Blabbermouths are finished in the fringe City if they are stupid enough to get noticed for it. So are those who too obviously con their employers.

C......., an ex-sharedealer of Harvard Securities, was living in a barn on a friend's farm in Kent, eking out a gipsy-like living by renovating rusty old cars.

He one morning received an unexpected phone call from a former colleague, now selling futures at DPR: 'Repairing cars won't pay your bills, C.......,' she said. 'It's only two weeks until the Financial Services Act comes into operation (27th February 1988). Afterwards you stand no hope of getting back into the City. Get a haircut. Dust your suit. And take the first train out of Kent. I've arranged an interview for you here at DPR. Remember this is your last chance . . . '

C....... landed the job. He then set about accumulating client records for use should he leave. His imminent departure was discovered and he was ignominiously sacked.

He retained contact with another salesman still employed at DPR, whom for the purpose of this book we shall call Peter, which is not his real name.

Peter was a poor salesman, but he hadn't been at DPR quite long enough yet to get sacked. He was an unconventional boy in his late twenties, with a fresh, youthful face. His hair naturally curled to his shoulders.

He made no bones about displaying his artistic temperament.

Indeed, he was both an amateur painter and a musician in a rock band that met at weekends.

His dress was not normal for the City. He wore no suit, but trousers, waistcoat and Paisley tie — fashion for the psychedelic movement of the 1960s. It was amazing that he got away with it.

When asked a question, instead of making the standard business response, he would say: 'Yeah, man' or use 1970s phrases such as: 'That's hip', or 'That's groovy'. He seemed to be a hippy in his blood.

Once C....... rang Peter at DPR and put to him this 'business proposition': 'You're an artist. I'll help you set up an art and printing business. I can get you access to office space in Mayfair. In return, you must get me as many DPR client coupons as you can. Stuff your briefcase. Stuff your pockets. Stuff anything, but get them out.'

Peter could not resist this. To set up an art and printing business had always been his pipe-dream. While he was getting it started, he decided he would try to hang onto his job at DPR. His side of the bargain, removing the client coupons, seemed no sweat.

He started staying late in the office, until 10.00 p.m. or later, pretending that he was contacting clients. What Peter did not realise was that he had aroused the directors' suspicion. All telephone conversations were taped, but his were now being especially replayed.

On C....... 's instructions, Peter's next step was to attempt a break-in to DPR's computer system, i.e. the leadbank. This proved unsuccessful.

C....... pressed him though to get more client coupons. He was now working for another futures broker, and wanted these both for his own business, and to put into a mailing list he would sell.

The DPR directors next discovered that Peter was stashing client coupons in the hollow behind a loose wooden panel in the men's loo. It was C....... who had informed Peter of this hiding place.

The directors laid a trap. One night they secretly told all employees, except Peter to leave early. By 7.30 p.m. Peter was there alone. Normally the others would remain for another hour or so.

Nonetheless, Peter in his eagerness didn't realise he had been set up. He made a beeline for the secret panel.

The directors watched him remove the coupons and put them in his briefcase. Here was the evidence they needed. Unsuspecting still, Peter left his briefcase on the premises as usual.

After he had left, they promptly searched it, retrieving a closely packed leadbank. The next morning Peter was sacked and escorted from the premises without being given a reason.

DPR's directors had evidence of C....... 's involvement too. They rang his new employers, stating that they would file charges

An ex-DPR executive, shown here working at Tudorbury.

for stealing leads unless they sacked him. Minutes later, he was out of the building.

One week several AEs were sacked from DPR for their inability to convey the concept of financial futures. Simultaneously, three other dealers left of their own accord, disillusioned with the lack of fresh client coupons.

An ex-DPR salesman had started at Stox, a new futures broker. He rang up ex-DPR dealers and said: 'Come over to Stox. There's not the same pressure on the dealing floor as at DPR, but you'll still make loads of money. They have fresh virgin coupons, not like those burnt out ones at DPR.'

'Who's running the show?' one asked.

'An ex-DPR pro,' said their former colleague. And they decided to join him.

In its short life, Stox was staffed by very young salesmen, sometimes teenagers. Green and overeager, they were distinctly optimistic to their clients over the telephone.

Some of the ex-DPR AEs couldn't take this 'kindergarten' seriously. When Stox went under it became a laughing stock. The firm had around £600,000 in the clients' managed accounts. 'This would have been a much larger sum if the salesmen had been any good,' argued one AE.

Following the implementation of the new Financial Services Act, licensed dealers dragged their nets to pull in a few of the old-style hard sell merchants. It was a last throw, before the whole game became too hot.

Tudorbury Securities agreed in principle to pay two ex-London & Norwich dealers £5,000 each up front to join them, such was their desire for hot-shot salesmen.

One dealer, desperate to work at one licensed dealer, was kept at bay because his arrival might have attracted press publicity. However, a female dealer struck a bargain with him. She would get him the job, if he gave her money and clients.

He agreed, and she set to work. She pestered the appropriate officer, several times a day over a period of three weeks. He was almost cracking when she said: 'I can't do any business unless he comes. I need him to motivate me.'

'I'll get him in,' said her boss, 'provided that you sleep with me.'
'Fuck off,' she said.

But the dealer was offered the job. Once he was there, she tried to exact his help in smuggling client records out of the firm to her home. Unbeknown to the firm, she was about to leave.

Once at her new work place she complained bitterly of how her style had been cramped.

She felt watched in her every deal. No cold-calling. No churning. No recommendations of stocks without a reason for it. In early June 1988, she was asked by a director how she had known to put so many clients into a particular Irish stock, just before the price soared on takeover bids. She explained that a client of hers had recommended the stock.

She couldn't quite tear herself free of the licensed dealing community. Her former colleagues accused her of bad-mouthing them. She felt pressured and persuaded her clients to sell out of stocks they'd picked up from various licensed dealers.

The way of life sharedealers aspired to was epitomised in the lifestyle of a Sultan whom a few Tudorbury staff once had the privilege of meeting.

RAI Hamilton, Tudorbury Securities' chief executive, took some of his dealers, together with a bombshell receptionist, to the prestigious club/restaurant Tramp in Jermyn Street. He ordered dinner for the group. One dealer asked for a hamburger. It cost around £7, the most expensive fast food he'd ever had.

The party met up with a Sultan and his daughter. These proved colourful characters. The Sultan was very chatty.

'What do you do for a living?' a dealer asked the Sultan. He puffed out his chest: 'I spend money.'

This is the ultimate way of life to which sharedealers aspire. One Harvard dealer, an American boy, was fortunate enough to get close to this quickly. By putting a wealthy client into some circumspect account trades, and so actually making him a lot of money, the dealer earned the client's gratitude.

The client set him up in his own office, with a Stock Exchange Automated Quotations (SEAQ) screen and access to all the financial press. The dealer was employed to make money in stocks and shares for that client. In return he was extremely well paid, and could use all the facilities for his own sharedealings.

Someone who put £50,000 into his licensed dealer's portfolio, and who let it be churned around ad infinitum, was likely to be testing what the firm would do with it. How much more money might he have had at his disposal?

Another dealer had instilled such confidence into some twenty punters to such an extent that they were dealing £5,000 a time on a long-term regular basis. He was managing to make them money. He achieved this only by disobeying his firm's orders that he should sell certain stocks at certain times, and by slipping in bargains here and there that were actually in the client's interest.

He later took these clients with him to Sheppards (Stockbrokers) where they dealt with him on a much larger level. This went to show that the full potential of a client was measurable only outside the licensed dealing fraternity.

One teamleader would occasionally keep his dealers behind after normal working hours. He would have them sell some peculiar stock, saying: 'They've given us this to get rid of, as we're the top team. Let's prove them right.'

It was only after they had offloaded the stock that the dealers would find out their teamleader had bought up large quantities of it himself.

Before the dealers could say Jack Robinson — let alone sell their clients out — their teamleader would have offloaded his own stock, making a handsome profit for himself. 'I knew you wouldn't let me down,' he would say, to his team.

He was under the impression the dealers didn't know what he was doing.

If one of this teamleader's clients said that another dealer had been trying to sell him stock, he would bellow: 'What's his name?' Upon extracting the dealer's name from the client, he would tear over to the culprit, who had usually been working quite innocently off a duplicate lead card. The teamleader would seize his collar, yelling:

'You speak to that client again and I'll beat your fucking head in, now give me the lead!'

He would tear up the lead card, and would storm back to his desk. He was the dealing room bully, and dealers quaked in their boots at the thought of being put in his team.

He kept a 'leadbank' for his team. Every dealer put his throwaway leads in it, only their leader occasionally forced them to contribute dealable ones. He would remove those for his own use, substituting his own dross leads.

Dealers came and went from his team almost weekly. One temporary recruit, a tall lean young black boy, sat whispering into the telephone all day. He never sold his day's OTC quota, and so his leader would shout: 'You'll soon be back on the fucking training floor.'

The black dealer eventually escaped to a stockbroker. From his comfortable desk there, he would look up from his *Financial Times*, and say: 'They're all monkeys at .... , just doing what they're told. It's pathetic. So what if they're earning more than me?'

Two young Harvard dealers who were sacked still owed two months' rent. Because they had squandered all their cash, they each had bank overdrafts of around £1,500.

In their last wage packets, Harvard did not pay the £2,000 or so each that they were expecting. The firm drastically reduced the sum totals on grounds of bad debts, fines, etc.

Their landlord visited them at the flat to recover back rent. The doors were bolted from inside. The two dealers escaped through a back window, after dropping their belongings down from the fire-escape.

Both dealers took the night train to a Northern province, the home town of one of them. They started a new job together, selling holidays. They tried to use the methods they had learned at Harvard until these were vetoed by their new boss.

They kept ringing up their former colleagues, making out they were selling the new Royal Life Unit Trust, that they had risen above OTC dodginess.

But their posing served only to disguise their dissatisfaction, as sharedealing had got into their blood. They started ringing up London recruitment agencies, such as Cambridge Appointments, asking if there were any sharedealing jobs around. The bug had bitten hard.

The former securities dealers did not, however, read the financial press and were unaware of the shake-up engendered by the Financial Services Act (1986). They could not now find their way forward.

Dealers would try to get other dealers sacked from rival firms, even if they had worked with them once. It was nothing personal.

One dealer urged a client not to pay for losses on roll-on account trades his Harvard dealer had put him into: 'Harvard'll never take you to court,' he said. 'They're still trying to get TSA membership. Just stick to your argument that the dealer said you'd make a certain profit. That way you should get the dealer sacked, and yourself in the clear.'

Share salesmen who were sacked from one firm were sometimes made welcome at another, sometimes not. Most licensed dealers could not resist kicking a man when he's down.

Dealers, sometimes surreptitiously encouraged by their firms, would go to great lengths to extract information from employees of rival firms.

In May 1988, Tudorbury dealers had the bright idea of fixing a football game with Harvard Securities. The match with 'Tom's boys' was scheduled for lunchtime in St James's Park. The Tudorbury lads saw here an opportunity to get information, and maybe even new dealers. Doubtless for those reasons Harvard banned the match at the last minute.

Bucket shops with more to hide are often more cautious when it comes to recruitment. They want only their own kind.

Of course, not all dealers are that way inclined. Many prove to be misfits, too honest for their job, or not enough on the ball to cope with its demands. This is why the drop-out rate amongst would-be dealers is so phenomenal.

Irish share-pushers Bailey McMahon, Dublin, in April 1988, refused to send out its newsletter or written details on stock sold to prospective salesmen. The material did not bear scrutiny. Any potential recruit knew the score. Either he took the first plane to Dublin, or he rejected them out of hand. Likewise he knew to take with a pinch of salt the recruiting officer's: 'We will get TSA membership. We've applied and foresee no problems.'

Anyone who joins a bucket shop swiftly enough grasps what's going on, even if he's been lied to. He becomes a rebel, a pirate, a leper. If he was this way inclined anyway, he will take to his new life like a duck to water.

The pressure can take its toll. One boy at Tudorbury Securities, who was finding the selling hard going, put his head in his hands, muttering: 'Jesus . . . '

A successful dealer sitting opposite him looked up: 'Yes,' he said. This was the most encouragement the boy got there, and it proved not enough to pep up his dismal sales figures.

Selling in bear markets to clients who have some inkling of it can be hell. So also is the underhand competitiveness of licensed dealers which makes individuals' possessions, jobs and their very persons unsafe.

An eminent stockbroker once observed that licensed dealers live and work in hell. If that is so, it is at least a hell of their own making, in which they can be gloriously themselves.

Chapter Three

Secrets of the Two-Minute Sale

Investments that appear to be too good to be true often are. To increase the public's awareness of this is a major purpose of this book.

The investor has been most likely to make his contact with a licensed dealer by selling shares from the government privatisations at an apparently favourable price. This proved a major source of clients for these firms. Few clients knew the probable losses they were letting themselves in for, were they to continue trading.

Indeed the government privatisations have saved many licensed dealers from going bust for lack of business. There are severe limits to the numbers of client lists that can be purchased. Furthermore, the process of converting names into dealing clients was time-consuming and costly, although it would have been far less economical still if the Department of Trade's regulations had been properly adhered to.

Dealers regarded the punters' concern to make a profit on, say, £500 worth of Rolls Royce shares with a contempt peculiar to the City whizz-kids they aspired to become. There was indeed method in their madness.

Small clients handled roughly from what sounded like a hectic dealing room got turned on by the apparent professionalism of it all, and often allowed themselves to be persuaded into buying almost worthless over the counter (OTC) shares.

The dealer would try to persuade the new client to re-invest not just the £500 he got from selling his Rolls Royce shares, for instance, but as much money in addition as he could be persuaded to part with, regardless of how far this was in his interest.

The dealer's first task was to get the client to agree to sell his Rolls Royce shares. His best way of doing this was somehow to lead the client into suggesting it himself. Then in case of recriminations afterwards, the client's own words would be safely recorded on tape.

'It's us or them,' one dealer kept saying, and this represented his firm's attitude.

The client would usually be looking secretly for guidance, and would be likely not just to sell out of his Rolls Royce shares, but to reinvest his original £500 with any profit, plus say £1,000 further capital in the stock proposed. A skilful dealer may get considerably more money than that out of the punter, by implying, sometimes even saying directly, that this OTC stock was a *better* buy even than Rolls Royce. The returns might be as quick and much higher, he would suggest.

The dealer would also imply that the client should come out of the new Rolls Royce issue *immediately*. His line would be something like this: 'You made money on the Rolls Royce, sir. With a little help, you can make a lot more money through share-dealing. I'm sure you'll agree it's a matter of going into the right stock at the right time. It's a good idea of yours to come out of the Rolls Royce while the going's good. Analysts are saying that the price will be static for a while, or might even go down. I'll put you down for 5,000 of this new one at 50p each, or could you manage 10,000?'

'I'd better just have £1,000 worth initially. If this does well, we'll look to doing some more business,' the client might reply.

A few days later, the dealer would ring and persuade his client to invest in another stock, on the grounds that for making money a portfolio of several shares was needed. He would never expressly suggest that one or two might go down, but would rather point to an accumulation of profits as deriving from several shares and not just one. He would work on the client by suggesting what he wanted to hear, and the client would be entranced.

The hardest sell of all was perhaps when the dealer said: 'You *will* do well on this. You can be assured of making a good profit.' Then he would qualify these certainties at the end, once the client had agreed to buy with something like: 'Of course, you'll appreciate that, as with any shares, I can make no absolute guarantees, but this is the best opportunity I've seen for a while.'

The dealer would usually get away with this, if tapes were checked, but clients were unlikely to complain, as they would recall the dealer's insistence that he could make no guarantees. Indeed, most clients would have shown their appreciation, at the time of sale, of the dealer's fairness in pointing out that he could make no guarantees. No clients wanted to appear ignorant about the market to their dealers.

Behind their backs, the dealer would call his clients 'suckers', saying: 'There's one born every minute', and, 'They just haven't got a chance'. This was his job satisfaction.

Clients who rang one licensed dealer and asked, for example, whether they should sell British Airways shares, assumed they would receive an unbiased opinion. It may be that from a stockbroker they would have done, although there is room for argument. It was possible, however, that from a licensed dealer they would be getting nothing of the kind.

For a start, most dealers were young and ignorant characters who before drifting into their present positions might have been on the dole, or at University, or in menial office jobs, at which time they probably didn't even know what stocks and shares were. It is a sad and generally unrealised truth that the client who had been investing for upwards of nine months, probably knew considerably more than a new dealer.

Even an experienced dealer would offer only limited advice. The bulk of his information would doubtless come from the newspapers, the same source his clients used. One slight distinction must, however, be outlined.

The client, even if financially unsophisticated, would probably read *The Daily Telegraph* or *The Times;* failing that, the *Independent* or the *Guardian*. Not so the dealer, who would be more likely to take a middle-of-the-road tabloid newspaper such as the *Daily Mail* or the *Daily Express*, as a source of more concentrated financial news, with a lay-out less taxing on his brain cells.

Some dealers read no papers except the least sophisticated tabloids like *The Sun*. These, at least until recently, hardly kept them up to date at all with stock market developments. Thus the dealers were forced to bluff the more, which amazingly, made them into more effective salesmen.

Of course, some clients too would read the *Daily Mail* and the *Daily Express*, in which case they would be as loathe as dealers to reveal the fact for similar snob reasons. This could cause problems, when, for example, a client read something nasty about Harvard in the *Daily Mail*, but did not feel able to mention it. For example, one client told his dealer: 'I happened to see an item in my secretary's *Daily Mail*.' The dealer, of course, would not mention unfavourable articles in any press unless he got asked.

The Daily Telegraph has printed numerous articles criticising the cold-calling techniques of licensed dealers, and their poor stock performances. The newspaper has a security-conscious approach antithetical to that of licensed dealers.

The *Daily Mail* has entered into the OTC market's spirit of enterprise, but has qualified this with constant awful warnings about licensed dealers and their stocks. The newspaper seems to specialise in witty opening lines. For example, here are the first lines of an article warning against OTC-traded Bio-Isolates: 'Watch out, watch out . . . The Bio bug's about: There are bugs that creep, bugs that crawl, sometimes bugs that hide in your bed. And there's a special kind of stock market bug — the biotechnology bug. He works on your wallet.'

Dealers were constantly pestered by journalists of national newspapers. They found this exciting. The most professional approach was to be polite but say nothing. This demanded an

Eyas Securities Ltd, 12 Borough High Street, London SE1 whose clients' boots were filled, metaphorically speaking, with incestuously linked shares.

articulateness beyond the abilities of most dealers. The *Daily Mail* printed an article headed, 'Slam down the phone on Eyas', querying the management of OTC-traded Crane Holdings and the credibility of this licensed dealer's directors. A further warning article followed shortly in the same paper. Eyas Securities got on the defensive: 'The article was misleading and the *Daily Mail* has apologised,' an Eyas dealer claimed to a potential client. Generally, dealing managers have had to bargain with journalists to keep their firms' names out of the national press.

Dealers at Harvard Securities found it amusing to ring up a client at 8.20 a.m. and to interrupt his shaving, breakfasting, or love-making in order to press him into buying stock. It also proved effective. Caught at such a weak moment, the client could not help feeling the situation was urgent, and was often more susceptible to persuasion. If the dealer backed his case with some item from that morning's news, he would appear thereby more on the ball. Of course, a tactless dealer irritated him even more at this sort of time.

Many licensed dealers' clients boast to friends of their broker, or their 'man in the City', who gives them tips. They believe, because they want to believe it, that he is offering disinterested advice, as best befits their needs. The skilful dealer does all he can to maintain the illusion, by, for example, saying reassuringly: 'My clients' interests are my own.'

Before selling, many dealers psyched themselves up. One dealer at Bailey McMahon, just before picking up the phone to speak with clients, would chant: 'I'll rip your head off. I'll shit down your fucking neck . . . ' Willpower often works — although it did not for Bailey McMahon, who found themselves on the receiving end of action by the Irish authorities.

Many dealers at Harvard Securities emulated this effective sales line for OTC stocks which a leading dealer introduced: 'What's wrong with this stock? Isn't it good enough for you?'

The more sales a dealer produces, the more revered he is by the rest. In the case of a female dealer, she is the more lusted after. A female dealer at Tudorbury Securities felt the hand of chief executive Roderick Alexander Innes Hamilton, affectionately known as RAI, sidling over her bottom as she was queuing at the SEAQ screen. She turned to him and smiled coolly: 'You wouldn't like me to size you up, would you?'

Share salesmen, even after A-Day, have upraised their status in the eyes of clients by quotation of imaginary praise from other clients, e.g. 'One of my clients is kind enough to say he's never had a bad tip from me.' If he is vague, it is impossible to prove he has lied.

In the licensed dealing game, impressions often counted for a lot. Sometimes dealers and clients alike wondered whether the whole thing wasn't just a game of bluff. Certainly, each party laughed at the other. Only, the last laugh was on the dealer, the client's sense of humour subsiding into resentment.

It was, after all, the dealer who manipulated the client, by giving him advice which was often biased to suit the requirements of his firm.

Despite being an ignoramus, the dealer who lasted even a matter of weeks would have a certain animal intelligence, as well as the true smooth operator's knack of twisting information to support the argument his firm insisted he presented.

At any given moment, he could present a convincing case for the client to sell British Telecom shares, reinvesting the proceeds, or to hang onto them and sit tight, or else to double up, or even to buy more shares in a distinctly dubious OTC stock, while hanging onto British Telecom. If he sounded logical and authoritative enough, the dealer would usually have his way.

To achieve this was a gift, and had little to do with how much he really knew. It is just as easy to sound authoritative if you know a little than if you know a lot. It is a question of personality, or more precisely how this is projected in the voice — down the telephone wires.

If for instance the market was temporarily down, following a sharp rise, a dealer would address the client with whichever of the following pitches both suited his sales needs and clicked with the client's mood and personality:

(1) *Buy another stock using fresh capital.* 'The market is down in the dumps. You'd be crazy to sell today. What I would suggest is that you seize the opportunity to buy . . . while the price is right. Make hay while the sun shines, you know. We'll cover the purchase by looking to coming out of your present holdings towards the end of the account, maybe today if the Index picks up . . . ' (N.B. If a client bought one stock today, and sold another tomorrow to pay for it, the time difference served as a cover for the dealer's churning. This so-called 'delayed churning' was commonplace.)

(2) *Buy another stock, transferring capital.* 'The market is looking grim. Quite frankly, we're worried how much further down it's still got to go. You'd better sell out of your holdings now, while you still can without too much of a loss. What I would suggest is a straight transfer into . . . which has resisted the general trend downwards, and should soon be moving right up. I'll do the exchange for you now. You won't be paying out more money. In fact we'll be sending you a small sum this time, for the difference.' (N.B. The dealer would do such a churn if he knew the client had no money from other sources.)

(3) *Pick up more shares in your present holding.* 'Hang onto your stock for goodness sake. The company's prospects are looking brilliant right now. The share price has only gone down because the market is generally down. Obviously the market is having an off day, and this is a marvellous opportunity for you to double your stake. You'll get shares today for far less than you paid for your present stake, and for astronomically less than their true value. What we're doing is called averaging out. The overall price you have paid for your shares is now . . . This is how the professionals make money in a bear market, you know. So now you've got . . . shares in . . . I'll ring you in the next account period, and I expect I'll have some very good

news for you.' (N.B. Buying more of the same stock seemed less like spending money, perhaps because it doesn't require the grasping of an entirely new situation.)

(4) *Sell out now. Buy big tomorrow.* 'Sell out of this now because you'll need those funds and a lot more tomorrow morning for a marvellous American stock we've got coming in. I'll put aside £5,000 worth for you. The shares should go quickly, so I'll ring you at 9.00 a.m. tomorrow. I don't suppose you'll be in the office earlier?' (N.B. The client may then say: 'You can catch me at home up to 8.30 a.m.).

(5) *Don't imagine I'm going to let you sell out of your holdings.* 'We're waiting for news on what we can expect the market to be doing tomorrow. Quite frankly, we're advising all our clients to sit tight, at the moment, and neither to buy nor to sell. I think you'll agree it would be counterproductive to act hastily at this stage. If it seems appropriate for you to sell, I promise you I will be back to you immediately. Are you in the office for the rest of the day, or are you going home? A good dealer might ring later and reassure the client. Many dealers would not bother.

The variations on these themes were endless.

One particularly effective line often used by dealers was as follows: 'Don't sell out this morning, sir. Wait until 2.30 p.m. when Wall Street opens. We're expecting good news from the States and there should be a knock-on effect.'

A person of conscience would never twist the truth in these ways, so the critics claim. The dealer's response was that every one of the positions was tenable, depending on which aspect of the truth was considered more important. In fact, total objectivity of vision is as much a gift as the ability to persuade people, and many dealers didn't have it. They believed, or almost believed, in what they were saying. They were often not interested enough to develop their own bona fide opinions.

The client who was not convinced and pacified by what his dealer said would not only refuse to trade further with him, but would not sleep easy at night, tormented by the thoughts of his investments tossing up and down like a rowing boat in a stormy sea. The smaller the client's investments, paradoxically the more bothered he got. Sadly the performance record of OTC stocks had little reassurance to offer him. The quickest way to discover this was often, sadly, the hard way.

The client who claimed he would rather know the truth was usually the type who would not. He who really wanted the facts had other sources by which he ascertained them, like his bank manager who invariably would advise steering clear of licensed dealers, and the OTC market in particular.

The streetwise client resorted to trickery, just like his dealer. If he

"We're virtually guaranteeing a profit! . . . It's as safe as Granny Bonds!"

said: 'I won't buy until I've seen written information on the stock', this frequently meant he had no intention of buying at all, and the astute dealer would pretend he was sending an Extel card (a written fact sheet on the stock) but in fact he would not bother. Afterwards, he could always claim that it was sent to an old or wrong address by mistake, or that it must have got lost in the post. Likewise the client who had received information could pretend it never came.

A client, to get a dealer off the phone, could say: 'I'll consider your proposition. If I'm interested, I'll ring you back. What's your number?' Once the dealer gave his number under these circumstances, he was submitting to the client's own terms, letting him off the hook.

Dealers would be taught to respond like this: 'We could do that. You'll appreciate though that with shares you've got to move quickly. What I would suggest is that you pick up 1,000 shares now at . . . There are not many guarantees I can make in this game, but one thing I can assure you of is that you now have 1,000 shares in . . . at . . . If you want to pick up some more, ring me back in the next twenty minutes. Don't leave it too late . . . '

(N.B. The dealer would himself ring the client fifteen minutes later, and would spin the following yarn: 'I've got just 5,000 shares left on my books. Take them!' A suggestible client would comply.)

Clients who have gone in for Public Issues often rue the day they chose to sell through a licensed dealer. Making money on speculative stocks was a far more remote possibility than on British Telecom or

TSB, although it might have taken them six months or longer to discover the bitter truth. By this time they might have gained a portfolio. They might well have got hooked. Their only prospect of immediate escape would be through selling everything, but the prices at which they'd do this might prove unexpectedly low. Their heads had been eased into the yoke, and they were now locked into the system.

A second stage would set in. Clients acquired a paternalistic interest in their stocks, started looking at profit figures and earnings per share, perhaps for the first time. They might ring up and ask why some of their share certificates had not arrived. They found themselves becoming increasingly dependent on their dealer's advice, at the same time sensing it might be fatal. Some clients pulled away by sheer willpower; many did not.

'Nothing ventured, nothing gained,' the punters told themselves. A few people were real risk-takers; these types were often company directors, and inveterate investors. They understood what they were going in for. Recognising sharp practice in their dealers from the outset, they would be less likely to blame them for huge losses. Sharp practice might even seem normal to some of them.

The majority of clients, it has to be said, were basic-rate tax-payers, educated perhaps, but too trusting. Many did not know the difference between a licensed dealer and a stockbroker. They were impressed by professional looking brochures. Even a name carried weight. For example, Harvard Securities may have reminded them of Harvard Business School, although no claims of any connection were made. Financial Planning Ltd sounded very orientated to clients' interests. The columns displaying prices of licensed dealers' stocks in the national newspapers did not always appear to be the paid advertising they actually were. Nor was it generally known that some newspapers had declined to accept such advertising on ethical grounds.

What was it about the stocks various licensed dealers traded in that seduced clients? The dealer's colourful stories captivated their imagination, made capital of their greed. The sales pitches were frequently exaggerated. Here follow some pointers that were actually used. Your author wishes to make clear that in no way are any aspersions being cast upon the firms involved.

(1) *Crane Holdings (Eyas Securities OTC)*
A Northamptonshire based engineering company, with a subsidiary that handles removal of asbestos.

Crane Holdings are what is left of Crane-Freuhauf, the well-known trailer manufacturers that used to be around.

MOD orders are coming through after a recent exhibition in Scandinavia.

With the looming British Steel flotation, Crane's services are much in demand.

Crane Holdings have just taken over Grey Rook PLC, which has a three year trading record. By this acquisition Crane can get a listing on the USM which is what the directors want.

You remember Parkfield Engineering, on the OTC briefly, then straight onto the USM, with a phenomenal rise in share price. This is what Crane Holdings should do within a few months.

Here are the real facts: Crane Holdings was in fact a highly speculative investment which in the event performed very badly. As its prospectus very properly pointed out, the subsidiary Crane Engineering Ltd was in receivership, but this fact was not pointed out to investors by Eyas dealers.

The subsidiary handling removal of asbestos was owned by a director of Eyas Securities.

Crane Holdings was no offshoot of Crane-Freuhauf.

The MOD reneged on its orders.

A reference to British Steel was something the punters would relate to, much to the dealers' amusement.

Crane Holdings did *not* achieve a Stock Exchange listing, but the share price collapsed when Eyas Securities, on A-Day (29 April 1988), was stopped from trading.

The shares, probably worth around 15p on fundamentals had been sold at various prices up to a staggering 45p.

(2) *Osprey Financial Trust (Eyas Securities OTC)*
A specialist in corporate finance, advising City institutions.

They have taken a major stake in Crane Holdings.

The shares trading at around 10p, should gain 50% in value on the back of figures due in December 1987. Come in big.

Osprey Financial Trust was the parent company of Eyas Securities, an Eyas being a baby Osprey. This link accounted for Osprey's directors' interest in Crane Holdings which was part of the same network. Investors were not told of these connections before they purchased the shares.

Figures were *not* released in December. Sadly the share price never saw the proposed gain. Clients unable to break even, let alone to sell out at a profit, found themselves locked in.

(3) *Waterslides (Harvard OTC)*
'They are opening the world's largest water-theme park, just outside Madrid. I can tell you confidentially that a well-known boxer who owns a company has been stake-building. I can't tell you his name . . . '

Investors who bought on the strength of this pitch saw the share price drop. Subsequently, a serious accident at the company's water-theme park in Surrey had a detrimental effect on its public profile.

Here is one client's comment: "On 30th October 1986 I naively, and reluctantly purchased 2,000 shares in 'Waterslides' from an 'enthusiastic' hard-sell Harvard salesman . . . . I have tried to sell the shares on several occasions through Harvard, having been told 'now is not the time to sell,' and 'best I can do is 5p.' Having paid 38p per share, I thought I would wait."

(4) *Rigby Electronics (Harvard OTC)*
'They've just brought out a device for checking whether a credit card belongs to a particular person or not. This is very much in demand, with so many credit card thefts going on at the moment.'

The above may be so, but it took a long while for anything significant to happen to the share price.

(5) *Bleasdale Computers (Harvard OTC)*
'The company has just arranged a major deal with British Telecom who will market and supply their computers. The share price is only 6p. It has previously been as high as 60p, and should rocket.'

This one proved a disaster, doing nothing significant, and the huge spread prevented investors from selling out except at a substantial loss. The fact that the share price had been 60p did not mean it would return to that level.

(6) *Hilton Mining (Harvard OTC)*
'Between ourselves, somebody may be picking up a huge stake in this company. In a week or two, the share price could be right up . . . '

Within weeks, the directors in charge of the dealing room were instructing dealers to prevent clients from selling out at all costs. The shares were suddenly suspended, and returned, worth almost nothing in the form of an investment holding company with plans to bring a Harvard director, Charles Mitchell, onto the board. Following this manoeuvre, the Harvard dealing director and dealers questioned the performance of Harvard's corporate finance department. Later, Clive Lawrence resigned from that department.

(7) *Spencer King (Harvard OTC)*
'They're a recovery engineering stock. They should be getting a lot of work through the Channel Tunnel project. They appeared on TV last night.'

Another poor tip, insofar as it has mainly lost clients money. The TV appearance was so brief that it hardly warranted comment.

(8) *Audiotext (Harvard OTC)*
'They are expanding their telephone lines dramatically, as they are getting several times the number of calls they had anticipated.'

Another failure in terms of making money for investors. Many dealers didn't think much of their recorded lines either.

(9) *Pacific Records (Harvard OTC)*
'They are major distributors of compact discs. Their clients include Virgin, Our Price, and HMV. They were tipped in the Investor's Chronicle . . . '

They were tipped as a recovery stock after investors had lost much of their money in a few months.

(10) *Thew Engineering (Harvard OTC)*
'They helped to lift the Mary Rose . . . '

Clients came in at 45p plus, only to see the share price drop rapidly to 18p, although it did later recover.

(11) *Weymouth Clinic (Harvard OTC)*
'They have the backing of the AMA who should be putting patients their way.'

An appalling 'short-term' investment, which it was sold as. Investors lost more than half their money on this one.
  Here is one client's comment: "I bought shares in Weymouth Clinic as a result of a concentrated selling spiel on the telephone. It was strongly hinted that "a dividend is expected in a few weeks time" which is equivalent to "a discount on the purchase price." Of course the company didn't pay any dividend, and has now been taken over by a firm making china and porcelain goods. I received a porcelain candlestick as a gift from this company last Christmas, and judging by the quality of that product, I doubt whether dividends can be expected from that quarter either!"

(12) *For Eyes (Harvard OTC)*
'They've got eighteen opticians, including a fantastic new one in Oxford Street . . . '

Too many shops too quickly, judging by their losses, and the takeover by Cooper Vision, leading to a drop in share price.

  One dealer would pitch Towerbell Records in this way. He would say to clients in his gruff, urgent voice: 'Have you heard of Bruce Springsteen?'
  'Yes' the client would say excitedly.
  'I didn't say that,' the dealer would continue. 'But Towerbell Records are signing people up, I can tell you, so come in heavy.'

The dealer knew full well that Bruce Springsteen was not signed up by Towerbell. He also knew how to sell shares.

Another dealer would sell an Australian goldmining stock, by saying: 'Do you want to be a millionaire?' His clients were entranced.

The tragedy of clients' huge losses is that they were sometimes led to believe they would make fortunes on the above stocks within a month or two, maybe within three or four weeks. As a long-term hold (i.e. at least six months) *some* of these stocks weren't so bad.

Harvard dealers were frequently selling shares in their own company. To some clients this seemed a cheek, but few regulars could resist the line: 'You've got the cart. Now buy the donkey that pulls it.' Besides, Harvard's own shares, when purchased in sufficient quantity, dispensed with the need for clients to pay the £12 administration cheque on their deals.

This is not, however, the perk it seems, as clients were perpetually dreaming and plotting to stop dealing with Harvard. If they had more efficient stockbrokers, they might indeed have broken away from Harvard long before. As it was, some struggled on, more often than not incurring further losses. Anyone who bought Harvard's own shares got effectively locked in, as it would take three months to sell out, on the matched bargain basis — a fact not usually explained to the client at the time of sale.

The riskiest OTC stocks can attract surprisingly intelligent investors. MENSA, the organisation for people with very high IQs, started an investment club which bought from one sharedealer an American OTC stock Biotech Capital Corporation. The share price promptly plummeted.

There were, occasionally, high performers on the OTC market. Leading Leisure and Corton Beach spring to mind. Dealers, after working in the business for a month, could pinpoint the good ones. So could the wiser clients.

At Harvard, to sell shares in Leading Leisure, for instance, was always relatively easy. Investors who had watched the company's share price climb often wanted to increase their own stakes, or were amenable to the suggestion that they should.

The power of the Press is dangerously high. Corton Beach were tipped in the national newspapers just before they left the OTC to start on the London Stock Exchange's third market. This led to frenzied buying orders.

When companies such as Airship Industries, who are known internationally for their airships in advertising and military defence, were tipped in the press, there followed a flurry of buying, without the dealers having to work at it. Dealers, normally reluctant to answer phones (to likely sell orders), then competed to take the calls.

Whoever received and processed a buy order would gain both the commission and a client, without having had to prospect in the first place. It was money for old rope.

Indeed, the author once took a phone-in for 100,000 shares in Leading Leisure, which netted him a substantial commission, although he had to fight off an unscrupulous colleague who had tried to seize the telephone receiver.

Clients would fare better if they examined profit figures, checked track records. Most OTC companies were all gas and promises, no substance.

Clients stupidly trusted their dealers. 'You're in the City. You should know,' one client said, and his attitude was typical. If he had been a little more aware, he would have realised that licensed dealers were largely excluded from the square mile, both physically and psychologically.

The many Harvard dealers who introduced themselves: 'This is . . . from Harvard Securities in the City of London' were perhaps sharing in their company's wishful thinking. No less optimistic was Harvard's attitude that employees should maintain the standards of dress appropriate in any 'City' firm. Harvard was not a City firm.

After Big Bang, private clients discovered that stockbrokers were offering them an increasingly impersonal service. During the market decline in August and September 1987, many brokers weren't even answering the phones. There were proposals for a telephone price information service at 38p a minute for private clients. Clients would then only have to phone stockbrokers to deal, so every phone call should generate commission. This, if implemented, would have led to a still more impersonal service. While such proposals were being mooted, it is no wonder licensed dealers were still in demand.

Licensed dealers offered a personal service, but this was marred by their self-interest. Amongst firms wound up early on, Prior Harwin was alleged to have mixed clients' money with its own, to have been mismanaged, and to have had insufficient indemnity insurance. Greenwood International Securities was said to have given biased advice. Trafalgar Capital took clients' money and vanished.

Nor was the OTC stock the only poor performer licensed dealers offered, although it without doubt put up a worse show than most shares traded on the Stock Exchange.

Licensed dealers also specialised in penny shares. A few of these were known to have galloped, often due to tipsheet promotion, and herd instinct buying, leading to an inflation of the share price beyond what the assets and figures justified. Indeed the chairman of Rotaprint, a penny highflier, publicly admitted in August 1987 that his company was overvalued. This led to a bursting of the bubble. Investors, some of whom might have earlier come out with a fortune were suddenly losing.

The penny share flourishes on the fallacy that if you get more shares for your money, you must be getting a better buy. The large spreads (up to 25%) and thin markets of many penny shares are reminiscent of the OTC market, and indeed most licensed dealers have traded in both.

The Stock Exchange's Unlisted Securities Market (USM) has not always performed well. Ever since Tom Wilmot won his historic battle with the Inland Revenue to deal in USM shares without incurring 1% stamp duty on every transaction, licensed dealers have welcomed and participated in the growth of this secondary market.

It remains relatively easy for a USM stock to obtain a listing on the London Stock Exchange. A three year trading record (sometimes not even that) is needed, instead of the five year record required for full listing, and advertising requirements are less onerous. Only 10% of a USM company's securities need be in public hands, as opposed to 25% for listed companies. The USM shares often have a very thin market like penny shares, so a few buyers will send the price right up.

The USM has had big successes, such as the Burford Group, a property investment company which came to the market in March 1986 at 80p, and in September 1987 was trading at 420p. In August 1987, top USM stocks under scrutiny for a new monthly rating by chartered accountant Deloite Haskins & Sells included: Burford Group, Glentree (Estate Agents), Rockwood Holdings (Electronic Components Distributor), Regina Health and Beauty.

It has proved possible to make a spectacular gain on the USM, but also a spectacular loss. Investors in the USM as in OTC stocks dealt all too often on grounds of glamour, as distinct from sound track record and figures. Some shares on the USM have outrageous P/E ratios. The momentum often subsides, leading to a tumbling of the share price.

The ride on a climbing USM stock such as Tyne Tees Television during the bull market was breathtaking. Spreads (i.e. differences between buying and selling prices) have sometimes been enormous, particularly if quoted by a Harvard market-maker when they would sometimes overreach the 10% level.

Licensed dealers have made markets in some USM stocks, and have dealt through stockbrokers in the rest. Many a Harvard dealer has needed to haggle with one of the market-makers in the adjoining room, in order to obtain something like a fair deal for his client.

If the market-maker of one dealer wanted to take back shares in a specific USM stock in order to balance his books, he would scribble 'bid only' over any quote slip the runner would present him on behalf of a dealer. If he was willing to part with stock as well, the market-maker would quote a two-way price.

He was not supposed to know whether the dealer was buying or selling on his client's behalf, but nonetheless he attempted to guess this from the runner's facial expression and comments. He was in a position to adjust his price to maximise potential gain for the firm, and to minimise it for the client.

He would sometimes ask the runner directly, before quoting a price. The runner would tell him in cases when the dealer clearly did not mind whether or not he would get the best price for his client.

For the dealer who *did* want a good price, the procedure became a matter of negotiation, and it paid him to buy the market-maker a drink sometimes.

Once TOPIC and SEAQ screens had been introduced into a firm, the dealer could check what approximate price he ought to be getting, to be varied by what the firm took off or added to quote its price 'net' of commission. That way he had a basis for haggling. If he did not haggle, he would sooner or later lose out, with a consequent loss for his client.

In the author's time, there was always a queue in front of the TOPIC screen at Harvard, although many dealers didn't know how to work its controls.

Which USM stocks did licensed dealers recommend? Harvard (1986-87) bought in bulk stocks such as Hobsons, Tyne Tees TV, Dewey Warren, Monument Oil and Gas, Derek Bryant, etc. Dealers have pumped these out to clients who often have an aversion to OTC (too risky) and to listed stocks (too boring). In the words of a Harvard director, they want something 'a little bit sexy'. Once Harvard had disposed of a stock, the price would often drop. This was because it was often bought at a high.

The individual Harvard dealer also picked his own USM stocks for trading. One dealer of the author's acquaintance was guided by a specialist journal from the Fleet Street Letter stable. Others relied on the weekly USM reports in the London Evening *Standard* (Fridays) and *The Times* (Mondays). One Harvard team for instance, punted out Campbell & Armstrong, and Rockwood Holdings on the basis of write-ups in *The Times*.

In their sales pitch for such stocks, some dealers would make out the recommendation hailed from their own research department, but by coincidence, *The Times* had seen fit to tip the stock as well.

Clients were invariably impressed by guff about 'our analyst', and 'our research team'.

Dealers who have left Harvard to go to other firms will tell their ex-Harvard clients that Harvard didn't in fact have that much in the way of research facilities, but clients were reluctant to accept this. Significantly many successful Harvard dealers have failed in later life.

Some dealers at various firms would sell specific USM stocks on the account immediately after they had bought enormous quantities of the same shares for themselves. A manager at one dealer did this regularly. He would, for instance, secretly buy 30,000 of a stock for himself on the account. He would then sell it on the account to all his big clients. Furthermore he would instruct all the dealers in his charge to do the same, on the grounds that a joint effort would shift the share price, and that, besides, the company's prospects were good anyway.

Due to a relatively thin market in the stock, the share price would climb. This unscrupulous dealer (now at a stockbroker) would then pull out of his own holding before the bubble burst, well within the account. On occasions when the whole dealing room was punting out the stock, the price might climb even further.

Anybody who 'ramps' or causes 'ramping' of USM stocks in this way cares more for the profits on his own transaction — profits possibly running into thousands of pounds — than he does for those of his clients.

Nonetheless, sometimes clients made money through such practice. It all depends at what stage the dealer chose to take him out. At other times, both the ramping dealer and the clients would lose out.

It was important for a dealer occasionally to make profits for clients, if he wanted to stay in business.

One dealer of the author's acquaintance would keep telling his clients: 'There's been a lot of buying this morning' when what he really meant was the dealers had been selling the stock all morning. He thus conveyed the false impression that it was in demand.

Another dealer would regularly punt out £40,000 or so worth of stock or so on the account to — wait for it — a school dinner lady. Another dealt a vicar 130 times in nine months, reducing a £30,000 portfolio to around £8000. He then brought up the £8000 to £18,000 by steering clear of the OTC, and the vicar was ecstatic that at last he seemed to be making some money.

The dealer moved to another firm and stuffed the client with £12,000 worth of a speculative American stock which ultimately proved a dud.

From his original £30,000, the client had finished up with around £6000.

One dealer would regularly say to his clients: 'I've just had lunch with the market-maker. I know he's anxious to move up the price.' This was usually untrue.

This same dealer would sometimes take clients out of many solid stocks to reinvest proceeds in just one huge holding in an OTC stock. As the bargains were all processed, records were kept of what he and other dealers were doing.

The dodgiest deals — discretionary, and big account trades — were done whilst the chairman of an OTC firm was addressing the dealing floor. Dealers would then whisper appalling things into the telephone knowing that they would not be monitored.

Harvard Securities introduced its own Personal Equity Plan Scheme (PEPS) which uniquely involved USM stocks. Like PEPS everywhere, this was slow to catch on, especially as dealers were forced to sell it for days at a time without getting paid commission for it, so most didn't bother.

Another reason for the lack of interest in PEPS is that its benefits were predictable and it tied up clients' money for at least a year. Clients of licensed dealers wanted *exciting* stocks, which would move *quickly.*

PEPS capital gains tax savings were of value only to those whose capital gains had in the given year exceeded the free allowance — not a predicament in which the average punter found himself.

Later, a carrot was offered to dealers who should sell Harvard's PEPS schemes. A fiver was paid in cash for every PEPS application form that a client sent back to Harvard.

This motivated dealers more than a previously introduced incentive to sell PEPS which had been merely an increase in dealers' OTC takeback allowance.

Still not much PEPS got sold. Harvard's dealing director started getting desperate. Finally, he shouted to all dealers: 'Ring all the clients that made money by coming into Helene of London on your advice. Pitch them on PEPS.'

Yet again the PEPS pushers worked pretty well in vain. So few forms came back.

The effective dealer always made a client feel that he had personally decided to go into any given investment. One way of achieving this was by closing each sale by some phrase like: 'It seems foolish to miss this one, but it's up to you.'

An ineffectual or inexperienced salesman would remind clients that he had 'put' them into their stocks. Clients didn't like being told they had been manipulated, and in the circumstances would be likely to terminate relations with that dealer.

Licensed dealers may offer facilities for trading in options. Harvard, for example, had its own options department. However, this form of investment has proved a dangerous risk for clients.

Once clients got launched into the option game by a licensed dealer, one of two situations developed. Either they became hooked on them, like gamblers to the roulette table — having no time, no inclination and no money left to invest in equities. Alternatively, they lost so much money so frequently on them that they became disillusioned with all options and by proxy any other financial instruments. In a word, they were *no longer* clients.

Of course, money tied up in options furnished just one of numerous excuses the client used to terminate relations with his licensed dealer. Another excuse was that he needed liquidity for a property deal or something of the sort, so a complete sell out would be necessary within the next month or so, albeit with the least possible losses.

The salesmen at one licensed dealer generally managed to persuade such clients to stay in their shares on grounds that the share price was perpetually due to move up, so they could avoid the losses they would incur through selling out at that moment.

Warrants were less addictive than options, and on the OTC market (except in rare cases like that of Corton Beach warrants) were no money spinner.

Warrants on shares rise and fall by approximately the same amount in pence as the share price, but by a much larger percentage of their trading price.

Dealers at one licensed dealer were instructed to sell specific OTC warrants on a specific day, just like shares. They would offer them as a high reward investment (playing down the risk) with all the liquidity of shares, and with a potential to convert into shares perhaps on one specific day each year.

The client who bought warrants often didn't understand what they were, although he would pretend to. This was hardly surprising as his dealers often didn't understand either. The client would puzzle out an explanation later, if he got informed by letter of his right to exercise the warrants. Then he might ask his dealer's advice.

By this stage, he who sold the client his warrants would probably have left the firm. If not, he would almost certainly be unwilling *and* unable to advise whether or how to exercise the warrants. The same could be said for his successor. After all, they got no further commission for such a service.

The client invariably had to make up his own mind, that is if he was lucky enough to be alerted to the exact opportunity. Some owners of OTC-traded warrants claimed that they had never received anything written about exercising them at all.

Often clients of licensed dealers who were genuinely interested in options would be easily led into warrants. There were clients who continually pestered dealers about their warrants. How did dealers not well versed in the technicalities of these cope?

One popular way was for the dealer to refer his client to somebody in the administration or accounts departments, or else to the director in charge of such details. The client then had to ring a different number.

Even if the phone was answered, the client might not get through to the person he wanted. If he did, he might not get a satisfactory answer. If the person promised to ring him back, he might fail to do so. The administrative backlogs and incompetence at certain licensed dealers became a nightmare for clients.

It was sometimes stated on contract notes that the firm, as well as the clients, owed interest when late in settling. One controversial licensed dealer often did not pay its interest due, although expected it from clients.

Further clients of this firm were often asked for interest payments they did *not* owe. How did they sort out the mess?

Dealers often advised pet clients to demand to speak to the chairman. Clients who did this suddenly found their complaints listened to.

Clients who withheld money they owed often achieved satisfaction on their particular bone of contention. Money counts with licensed dealers. As a Harvard director once put it, 'Money talks, bullshit walks.'

The Harvard dealer was on the sharp end of clients' complaints. It was he who had to listen to how the clients could never get through on the telephone, how they were chased by debt collectors even when they had paid, how they could not find up to the minute share prices, etc.

The good dealer was something of a social worker as well as a salesman, developing a very intensive relationship with clients who didn't mind being churned every day. Sharedealing developed into the pretext for regular human contact on the part of lonely clients who carried on trading because they could not live without that friendly familiar voice on the other end of the telephone.

Some dealers derived pleasure from the clients. It would boost their egos to talk to a director of a leading bank, or a key man in a well-known company as an equal, and it was incredibly revealing how little such high up people seemed to know about shares, how desperately motivated they were by greed.

When the London Stock Exchange's new third tier market started up, most punters were interested. Here was an OTC style casino, only with official back-up. Most held their breath and tried a punt or two on the third market stocks their licensed dealer recommended, which in some cases had been quoted on the OTC market earlier. Some dealers tried to convey the false impression that the two markets were in cahoots.

Prior to the 1987 stock market crash, the third market went through lean periods. The share prices of Catalyst Communications and of Corton Beach, strictly on a temporary basis, dropped back; these erstwhile giants of the OTC market seemed to have come a cropper.

'You'll be better off investing in OTC stocks,' Harvard dealers urged; they were paid a higher commission on OTC than on third market sales.

The Third Market had considerable advantages over the OTC. Liquidity was better. Third market companies had to find a member firm to sponsor them who would ensure not only the suitability of the company for trading, but also that the company's decisions were communicated to the shareholders, and that there was an effective and orderly market in the shares.

Third market companies remain 'gamma' or 'delta' securities for the purposes of SEAQ and TOPIC. This means a punter can follow the price movements himself, or obtain up to date prices from his stockbroker. Likewise, transactions in third market stocks must be trade-reported, and are subject to publication in the Stock Exchange Daily Official List on the following day.

The Third Market, like the USM before it, doubtless owes its existence in part to the competition posed by Harvard Securities and the OTC market. Despite this, the new market must have met a demand as its performance was soon outpacing the FTSE 100 index. This is in spite of a poor start, in which the Irish based Eglinton Oil and Gas performed unpredictably.

The OTC traders have gained an enormous amount of extra business from the Government's Business Expansion Scheme (BES). This has, however, dwindled since investors have found increasing access to a form of BES unshackled by the OTC.

The BES originated in 1981, offering tax relief to investors in the form of the Government's Business Start-Up Scheme. The scheme probably led to no more than £20 million being invested, and so a more attractive plan was formulated.

Under the BES that has succeeded it, UK residents can invest up to £40,000 in one or more UK resident companies. There is a minimum investment of £500 per company. Relief is paid at the tax-payer's top marginal rate of income tax, provided the investment is retained for five years.

After this date, the shares may be sold without losing relief, although capital gains tax is payable, subject to the usual free allowance. If the shares are sold before five years are up, there is a clawback of tax relief.

The higher rate tax payer has found the entire scheme irresistible to such an extent that he has invested in companies he would otherwise not have touched. Is this sensible? If he loses all his money, it is no use his having saved tax. After five years, there is no guarantee BES sponsored companies will survive.

What sort of companies have attracted BES support? There have been some very diverse schemes, including a wine company that after five years would offer investors a taste of the booty. Amongst other BES companies, we have seen a school in St John's Wood, and a company proposing to use investors' money to breed pedigree mohair-producing Angora goats, and to produce an Angora 'super-goat' through cross-breeding.

The BES fund is an alternative that has been made available to investors. Such funds usually offer less flexibility than individual shares handpicked by the investor. If one share in a client's portfolio is relinquished, tax benefits can be retained through the remaining shares. If a client sells out of a BES fund — no easy matter — he loses his entire tax savings.

It was quite common for an affluent client to insist: 'I'm only interested in BES schemes', although a skilful dealer would tempt him into a short-term punt in a stock outside the BES.

If an affluent investor had invested in a poor stock, he might not object as he would enjoy setting losses against capital gains for the year. This would appeal to his sense of order, even if he should lose out financially.

Dealers were told to say to clients: 'We're getting involved in the BES next year in a bigger way.'

This did not in fact happen, but the earlier suggestion of it kept some of the wealthier clients on tap.

In the 1987 budget, a 'carryback' was introduced for BES investors, enabling them to carry back to the previous tax year relief on up to £5,000 invested. The purpose was to prevent crowding of BES issues at the end of the tax year, but the ceiling limit meant that investors putting up the full £40,000 still made most of their investments as near as they could to 5th April.

A survey published in September 1986 by accountants Peat Marwick Mitchell revealed that out of a total of 213 British companies seeking a flotation on the OTC markets by August 1st 1986, 80 raised money under the BES terms, and more than half the OTC entrants were BES schemes.

Obviously BES depresses the liquidity of the OTC market, since sellers of BES investments would lose their tax relief. As a result of this, upward mobility in the OTC market has been adversely affected. A company seeking a flotation might be better off skipping the OTC and starting out on the third market or USM.

The OTC market in America is taken seriously. Top American brokerage Weedin & Co has constantly rejected the New York Stock Exchange for the American OTC market, which it considers superior, and this attitude is by no means uncommon. Literally hundreds of US companies that have qualified for exchange listings have elected to remain on the OTC, preferring a more competitive system of market making to a single exchange specialist.

One or two OTC dealers in order to present an aggressive American image, as well as to convey by implication a market of the status of the American OTC, toss around American phrases and terms in their sales presentations. These are perhaps more appropriate when offering an American OTC stock. References to 'poison pills', 'shark repellants' and 'golden parachutes' irritate some investors even as they impress others — and they flummox almost everybody.

Some dealers would do well to heed the advice offered by Mark McCormack in his book *What They Don't Teach You at Harvard Business School* — 'Awareness of when you are imposing can be an important asset.'

The NASDAQ system has increased the American OTC market's liquidity. There is no evidence that the UK OTC market will ever attain its size and respectability.

Clients will never love the UK OTC market, or at best will only love an isolated stock or two, like Hard Rock Cafe, which achieved a proper stock market listing in the UK and in the United States, and which was taken over by Pleasurama in July 1988. Compulsive investors in the UK's OTC market enjoy at best a love-hate relationship with the stocks, the dealers, and the whole manic unpredictability of it all, weighted against their interests though it is.

Clients who are truly hooked will go to any length to meet their dealers' demands. They will take out overdrafts, empty their building society accounts, even sell their second houses. Licensed dealers will hold surplus money on deposit from them and take every penny they can. However, nobody seems to blame the clients for falling prey to their own greed and stupidity.

In April 1988, just before A-Day, a top dealer set new standards of ruthlessness. He got clients into his grip and pressed them to buy shares in huge quantities. They begged him to let them off this time, but he rang back hour after hour, day after day: 'Sell your car. Mortgage your home. Get an overdraft.'

Clients settled for amounts they didn't have. They just dug it out from somewhere.

The attitude of another dealer was almost more callous. A client bought from him a large quantity of shares in an infamous OTC stock which went bust. The client lost money he could not afford. He rang up his dealer, almost deranged: 'What shall I do?' he ranted.

'How the fuck should I know? Go and jump in the Thames,' said the dealer. The client was heard from no more.

The relationship between dealer and client is not always divorced from the occult. A salesman at one licensed dealer used to read his clients' horoscopes for them. He would then say something like: 'The sun is in Pisces. It's your lucky day today. And this is the share you should be going for. Come in big . . . '

Even FIMBRA members have succumbed to the continental share

sharks. Professional investment analysts and advisers are sometimes attracted to the OTC market like bees to the proverbial honeypot, and significantly seem no more interested in figures and ratios than the common or garden punter.

Accountants sometimes pretend interest in the figures, but this subsides when the dealer tells them what they want to hear: 'I earn my living by making people money. If you want to make money, just listen to what I say. Don't worry about P/E ratios and profit figures. Put in £5,000, and sit tight for eight to ten weeks.'

Oil stocks are particularly easy to sell, because a dealer can twist the latest news to substantiate his pitch, e.g. the situation in the Middle East indicates that there will be a massive rise in oil prices. He can waffle on about OPEC ad infinitum, and most clients won't know what the hell he's talking about, but they'll pretend to agree with him and will buy on the strength of what he says.

Furthermore, the dealer can point to the oil stocks that have made investors good money, e.g. Monument Oil and Gas, Clyde Petroleum, Cluff Oil, Britoil. He can claim, whether truthfully or not, that he had recommended clients to come in at exactly the right times. He need not mention any of the failures.

The only time the ace dealer comes a cropper here is when he stumbles across a client who works in the oil trade. One dealer at a London based sharedealing outfit was selling an unknown oil and gas stock to a client who replied: 'I work in the oil industry myself, and these speculative situations, I know, can go badly wrong. I'll pass on this one.'

Many see oil stocks as too risky. For instance, a sales pitch claiming that a major discovery has been made in the North Sea sounds suspect to the investor who has lost out several times in the past.

Some dealers find it hilarious when clients take their investments so seriously that they investigate the OTC companies personally. Their comments, although not always fair, are heartfelt. One client of a Harvard dealer visited the premises of a medical clinic, then got on the line to his dealer grumbling: 'There's nothing to it.' Another client was not particularly impressed with the new Oxford Street branch of For Eyes the opticians. Yet another who went into a Scoops (now Staks) Reject China Shop described the stock in less than enthusiastic terms, although this was doubtless sour grapes over the sluggishness of the share price at the time — contrary to what his dealer had led him to expect. Somebody who claimed to have visited Punters wine bar in the City said he found it 'virtually empty'.

The telephone lines of companies such as Thew Engineering, when the share price was going down, have been constantly busy with shareholders trying to find out what's going on. The suspension of an OTC stock for optimistic reasons (like Thew Engineering, Rigby

Electronics) or for pessimistic reasons (like Weymouth Clinic, Hilton Mining), has led to investors ringing Harvard constantly to ask what's going on.

The newsletters issued by licensed dealers, whether written in house, or anonymously by stockbrokers, tend towards propaganda. Some of the recommendations may be bona fide, but slipped in will be those of stocks the firm wants to offload.

It is a fact of life that a client who spends real money will be better treated than the rabble that doesn't. Somebody with a £100,000 portfolio who deals £5,000-£10,000 worth of stock at a time will be protected from the worst stocks, doubly so if he is lucky enough to be in the hands of a dealer with a longer-term commitment to his profession than average. He may never appreciate the VIP treatment he is getting. Clients who make money with licensed dealers, by accident or design, imagine this is what usually happens.

Naturally, friends of dealers tend to do well on their investments. This may be technically insider-dealing, which is far more rife in the City than people have generally been led to believe.

Salesmen discriminate between clients in their own ways. One successful dealer distinguishes between his 'dustbin' clients, i.e. occasional or stupid, or with limited financial resources, on whom he off-loads OTC shares, and his 'regulars' whom he treats more carefully.

For shareholders in Hard Rock Cafe, originally Harvard's best OTC stock, a perk was permission to jump the long queue outside the Hard Rock Cafe off Piccadilly. Harvard dealers were granted the same perk and for that reason kept it concealed from clients, even if it would swing the sale. Dealers' young girlfriends were always impressed by a visit to Hard Rock Cafe.

Dealers sometimes work in pairs, which can lead to a double efficiency if the talents of one complement those of the other. For example, if the soft sell chap fails to wheedle his client into buying, his partner can ring him up and say: 'My colleague's at an important meeting, but he asked me to call you about this stock. We've saved you 10,000 shares . . . '

This dual approach often works, proving that two heads are better than one. Likewise, one's workmate can take awkward calls, e.g.: 'My colleague's not in today, I'm afraid. I'm a senior dealer and I work with him. Perhaps I can help you . . . ' If he pacifies him skilfully enough, he might even make another sale on his colleague's behalf.

The term 'senior dealer' was generally understood to apply only to those who had achieved certain levels of business which would usually take at least three months. This term has, in practice, been used generally by dealers who want to impress their clients. It gives

Hard Rock Cafe, the popular Piccadilly restaurant where Harvard dealers had been known to use their influence to jump the queue.

the impression of long experience. If a dealer has worked in the business for only a few weeks, the client has no way of telling whether he is senior or not, and some licensed dealers have taken advantage of this. This is yet another example of how the business most dealers attain is a tribute to their capacity for sounding convincing. Indeed, claims by inexperienced dealers to be senior dealers became a matter of complaint by aggrieved clients.

Success to certain media people means earning your age in thousands, e.g. £30,000 a year at thirty years old, etc. Good dealers in shares and futures would laugh at this yardstick. Earning twice that, they would challenge their 'Greypower' critics with a fist in the face. Older people, or 'wrinklies', are just cardboard cut-out figures to them.

Dealers feel an instinctive dislike for Stock Exchange member firms where position is awarded according to age and experience. They feel this is old-fashioned and stultifying.

They regard stockbrokers' work as tedious. Understanding of figures and a modicum of research seem called for. The hours of work appear sometimes ridiculously long. Such sentiments are confirmed by reports from the few dealers who make it into stockbroking offices.

Stockbrokers never more than now lack enthusiasm for the small client. They fail to keep him informed, and to advise at crucial times, such as takeovers. They give him poor tips and charge high commissions. Their settlements are not always on time. Moreover, they are difficult to get through to. Despite their prestige, they seem to have less to offer the private client than licensed dealers. On balance, provincial brokers seem to offer more of their time, although giving no higher quality advice than their London rivals.

Nor do banks and building societies provide satisfaction. Their saving schemes, if safe, are boring and investors get alarmed by the low interest rates. Many, despite their bank manager's warnings, plunge into speculative shares whose prices are likely to make them lose all or most of their money.

They hear, most usually from the share salesmen, the most amazing stories of quick and fantastic profits. For instance, shares in OTC-traded Burrough, the Beefeater gin business, leapt from 445p to £12, after the company had been bought up by Whitbread.

The skilful dealer represents such rare gains as a regular occurrence. He does this more by implication than by direct statement.

Licensed dealers still deal in certain shares the punter reads about in the tip sheets. There are some unsavoury tie-ins at work here. Punters are just crazy about penny shares, and their blindness, some might argue, is only too readily exploited.

Punters who rely on the tip sheets must get into stocks early, and maybe sell out quickly. They must form their own judgments, from a variety of sources.

Those who depend solely on their licensed dealers to find them another Polly Peck (probably the most spectacular penny share success ever) are probably doomed to disappointment. If they are lucky, they will be the blind led by the blind. More often, their dealers will be all too clear-sighted in losing them small fortunes. It may take a while before the clients cotton on to what is happening. Even then they will have no evidence — unless perhaps they tape all conversations with their dealers, for themselves.

Clients equate reward potential with risk, a fact dealers exploit, but the two may not coexist proportionately. Only by researching stocks thoroughly or by taking skilled impartial advice can a client ensure against being misled. Laziness is a greater cause of failure to make money in shares than bad luck. Don't the share salesmen know it!

Some clients, usually the more ignorant ones, stupidly assume they are experts. They rely on hunches that are based on their cravings rather than on hard facts. Disappointment, again, lies in wait for them. The dealer will agree with his client's proposals, even offering what evidence he can muster, provided he gains business this way. He will be laughing at the client behind his back.

One dealer wrote on his client lead card: 'Likes to think of himself as a professional. Will take no crap from dealers. Send info.' Such a client will prove eventually manipulable. In truth, he is begging to be convinced.

Client record cards are not necessarily helpful to a dealer who inherits them, however. Witness this comment from another one: 'He's died. Gone to meet his maker. He's propping up the daisies. He's fucking snuffed it.' In actuality, in this particular case, the widow of the deceased, when offered the apparent investment of the decade, certainly spent something.

This leads the author to conclude that shares not suitable for widows and orphans are often sold more easily to widows and orphans than to anyone else.

Although dealers have been sacked from their firms for hard selling to the aged or infirm, it is usually only when complaints are made. New dealers are then brought in to replace the dishonoured ones. As an ex-Harvard dealing director once pointed out, 'Dealers are two a penny nowadays.'

This is manifestly untrue of the good ones, but mediocre young men on the make are proliferating. As one manager wryly remarked of his firm: 'All aboard the pirate ship.'

Futures salesmen are a tougher breed than share salesmen. The best earn a great deal more money. They seem born to the hard sell ethos although new severe regulations against cold-calling and for 'knowing the client' are forcing changes in their attitude.

The overlap between dealers in futures and dealers in shares is nonetheless considerable. Both sell financial instruments, and can be ignorant about the markets. But the equities salesman who goes to work for a futures dealer may find the going hard.

Most private investors do not understand the concept of futures, whereas shares present no problem. Furthermore, the risk warnings for investment in futures put many punters off. Yet Account Executives (AEs) push them into investing in futures capital they cannot afford to lose by underplaying the extent of the gamble, emphasising the potential gain.

Before blaming AEs too harshly, it is essential to understand the tremendous pressure their directors have put them under.

AEs at one futures bucket shop cheered or hissed colleagues in the early morning, according to their individual sales figures on the previous day. A large wall chart tracked commissions earned by each AE per month.

Salesmen who underperformed even over a short period at the futures bucket shops, were put on 'terminal'. The ultimatum was as follows: 'Get in X number of clients next week, or get out.'

The loss of face that would result from getting sacked served to spur on the AE. In the heat of the moment, he might slacken his moral principles.

Selling methods at DPR were moulded on those proven at LHW. AEs found the negative sell easiest. The DPR client was left feeling that DPR did not need his business, it was prospering so much. It did not usually occur to the client that DPR might be prospering from his losses.

AEs find the hard sell more difficult. Inexperienced AEs attempting the hard sell will often have 'blow-outs', i.e. cancellations, on their hands.

A former AE of a major futures bucket shop here recalls using hard sell techniques on a visiting client: 'One day, he came to lunch with me, and I became quite drunk while he stayed determinedly sober. Over coffee back at the office I tried to pull myself together and sell him a traded option in copper which would, as it turned out, have made him quite a lot of money. I was with him for four hours and got nowhere; I requested colleagues to have a crack at him all to no avail. After this episode I stopped telephoning him, only to find he enjoyed the game so much that he began calling me.'

This AE recalls a sales manager who tuned in to AEs' telephone conversations, thereby gaining snippets of information about their private lives which he would not hesitate to use.

The AE at such firms as these had to get in a minimum number of clients per week. The level of their investment was not at that stage important. Clients once opened up were handed to the Senior Account Executives (SAEs) who would squeeze them like lemons out of their very last pennies.

The Senior Account Executives (SAEs) at DPR Futures were dealers who had graduated from the ranks of the accounts executives due to their exceptional sales performances.

When an executive had been thus promoted, his style and approach would become refined. He was then a smooth operator.

After a new client was ushered onto the market by the AE, the SAE would then assume responsibility for looking after the client's market positions, and for obtaining future business. Normally, the first trade was done for about £2,000.

The SAE, two or three days later, would ask the client to pay ludicrously high sums of money for additional contracts. Unlike the AE, the SAE would inject subtlety into his hard sell tactics.

He gave the impression of being a high-up executive who had years of experience in advising investors. He often wore pinstripe suits and braces, coordinated with a smart shirt and tie, like the outfits portrayed in the film *Wall Street*. He was the cream of the crop.

One SAE of DPR, who for the purposes of this book shall be called Oliver, was known to have earned around £19,000 over one Christmas period.

He was brilliant at handling the most difficult client. These high earnings, however, confounded the directors, as he achieved them while the markets were quiet, and while business was usually slow, at a period when morale was low from the market crash a few months earlier.

His clients were normally able to come into the market with at least £10,000 each per trade, and sometimes as much as £100,000.

The competitive instincts of AEs at DPR were unleashed by the allurement of cash prizes.

The £50 offered daily to the first AE to get a bike back with a client's cheque, seemed to the world-weary AEs worth more than three times the equivalent, as paid at the end of the month. They were not convinced of delayed payment until they saw it. They could lose their jobs, or DPR could go bust, without warning.

A weekly competition at DPR awarded £100 and a bottle of champagne to the AE who got in the largest amount of money over the five days. Perhaps four or five, out of thirty AEs, were realistically in the running. The rest put money on whomsoever they thought would win. The betting would start on Monday. By noon on Friday, the competition would become heated. There might be three candidates or so left, bulling into clients.

DPR's competitions stimulated most AEs to greater effort by instilling purpose into the dealing room. The few AEs who were distracted were unsuited to their roles in any case.

The good DPR Futures AE could squeeze money out of real 'stingebags' and 'whiners'. He could tackle clients whose records contained comments like this: 'He has lost £50,000 with LHW, and is not interested now. Keep in touch . . . send brochure first. Will read. Get back to him in a fortnight . . . He doesn't understand futures, but he knows they're bad news. He'll discuss the proposal with his wife . . . Has dealt with other futures firms such as Bailey Shatkin. Isn't doing anything now . . . '

The national press has brought DPR's hard sell techniques into the public eye. At one stage, AEs found that the very mention of DPR's name almost guaranteed no sale. So they were told to introduce themselves like this: 'I'm calling from Deller Page and Rycott Ltd in the City of London.' This sounded respectable, and many punters failed to make the link. AEs also took to answering the telephone with: 'Deller Page and Rycott.' Executives amongst themselves called it Deller Page and Rip-off.

The strongest selling point for AEs at DPR or LHW was the 'limited liability' concept, which meant clients could lose no more money than they put in. Many a more respectable futures dealing firm did not offer this. However, the cost to DPR of providing this facility was only between $60 and $90 and the stop loss level was set so close to the market price that many contracts were very quickly wiped out, since all the investors' margin was used up.

DPR AEs sent out to clients a glossy brochure entitled 'Opportunity Unlimited' containing a photograph of a glamorous country house with a Porsche parked in front of it. Underneath was this dazzling byline: 'The rewards can be greater and faster than any other form of financial speculation.'

AE's sometimes addressed themselves to irate people who said they would *never* invest in futures, let alone through DPR. Typically the punter would say: 'One of your crew rang me three months ago. Scratch me off your mailing list. I'm tired of you lot pestering me. I have no money. Your firm's methods are always being exposed in *The Times* . . . '

After an earful of this, the AE might laugh, and write on that client's coupon a misleading comment like this: 'Has been in hospital. Recovering from a minor op. Call in three months and bull into him. Will be ready with £5,000.'

Such faked coupons were handed to trainees. When they pitched these clients, trouble sometimes arose. The beleaguered ones might threaten complaint.

In early 1988, DPR were prone to particularly vigorous sales campaigns ahead of trade figures, or on significant movement of interest rates, as opposed to all the time. This self-imposed limitation was attributable to their desperation for AFBD membership. But AEs who could hard sell were still valued the most in the firm.

The American trade figures were generally the high moment of the month. On the morning of the days on which they were due to be announced, the dealing manager of DPR Futures would scream at the AEs: 'This is it. Get 'em in. Get as many as you can for the trade figures. We've got our forecasts right this time . . . If they're afraid, get 'em in for the minimum. Bull up. Bull up.'

The AEs would scramble between their dealing screens and telephones, negotiating afresh every minute. Their voices conveyed urgency. Furthermore, the infamous cassette tape recording of open outcry on a real trading floor was turned right up to impress clients, so the AEs had to shout loudly to make themselves heard.

DPR often appeared to get its forecasts wrong. Days before the trading figures were due, when it should have recommended a long position, the firm was likely to recommend going short.

After a succession of incorrect forecasts, DPR suddenly switched tactics. One of the bosses announced: 'We don't know what the real trade figures are going to be. This one's really difficult to judge. Let me suggest a new way to handle your clients. Talk to them from Monday about the trade figures due out on Thursday. Tell them the company hasn't taken a stance at all, that our analysts are still working on it.

Insist that they are ready on Thursday afternoon to go in either direction, long or short, that the company takes.'

Executives started to smile. This sounded like a psyching-up treatment that clients would respond to. The boss quickly interjected: 'This is the best time to get new clients on board. They may not understand the Deutschmark or live cattle, but even idiots know about the Yankee trade figures. They are talked about everywhere. They affect the grannies . . . '

One executive opened seven new clients for the next American figures. In his polished accent, he informed one new client who was sceptical: 'Sir, you have nothing to fear. You are in my capable hands. If DPR takes a long position, I'll press a red button. If a short position, I'll press a blue button. It's as simple as that. Everything's computerised, you see. You'll be in and out of the market before you can bat an eyelid.'

Unknown to the client, DPR's facilities were far from being computerised. There were no red or blue buttons to push, only a lot of paperwork. The controls signalled a dozen dealing screens, but only three were in use.

DPR's actual trading room consisted of a matchbox style office in which two overworked traders would place the company's orders to brokers situated in London, Chicago, or New York.

DPR demanded funds in immediately, but, paradoxically, took their time about executing the clients' orders. Executives led clients to believe they were being put on the market immediately, and, indeed, this was what they themselves thought was happening.

One executive smelt a rat when a new client queried a contract note. The executive took care not to let it slip out that he had never seen a DPR contract note.

The client stated his contract had been executed at an unexpectedly high price. The executive checked the documents, and noted that the order should have been executed at a much lower price. The difference in price suggested that the client's order had been executed a full day after it had been placed.

Imagine yourself in the role of a client. Would you be happy with this sort of practice?

Chapter Four

Bucket Shops Galore

Some licensed dealers have at times sailed extremely close to the wind.

However scandalous the UK dealers seem, the continental ones are more so. One ex-Harvard dealer at Dublin based Bailey McMahon quarrelled with his 23 year old dealing manager. He resented taking orders from a younger man, for whom he had no real respect.

He upped it one day, landing on his feet across the Channel. Later in June he rang one of his old Bailey McMahon colleagues. He was now working from a switching office near the Arc de Triomphe in Paris. 'I'm ringing clients up, telling them I'm phoning from Geneva. I sell American pink sheets stock on behalf of various firms, getting up to 30% commission on sales,' he said. To get this commission in perspective, it was around fifteen times what Tudorbury Securities or Harvard offered their dealers.

He explained further how the whole operation worked: 'Clients ring a given number in Geneva, which unbeknown to them, is a forwarding number. They are told their dealer is in a meeting, and will ring them back. The office immediately facsimiles or telexes a message to the dealer concerned in whatever country he is working from — usually Spain, France, or another part of Switzerland. The dealer then rings back the client.'

All contract notes were forwarded from Rotterdam, or elsewhere, to Geneva in a big bundle, then were sent out from Geneva so they looked as if they came from there directly.

The spread of offices at secret addresses throughout Europe acted as a safeguard. For instance, the Swiss authorities might raid a premises in Geneva, and find nothing significant. They would probably have no inkling of a back office in Spain.

American pink-sheets stocks pushed by such bucket shops allow for a minimum 10%, often more than 30% commission accruing to the dealer. Much of this would be lost, however, in client cancellations. Furthermore, dealers might spend much money travelling across continents every week, for business and pleasure.

These pink-sheets stocks are listed and priced in a salmon-coloured directory numbering 400 pages per day, which is published by the National Quotation Bureau in Jersey City, New Jersey. There are 11,000 pink sheet stocks, and they do not meet the listing requirements of the National Association of Securities Dealers' Automated Quotation (NASDAQ), which is effectively America's over-the-counter market. The requirements for listing are minimal. Market-makers fill out a form indicating the company's purpose, number of shares outstanding, and the price. The information is then sent on to the Securities and Exchange Commission (SEC). If the Agency raises no questions within forty-eight hours, the company is listed. The National Quotation Bureau does not discriminate between stocks. Market-makers pay $7 a month to list up to 10 stocks, and subscribers pay $46 a month. Many of these stocks are unsellable, and some, upon investigation by the SEC, have proved instruments for unscrupulous money making.

Dynapac Inc., an investment company that dabbled in a gold mine, a TV game show, and an electronic folding sofa-bed, was a case in point. Its share price within months almost doubled, reaching approximately the $8 level.

The SEC investigated. A ramp was detected. Dynapec's assets and business connections had been exaggerated out of all proportion. Trading in Dynapec was suspended, and the SEC's charges were largely uncontested.

Such operations are as old as the hills. Share selling bucket shops have a chequered history. Shortly before the Second World War they flourished in the UK and abroad. Unlike Stock Exchange member firms, they were allowed to advertise openly, as much as they liked. All sorts of unsavoury characters were buying up lists of potential investors and setting up a share-selling operation, perhaps from nothing more than an accommodation address.

The early Prevention of Fraud (Investments) Act had put a stop to unsolicited recommendations, but there remained a perfectly legal means to continue. A firm could advertise, the potential client then responding on his own initiative.

Some bucket shops operated under the cover of a respectable firm, which they had bought up to use as a base for pushing dodgy shares. Clients were persuaded to sell their sound shares — a very liquid form of investment — and to use the proceeds to buy up rubbish.

Sometimes when clients' funds had been gathered in, directors of the dealing firm would abscond. If they acted at the end of the week, no discovery could be made until well after the weekend.

If clients were foolish enough to accept unsolicited cheques, they were bound to further payment. Typically, they were sent one bought contract note, followed by one sold, at a small profit, and a cheque for the sum owed. Clients who encashed this cheque were accepting a false transaction. The next two contract notes might show a heavy loss which the client would be bound to pay.

Of course, not all dealers operating in the 1930s outside the auspices of the Stock Exchange were bucket shops. In his fascinating memoir *Before The Big Bang* (Milestone Publications), Stock Exchange veteran Donald Cobbett recalls that Nicholson's of Sheffield, with its sizeable clientele and continuous, two-way prices, was a kind of precursor of the present-day OTC market. Cobbett describes the firm as a 'reputable and formidable' competitor of the Stock Exchange, pointing out further: 'It appeared at one time to rival London in certain low priced industrial equities. Indeed, it claimed to be the biggest market in the shares of Low Temperature Carbonisation, precursor of the present Coalite Group.'

Just as satisfaction with a good investment can be high, there is nothing worse than having put money into an obvious dud. In Charles Dickens' famous novel *Martin Chuzzlewit*, Martin, the hero, invests in the Eden Land Corporation. A plausible managing agent had led him to believe that Eden was 'the most powerful and highly civilised dominion that has ever graced the world'.

Here is Martin's first glimpse of the 'flourishing city': 'At last they stopped. At Eden too. The water of the Deluge might have left it but a week before: so choked with slime and matted growth was the hideous swamp that bore that name.'

The first Edener they saw was 'pale and worn' from fever, with 'anxious eyes' that were 'deeply sunken in his head'. Furthermore, 'His dress of homespun blue hung about him in rags; his feet were bare.'

Phineas Barnum once said, 'There's a sucker born every minute' and his pessimism — or optimism, if you like — seems verified by history.

Swindles are always more disastrous when many are involved, such as in the legendary South Sea Bubble of the early 18th century. The public was persuaded to make huge investments in the South Sea Company, so that National Debt could be paid off. The venture was proving successful, with investments soaring in value.

In its wake, hundreds of other investment companies sprung up, claiming situations as good. Companies offering shares for sale were engaged in such varied activities as planting mulberry trees, breeding silkworms, building pirate-proof ships, importing jackasses to improve the quality of British mules, and insuring girls against losing their virginity.

By 1720, the South Sea Company was heavily in debt from unwise trading, but put up a new share offer instead of going under. The share issue was successful, but the truth then started leaking out. There was an amazing rush to sell the shares, and what can only be described as a national panic.

In the frenzy, it was made illegal for firms to trade without a licence.

Many firms immediately went bust, and investors everywhere committed suicide. Jonathan Swift put it like this:

> Subscribers here by thousands float,
> and jostle one another down;
> Each paddling in his leaky boat
> And here they fish for gold and drown.

Fortunately the Prime Minister, Sir Robert Walpole, arranged for the Bank of England and the East India Company to take up much of the South Sea Stock, and for surplus funds to be divided amongst damaged shareholders.

There were those, of course, who had got in and out of the bubble quickly at a profit, such as Spencer Compton, Speaker of the House of Commons. Also, some of the investment schemes proved sound; insurance, pension, and other saving schemes in particular.

Charles Lamb speaks for the majority when he says of the South Sea Bubble: 'that tremendous *hoax*, whose extent the petty speculators of our day look back upon with the same expression of incredulous admiration, and hopeless ambition of rivalry, as would become the puny face of modern conspiracy contemplating the Titan size of Vaux's superhuman plot.'

It is easy, of course, to be wise in retrospect.

Worse than this sort of mess is the share fraud that was intentional from the start. There springs to mind the case of an American businessman who was arrested and charged with attempting to sell at least $385 million in Peruvian Securities that later proved worthless.

Kenneth Hocking, president of the International Industries Development Corporation, Illinois, had obtained the notes while promising to build low income housing projects under a US Agency for International Development (AID) loan programme.

Mr. Hocking marketed the notes in investment packages that he claimed were guaranteed by AID, although the Government had never in fact approved the projects.

This was a major disaster, particularly as it took time to recover the dubious securities, and people were getting loans based on them. One Secret Service official called the case the largest financial document investigation, in terms of money, in which the Secret Service had participated.

Investment propositions have been made on promises still more dubious than the above. At much the same time, a gentleman by the name of Jeffrey Cohen was claiming to potential investors of the Camp Springs area in St. George's County that he was a million-dollar shareholder and licensed broker for Kendall Mining International Inc. (KMI).

Punters were told that KMI was a company dealing in gold, silver, and precious metals, as well as in oil, and was 'a very lucrative investment'. At a meeting, Cohen distributed outdated brochures describing these operations. He proceeded to offer 'clients' an opportunity to buy unlimited shares at 8 to 16 cents a share.

Some $30,000 was invested with this man, and investors only started to complain when share certificates did not prove forthcoming. One victim who contacted Cohen was told that the money had been used to bail out a failing car-dealership.

Jeffrey Cohen had been posing as heir to Giant Foods Inc. But Israel Cohen, partner in the firm, commented: 'This man is not affiliated with Giant Foods in any way . . . As far as I know I only have one son, and he's in Florida doing well in the automobile business.'

Cohen was eventually discovered at the Hilton Hotel in the USA, and arrested. There are, however, other deceitful share-pushers who get away with their game for longer.

Decades earlier, the infamous Horatio Bottomley made a fortune from gold mines and other companies. Investors flocked to his ventures, lured by the prospect of high dividends. Once their prices had risen high, Bottomley sold the shares profitably. When a company's luck turned sour, this swindler would launch a takeover through a new company, backed by yet more of the shareholders' funds.

All this proved a springboard for the inauguration of Bottomley's Victory Bond Club in 1919, a scheme whose popularity with the public was in its extremity matched only by its unscrupulousness. Investors' monies were set aside for private usage.

The good faith of investors was similarly exploited by Jabez Balfour, a Victorian MP who was renowned for inventing the snowballing method. The public trusted in his companies which regularly paid out 8% dividends, and everybody queued up to invest with him. Unfortunately, these dividends were paid out of monies invested, and not from company profits. When in 1882 one of his companies went into liquidation, Balfour's incredible swindles were revealed.

Balfour was sentenced to fourteen years' imprisonment, and the judge, Mr. Justice Bruce, said: 'You will never be able to shut out the cry of the widows and orphans you have ruined.'

After a similar fashion, the plausible Swede Ivar Kreugar coaxed millions of pounds from a credulous public, into his network of companies that supplied most of the world's safety matches. He compiled his own company reports, and presented dividends from his investors' monies.

Less malevolent, although equally destructive, is the type of fraudsman whom Dr. Michael Levi in *The Phantom Capitalists* declares to be on the 'slippery slope'. He starts off honestly, but lapses into deceitful ways in order to save his business from insolvency.

A certain David Langford demonstrated how this could be done.

He specialised in 'bond-washing'. This entailed public investment in local authority bonds, which were then sold midway through their lifespan, so the proceeds could be reinvested in a new bond. This roll over enabled the profit from the sale to be assessed as capital gain and not as income tax. It was an attractive, apparently safe investment, and found many takers.

However, Langford was already plunged into financial problems due to his mishandling of investors' funds in the past. As his new company collapsed, he went away, and was reported missing for a full three months. Then he gave himself up to the police.

In his book *Too Good To Be True*, Rowan Bosworth Davies, ex-detective in the Metropolitan Police Fraud Department, records how a retired gentleman from Swansea had seen bond-washing written up in a magazine and so had arranged to meet Langford.

Impressed with both the man and his offices, he gave him £5,000. He received for this a contract note, evidencing his acquisition of a local authority bond. A friend of this same gentleman invested thousands of pounds in a similar way.

In the end, the two men got their money back with interest, from the Department of Trade and Industry (DTI), after they had embarked on the most amazing and wearisome campaign for justice conceivable.

They had contacted their MPs, and finally their complaints reached the Parliamentary Under-Secretary of State for Consumer Affairs. The great man considered that the department's actions had, in the circumstances, been reasonable. So the two unlucky investors took their complaints further to the Parliamentary Commissioner for Administration: in other words, the Ombudsman.

The Ombudsman found some behaviour of departments involved 'surprising' and 'extraordinary'. Various failings 'merited criticism'. Furthermore, he denigrated the DTI for its failure to act on repeated requests for further information. Why had it been necessary to carry the complaint this far, before justice was done?

Indeed lack of regulations has permitted continental crooks to filch the investing public's money, in return for over-valued or worthless shares. The bucket shops in question operate from all over the world, but their most notorious haven is Amsterdam. Here con men operate from dingy cramped offices, often situated around the Red Light District.

In Holland as a whole, there were until recently perhaps fifty to a hundred such outfits, often staffed by hard-nosed Canadians, and selling stocks to investors both in Britain and elsewhere.

Sharedealers from Amsterdam and other continental bastions were promoting shares in Kanbrik Airlines, and in European Computer Group. However, Kevin Fuller, the director of European Computer

Group, commented at the time that his company was going through a difficult period, and that this was not the best time for investors to be buying shares in his company.

In fact, Fuller had not even known that the shares were being sold, although they had been described as a pre-subscription offer, and although it had looked as if European Computer Group itself was selling the shares.

Investors who had received a share tip sheet through the post called The Tower Report were persuaded by telephone salesmen of Amsterdam-based Tower Securities to buy shares in European Computer Group.

Once a sale is agreed, investors are legally bound to the contract. What does this let them in for?

The investment might, of course, be good. The emphasis is on 'might'. A few continental dealers have pumped out a small line of Stock Exchange quoted stocks, a welcome antidote to their more speculative offerings.

Indeed even the most unscrupulous sharedealer offers good stocks at one time or another, if only to lull its clients into trusting it. An obvious example of this malpractice occurred in the sales campaign for sharedealing in a reputable company called AC Scotland PLC, as organised by Chartwell Securities AG Ltd.

AC Scotland PLC had been formed to promote the renowned AC sports car, by way of building new cars under the old name. The company was to prove as sound an investment as it had appeared from the start. In fact it was exactly the above board sort of share offer that Chartwell Securities AG Ltd needed to start the ball rolling.

Shares in AC Scotland PLC were originally marketed by London Venture Capital Market Ltd, which operated under the wing of the Ravensdale Group PLC. This holding of shares was bought up by Neil Bruckman's Trafalgar Capital (UK) Ltd, as London Venture Capital could no longer afford to sustain a market in them.

Neil Bruckman originally had been refused a representative's licence, and for Trafalgar Capital (UK) Ltd, a principal's licence, but he had nevertheless been successful in obtaining membership of the Association of Stock and Share Dealers, which was recognised by the DTI in its own right.

Next another company, called Chartwell Securities AG, was set up in Zurich, and also in Munich and Dusseldorf. Chartwell enjoyed a defined business relationship with Trafalgar Capital (UK) Ltd. Amongst the directors of Chartwell Securities AG was one Rochelle Rothfleisch, who was the wife of the infamous Thomas F Quinn.

Thomas F Quinn had been disbarred from law work in America and imprisoned for six months after he had been convicted of selling dud securities in Kent Industries Inc, to the tune of $380,000. He was later in trouble with the Securities and Exchange Council (SEC) in relation to the underwriting of Sundance Gold Mining and Exploration Inc., a valueless stock.

Shares in AC Scotland plc proved incredibly popular. One hundred and fifty telephone salesmen raised some £20 million from their offices in Germany, Switzerland and Liechtenstein. 20,000 interested investors were tapped. Partly because they were aggressively promoted, the shares soared in value until they were regarded as overpriced.

Nonetheless, the company's business started to thrive. David MacDonald, AC Scotland's chief executive, said that his staff were having to work sunstantial overtime to fill an American order for two hundred cars a year for the next ten years.

When Chander Singh's Ravensdale Securities offered to buy the shares at 35p, the *Daily Mail*, and various investment advisers, recommended to sell, as the shares seemed overvalued, even though such action would surrender the BES tax saving.

Investors were introduced to the OTC market on the back of the well-established American OTC. Amongst the colourful shares in which Trafalgar Capital (UK) Ltd made a market was North American Bingo, a company formed to build bingo houses on Indian reservations. At one stage Trafalgar Capital (UK) Ltd was quoting prices in eighteen stocks. Many of these were later to prove worthless.

Next, Neil Bruckman organised promotion of shares in Derby Vision PLC, a revamped version of the notorious Video Turf Inc.

The prospectus for Derby Vision PLC offered warnings of 'no guarantee of increased customer response', also pointing out the likelihood of 'unforeseen technical problems'. There was also printed an ultimate warning: 'Trafalgar Capital (UK) Ltd will endeavour to make a market in the Ordinary shares of Derby Vision on an over the counter basis. There can be no guarantee that such a market will be developed or maintained. Investors may accordingly not be able to realise their investment.' Unfortunately, this prospectus was not circulated to all shareholders.

To crown it all, Mr Arnold Kimmes, a convicted fraudster, was made sales force leader of a branch of Chartwell Securities AG, where he introduced incentives such as having $500 attached to the wall, to be claimed by the best salesman of the day.

The police closed Chartwell's offices down and Trafalgar Capital (UK) Ltd started sorting its affairs out. An accountant who told Trafalgar's management that they were losing money through the conversion rates was told to mind his own business, so he alerted the police.

Thomas F Quinn, confronted with the report of another dissatisfied accountant, said: 'Who is this guy? I'll break his fucking legs.'

Soon, Trafalgar Capital (UK) Ltd was suspended from membership of the Association of Stock and Share Dealers, thus forfeiting the right to sell shares. Neil Bruckman himself returned to America, where he was arrested in respect of other matters.

A time honoured method of enticing the punters' money is to recommend they trade in their new issues or blue chip investments for speculative rubbish.

In a flamboyant gesture, BA Investment Advisory Services of Prinsengracht, Amsterdam, was distributing a circular strongly recommending a sale of Guinness shares. Gary Anderson, BA's director, said that they were overpriced, and that he recommended Commercial Industrial Minerals, 'even though it's a different quality to Guinness.'

Commercial Industrial Minerals was an unknown, unquoted Canadian company. BA originally tried to call the company ICI, until the chemicals group complained. Guinness said: 'The whole purpose of such a mailing is to encourage investment in speculative businesses promoted by a foreign group, by running down quality companies, and so encouraging the release of cash.' The British Press warned the public against dealing with BA's boiler-room operation.

Guinness called in the DTI and the Stock Exchange to investigate, although it seemed they could not prevent the recommendation to sell Guinness shares being made.

This was a precursor of the way holders of Jaguar shares were urged to trade these in for more speculative alternatives, by another Amsterdam based securities dealer. Soon, BA were driven out of Amsterdam, and some £1 million of BA's money had been frozen in the Isle of Man.

What sort of companies did BA offer shares in? Global International, with shares at $5 or so each, was not listed anywhere. Sherlock Securities was sold with a patter about their inventing a lock so strong that the first person to open it would receive £1 million. Marco Resources, listed in Vancouver, and Commercial Industrial Minerals with a limited availability of shares, were considered perhaps better propositions. What is it that shares like these have in common?

A colourful story, one way or another. An aggressive promotion scheme. The appearance of a swelling demand. Young companies in most cases, with track records and figures that do not bear scrutiny. These are often American pink sheets shares.

Rodrick Casander of Casander & Partners, Amsterdam, has been directly involved in the winding up of both BA, and another notorious securities dealer, Financial Planning Services (FPS).

FPS pushed shares such as Portinax and Federal Ventures which have been described as seeming to have little value, as well as better stocks such as Nighthawk, which may have had a Vancouver listing.

Capital Venture Consultants, also Amsterdam based, was closed by the Dutch police. In the same year, Amsterdam based Tower Securities was raided and closed.

First Commerce Securities, another Amsterdam based operation, regularly sent out an impressive looking newsletter called *Investors Alert*, then followed up the mailing with phone calls.

Their premises were regularly patronised by one Mr. Irving Kott, a convicted swindler who had been heavily fined by a Canadian court in 1976. Kott's son, Michael, worked here as a telephone salesman, using a variety of pseudonyms.

First Commerce Securities was declared bankrupt, and possibilities for criminal proceedings were investigated. Some of First Commerce's clients had invested also with Trier Investments, which was raided and closed down by the Dutch police.

Another such company, York International Securities, was expelled from Holland by the Dutch authorities, only to resurface in Nicosia, Cyprus. Some investors have been left holding shares in companies such as Biomedica -- which combines drugs and computers, old favourites of share-sharks. Biomedica is unquoted anywhere in the world.

Nicosia's Central Bank revoked York's licence on grounds that the dealing firm was breaking rules by taking deposits from the public, in addition to acting as brokers. The Cyprus authorities have now shut the firm down.

Another sharedealer that has recently suffered this ultimate fate was United Consultants of Amsterdam. Many investors in a company called Colt Computer Holdings apparently lost their money in the subsequent reckoning.

Mr Thorpe and Mr Johnson who owned Colt Computer Holdings, sold 45% of this company's shares to a Swiss Bank, which sold them to United Consultants.

The British-based Colt Computer Systems of Hounslow was the sole asset of Colt Computer Holdings. The parent company was located in Liechtenstein, outside British jurisdiction.

What is the main complaint that has been directed against these Amsterdam outfits? According to Mr. Reinier Fuchs, secretary to the Amsterdam Stock Exchange, the biggest problem for investors has been inability to sell back stock. How does this fit into the typical sales campaign embarked upon?

Here is the way it works. Dealers first 'paper' clients, i.e. send out sales brochures. They then ring and hard sell stocks. 'This is the first time we've traded, so I'm anxious to do a good deal with you,' they say. They will often guarantee extraordinary quick profits, and may offer stock at apparently special prices.

After the first sale, the 'loaders' or 'dynamiters' contact the client. These are the second line salesmen who, like leeches, suck all the money from clients they can.

If clients, ignoring urgent recommendations to the contrary, succeed in selling out, they often find they get only a quarter or half of their money. This may be due to a price slump, a wide spread, or delaying tactics on the part of the dealers. It may be due to any combination of these factors. *The Sunday Times,* has reported typical experiences of two investors.

The first one, following phone calls from First Commerce Securities, bought shares in De-Voe-Holbein, understanding the shares would reach $12 within weeks, and $30 within a year.

De-Voe-Holbein, with its technology that was based on metal capturing compounds, had made a net loss of $1.4 million in a period of ten months. A price of $30 would have given the company a value of $639 million, roughly equivalent to Rowntree Mackintosh's 1985 capitalisation.

Feeling uneasy, the investor tried to sell. Ringing sell orders at prices quoted over the phone, he confirmed by telex. He went through this procedure twice, only to be told there was no record of his sell orders anywhere.

He then found the market shut down over the Christmas holiday period. he finally sold later than he had wished, at just under $5 a share. His loss amounted to $12,000. Mr Walter Bonn, managing director of First Commerce Securities, explained the fall in De-Voe-Holbein's share price as a consequence of panic-selling after bad publicity in England.

The second investor bought shares in Techno Scientific from Tower Securities, on the understanding that they would go to $9 or so within two months, in accordance with the dealers' inside information.

When he asked the stockbroker Merril Lynch, and his bank about Techno Scientific, neither could find any information. He sold back through Tower Securities, but his telex got lost, despite the call back signal confirming it had arrived. He finally sold Techno Scientific at $2.75 a share. His loss amounted to $3,000.

Harvard Securities in the UK offered to buy shares of reduced value at a nominal price with a dealing charge, so losses could be established for tax purposes. The *Daily Mail* described this offer as making sense.

The UK-based Harvard Securities disassociated themselves from Harvard Securities in Cologne, renamed Nova International, which was closed down. Books and cash were seized. No charge was made, but Harvard also closed its Munich office. Controlling shareholder,

Morty Glickman commented: 'It's a total obscenity. We're operating a legitimate business.'

The ruinous practices of the continental share-pushers has, of course, stemmed in part from lack of legislation. On November 21st 1985, the Dutch Finance Minister had introduced moves towards looser, not tighter controls. This was because other countries such as Germany, Switzerland and France were winning financial business from Holland.

Later moves by the Dutch Ministry of Finance advocated that securities not quoted on a recognised exchange should be accompanied by a 'clear' prospectus, but changes have been slow to come about.

The smoothest operators traditionally come from Canada, or are trained there. They have a reputation worldwide, and are working all over Europe.

One pioneer was the seventy year old Murray Libman who found investors for a non-existent company based on a Costa Rican gold mine. His partner Robert Colucci took £65 million from investors in the 1960s, in another share fraud.

Canadian Business, exposed the fraud involving the Tres Hermanos (Three Brothers) mine in Costa Rica. Machinery and rocks were available there to deceive casual visitors, as indeed they did. The Canadian Mounties, not so easily fooled, just found mainly crumbling walls within the mines.

Another haven for share-pushers is Madrid. Timezone operates from there, selling often obscure stocks to private British investors.

One investor with Timezone who asked for his money back in Beaconsfield International shares, was permitted only to exchange his investment for shares in Vanguard International.

The *Sunday Times* advised this investor of the following concerning Vanguard International: 'It is based in Fort Lauderdale, Florida, as is GSS Venture Capital, the subject of a number of warnings in this column; it is represented by a Chicago Public Relations firm, Campbell and Associates, as are GSS and Sherwood Financial. It has recently . . . been the subject of action by the US Securities and Exchange Commission, which ordered a suspension of trading in its shares pending further investigation.'

The newspapers and specialist financial magazines do their best to safeguard private investors from their own folly. *The Observer* told of an eighty-four year old investor who was unable to properly sell his 1,000 shares in Vyquest International, which he had bought from Timezone for £1,530.

Timezone had informed him that his shares would fetch just $100 in total, unless he accepted a 'contingent order', by which they would give him $3,000 for his Vyquest shares if he reinvested in another company, viz GSS Venture Capital. This pensioner had been told that Vyquest was about to acquire a German company Hexagames, but this acquisition never took place.

Previously, Timezone, and FMS, a securities dealer which had been closed down by the Fraud Squad, had told investors that GSS had acquired a company called I-Point which had developed a freshness monitor for foods. But this acquisition had never taken place.

Another proposed acquisition was that of GSS by another American company, Sherwood Financial. This too fell through. According to the Timezone newsletter *International Dateline Report*, the management of GSS Venture Capital cancelled its proposed merger with Sherwood Financial, the insurance and travel agency from the UK.

The Observer pointed out that Sherwood owned no UK insurance and travel agency companies, and furthermore that it was the Securities and Exchanges Commission — not GSS — which called off Sherwood's acquisition of GSS by getting court injunctions, on the grounds that it was part of an allegedly fraudulent scheme.

Timezone has appeared part of a European sharedealing network including not just the now defunct FMS, but also Chelsea Securities of Rotterdam and Geneva, and Falcontrust Financial of Geneva.

Vyquest GSS, Datalink Systems, and Transworld Network (another company recommended by Timezone) were connected with American Carl J. Porto, and Abraham and Robert Margolies.

Abraham Margolies was a shareholder in the now defunct Ravensdale Group. A warrant was once issued for the arrest of Robert Margolies on grounds of VAT evasion. The Margolies brothers have business interests connected with the jailed leader in New York's Genovese Mafia company, Matty Ianello.

Chelsea Securities have also sold shares in ICA Investment Capital Associates whose subsidiary is Falcontrust Financial. ICA and FMS shared London premises which Thomas F Quinn frequently visited.

Commonly, investors received unexpected phone calls from the continental dealers. *The Daily Telegraph* told of an investor who had been phoned by a dealer from Chelsea Financial, Basle, on the basis that one of the dealing firm's clients had recommended him. When he asked for the name of the client he was told that Swiss Banking Law prevented disclosure of this.

The salesman also claimed his company was connected with Chelsea Financial in Salt Lake City, Utah. This was later denied by Newport Beach based Chelsea Securities, which has an office in Salt Lake City.

Gibraltar based Griffin Hayhurst were pushing on to UK investors shares in a US company called Kinesis, which claimed to have invented a sole for running shoes which would enable professional athletes to run much faster and so break world records.

More recently, Griffin Hayhurst's British clients were about to invest £3 million into Kiga Industries, which was supposed to be marketing a food preservative that rendered freezers obsolete. The London Fraud Squad intercepted their money before it left the UK.

Medatlantic Investments, also responsible for selling Kiga Industries, had an organisational link with Griffin Hayhurst, the exact nature of which was obscure.

Promoters of one crashed bucket shop have traditionally moved onto the next. For instance Dutch computer programmer Phillipe Hijmans, used to run the Amsterdam based Tower Securities. This was closed down by the police so he moved to Timezone.

Directors of these firms can have still more dubious backgrounds. In charge of Gibraltar-registered International Finance and Management (formerly Universe Finance & Management) for instance, is Bernard Klavir, who has a warrant out for his arrest in Los Angeles for violating the Securities laws.

The Amsterdam-based BA Investment Advisory Services was run by Barnet Altwerger, who had a criminal record of forty years standing. Mr Altwerger used aliases such as Barney Ames, Barney Auld, Archie Bennett, and others. BA's liquidator, Rodrick Casunder, recently seized some of Altwerger's money, hidden in Lloyds Bank and Midland Bank accounts on the Isle of Man.

From June 1988, the National Association of Securities Dealers (NASD) in America has started clamping down on malpractices in the trading of American pink sheets shares. Market-makers have to report the price, volume, and significant trades in pink-sheet stocks daily to NASD. In this way, people ramping the price through buying the stock excessively, then dumping it at inflated prices, can be detected.

For the future, an electronic bulletin board on which pink sheets stocks have a mandatory listing is planned. This could however lead to the quotation of unrealistic prices, dating back to when the shares last changed hands.

Although many US brokers dismiss them as garbage stocks, the pink sheets stocks, like the UK OTC market, can claim a few successes. The market for that reason remains a plausible haven of hopes and dreams for transcontinental speculators. Xerox and Doubleday, for instance, started life on the pink sheets.

Under the Financial Services Act (1986) commodities dealers have been getting wiped out, including Stox and DPR. These outfits, however, appeared as clean as a whistle compared to Exchange Securities and Commodities, earlier set up by Keith Hunt.

Hunt was offering his professional advice in return for a proportion of his clients' profits. For a period of four years, he seemed to be offering 93% annual interest.

The 'index bet', i.e. betting on the market through a bookmaker, not a broker, was inaugurated by him, and has since caught on in the UK. Profits via this investment method are categorised as gambling gains, thus offering extra tax savings.

Hunt's firm collapsed, after the Department of Trade & Industry (DTI) had established that he had not been doing any trades for the past six months.

Exchange Securities & Commodities was a front which had brought in £18 million worth of clients' funds. Keith Hunt subsequently vanished, with some £10 million in tow.

A similar technique was used by one Jerry Dominelli, who transferred his commodities firm J David & Co to the City of London, under the name: 'The J David Banking Corporation.'

Dominelli boasted that he had shown his American clients a consistent 40%+ return over the previous three years. Now he was purporting to offer British investors a slice of the cake . . .

The Bank of England objected to Dominelli calling his company a 'banking' corporation, so he changed the name a third time to J David International.

He was turned down for membership of the London International Financial Futures Exchange (LIFFE), even while LIFFE was seeking new members. He was turned down later too when he tried to buy his way in. All this was a bad omen.

Soon Dominelli's operation was revealed. All clients' funds had been getting secretly channelled into his own pocket. He was tried and found guilty of fraud.

More original was the scheme of Harold Goldstein, the California based options trader who made his name in the 1970s, when his rise to multi-millionaire status was meteoric.

Goldstein offered his clients an investment package which combined the high risk of commodities with insurance bonds to insure against loss. His claim was that clients would at worst break even.

Shockingly, the insurance bonds on the contracts proved non-existent. The entrepreneur was jailed for fraud.

Despite increasingly stringent regulations, there will always be fraudsters, or those operating just within legal, if not moral limits — to whom gullible and greedy investors will fall prey.

At the same time, a few investments in the unregulated markets have been known to turn out to be good. Anybody who makes an unwise investment might just be accepting opportunity with the risk. If in such cases he is not victim to real misrepresentation or fraud, then he must hold himself responsible for the consequences.

The client, as a charming salesman from Swiss based Kettler AG once put it, must 'paddle his own canoe'.

Chapter Five

A DEALER'S LIFE IS FOR ME

Dealers in shares and futures at bucket shops are an unhealthy hybrid of City yuppies, Bohemians, and layabouts, although they would not define themselves as such. Instinctively anti-establishment, they find the free-for-all atmosphere of their dealing rooms most gratifying. For ex-public school dealers, this is the state school they never had.

The day kicks off with breakfast. Only small firms with well-established dealers can cook the Great English Breakfast on the premises. Dealers of most firms might pick up coffee and a bacon sandwich from the nearby breakfast cafe, and bring these into the dealing room in good time for the early start.

Harvard dealers often used to earn much more than their largely better-spoken, better-qualified counterparts who were working for top stockbrokers. They did not know as much, they were just more ruthless.

Dealers in bucket shops, unlike their counterparts in more respectable firms, make a habit of boasting about their earnings, but only in casual asides, so as not to appear patronising. They might hint at their income during parties. Throwing around money as opposed to talking about it is the outward manifestation of their inner beings. It is their status symbol, and they get most irked if people are not obviously impressed. Where does their money go, and how easily do they save it?

Team leaders at Harvard Securities were given company cars, a perk rather than a necessity. The rank and file dealers had to buy their own. Many craved flashy sports cars. One female dealer at Harvard Securities became the envy of the rest because she had acquired, for around £16,000, a jet black second-hand Porsche. That vehicle became resented by colleagues who had set their sights on a Golf GTI or a BMW, which was somewhat lower than she had actually achieved.

Directors and managers of licensed dealers get the best cars, whether by courtesy of the firm or by dipping into their own pockets. Neil Miller, when made director of London & Norwich Investment Services Ltd, was given the use of a new Mercedes. In the dealers' eyes he had become cock of the walk. This was a sign that he had made it. Managing directors sometimes have Rolls Royces complete with cap-touching chauffeur. Car phones, real or fake, add an impressive touch, and if real are used a lot for effect.

Some licensed dealers have their own private car parks; others do not. Dealers of Harvard Securities used to regularly retrieve their cars parked in a public road behind the office block after work, only to find tickets slapped on their windscreens: they resorted to several tried and tested responses. Some saw the £10 fine as a necessary daily expense for the privilege of working at Harvard Securities. Others simply fought every fine, where they could get away with it, refusing to pay. One dealer even removed the tickets, putting them on the windscreens of cars parked nearby.

Dealers at Harvard Securities would sing themselves through the day. The Harvard Shuffle was often sung by dealers during occasional breaks, or particularly while they were looking through leads, seeing whom next to ring.

A few dealers would stand up, inspired and would burst into song, to the tune of Hokey-Cokey. The Harvard Shuffle, went as follows:

> Put your clients in, take your clients out,
> Put your clients in, and then churn them all about.
> Then do the Harvard Shuffle, and you turn yourself about.
> That's what it's all about.

Meanwhile they would indulge in the most extraordinary gyrations — to represent the agonising lengths to which they manipulate their clients.

Unshaven dealers, with cigarettes hanging from lips, would soften to the Harvard Shuffle and join in. It cut through to the very core of their being. This was the one thing that made some smile with deep emotional pleasure. One dealer said: 'Ooh, this really gets my rocks off.' Regretting that he was not of the hardcore calibre, he tried desperately to fit in.

There was another ditty that was sung by dealers every hour or so, to the tune of the American Marine Corps drill march, and most merrily in times of a falling market, or when an OTC-traded company had just gone bust. The words were as follows:

> 'Buy at six and sell at four.
> This is what we're looking for.
> Buy at six and sell at four,
> What a pity you didn't have more.
> In at five and out at three,
> Sorry that's the way it'll be.
> (Chorus) Sound off 1, 2.
> Sound off 3, 4.
> Bring it on down 1, 2, 3, 4.
> 1 - 2 - 3 - 4 !!!'

Dealers joined in with gusto, often to the accompaniment of riotous dancing. Serving clients became confirmed here as holiday-type fun, a game of wits. Not really like work at all.

The sing-song was a bug that bit some dealers hard. First thing in the morning before one of the managers rolled in with a hangover, the trainees sang out:

'This is the way we ring the coups,
Ring the coups,
Ring the coups,
This is the way we ring the coups,
Early in the morning.'

Coups referred to clients' coupons or leads.

After lunch, Harvard dealers staggered back from the pub, drunk and beaming, arms round each other's shoulders. They were like a rugby crowd. Here is what they would sing:

Roll out the barrel,
We'll have a barrel of fun.

This rolling of the barrel signified *churning*, i.e. taking clients in and out of stocks at a furious rate, so generating further commission for dealers. Officially forbidden in most firms, churning was in fact tacitly condoned. The only way for a dealer to hold his job down was to overtrade his clients.

This unofficial version of 'Good King Wenceslas' was penned by a Tudorbury dealer for private circulation amongst his colleagues shortly before Christmas 1988:

1. Old mug punter he was phoned
With a view to dealing.
His dealer gave him a tip,
Made it sound appealing.
'Swanyard is its name' he said,
'It is set to double'.
So he bought ten grand's worth,
God now he's in trouble.

2. One week later he phoned up
To see how they were faring.
'What's the stock?' his dealer said,
His voice sounded so caring.
'Swanyard was the stock I bought,
Yes, 2p bid at present.
I got in at 4p net,
This is not so pleasant'.

3. 'Never mind' the dealer said,
'Not every one's a winner'.
'But' said the client 'money's short,
My wedge is getting thinner'.
Here's a churn the dealer thought,
I'll stick him into Norton.
'Buy these shares and sell Swanyard,
You never should have bought 'em'.

4. One year passed, the client was
In reduced circumstances.
He'd finally sold all his Boms
Given them enough chances.
So upon the train he got
And did his shotgun load.
His dealer'd decaked him too much
So he was up the road!

Harvard dealers would sing another hymn to churning, to the tune of the themesong of Rawhide, a cult Western of the late 1960s, starring Clint Eastwood:

Churn in, churn in, churn in,
Keep them clients churning.

Another rhyme, delivered in an ordinary voice this time, was: 'A churn a day keeps you in pay'. Dealers used these songs to ease the pain of what they did. It was like a hot toddy.

Dealers of various firms would sometimes sing to the tune of 'We Three Kings of Orient Are':

We three dealers of ------ are,
Sell your house, get rid of your car,
Think it's funny,
Lost your money,
Oh what a cunt you are!

Clients never suspected that dealers were putting them in a queue to be churned. If they had only known!

Harvard seemed particularly concerned with malpractice which lost the *Company* money. For instance, a director patrolled Harvard's dealing room, shouting '£25' to any dealer who had not written out a bargain slip correctly. This was a fine, to be deducted from his wages.

The dealers got plenty of fines. Many took nothing about their jobs seriously.

Their attitude was manifest in the nicknames they had found for stocks. Scoops (later Staks) became 'Scooby Do'. Rigby Electronics was 'Eleanor Rigby'. Charles Baynes was known as 'Charley B'. Wheyway was called 'Wee wee'. Over familiarity it seemed, bred contempt.

The nicknames by which Harvard dealers became known generally reflected their characters. Prominent at Harvard was a dealer nicknamed 'Foreign Legion'. He was an eccentric ex-public school man in his mid-twenties who had actually spent three years in the Foreign Legion.

'Foreign Legion' did an amazingly high turnover of business. He had two clients who would deal in excess of £250,000 each per account. One of these clients had supplied him with a mobile phone to call him on. During any one day, this spectacular share salesman would be seen using three telephones: the ordinary ones, the brown internal ones, and the mobile one.

He would dive under the desk and work all day from the floor. His voice would drone muffled through the room like a ghostly echo of the dealers pitching over his head. Upon dealing, he would throw his completed bargain slips upon the desks. Any leads he could not open, he sent sailing across the desks, to land perhaps in some dealer's lap.

From his vantage point, Foreign Legion's exact words were not all heard by his manager, which may have worked to the benefit of his sales figures.

By the end of the day, the area around his desk looked like the aftermath of a drunken celebration. Client cards lay everywhere, with empty cans and sweet wrappers. Coffee would be leaking from his military flask. But Foreign Legion's heyday was yet to come.

Moneyspinner, a Channel 4 TV programme, had presented Mr and Mrs Loveday, an old couple who were complaining about their dealings with Harvard Securities. They felt they had been unfairly treated in connection with the husband's purchase over the telephone of shares in OTC-traded Scoops (now Staks). The situation was that they had sent a letter of complaint to Harvard. The letter had been answered and Harvard director John Harris had suggested the Scoops bargain should be cancelled, with the money reinvested in another OTC-traded company.

The day after this television interview, it was revealed that it was Foreign Legion who had handled the Loveday's account. The tapes of the whizz-kid's sales pitch were replayed for all the dealing room to hear.

The pitch *was* in order. The dealer had neither lied nor exaggerated. The client had agreed to settle for the shares in the normal way and all the dealers clapped him. He had emerged clean, and was briefly Harvard's golden boy.

It was this dealer who had introduced to Harvard the 'down it in one', a trick he'd picked up in the Foreign Legion. In the evenings, trainee dealers would flock to the local pub in droves. They would congregate around the edge of the bar with their small glasses of spirits.

Their trainer would smack his hand on the bar surface and shout 'Go'. They would lean down and pick up the glasses with their teeth. They would down in one whiskies, gins, vodkas, or brandies, without using their hands. The first to finish his drink scored a point. The contest could contain up to fifteen rounds. Sometimes the trainer joined in, in which case the rest might club together to pay for his drinks.

Once, the dealers played 'down it in one' at lunchtime. They came back into Harvard the worse for wear, and started doing some pretty inspired selling. Harvard brought out the breathalyser.

A high profile dealer at one licenced dealer was always on the verge of being sacked for dodgy dealing. He did a little discretionary dealing, to which his clients assented, complaining after the event when the share prices often seemed to go down. He was fined but never quite sacked when clients complained. He was, after all, a good salesman.

This dealer was secretly married. His wife made jewellery which he used to hawk round the dealing floor. Returning home from work, he occasionally even sold to commuters on the tube. He added watches and coats to his repertoire.

He ended up at another licensed dealer, where he would stroll into work wearing a slimey green mackintosh, pointed shoes, and a white or checked suit fit for night-clubbing in the West End.

He wore bracelets, rings and earrings. He was his own clothes model. Right down to the space age aluminium briefcase in his grip, the Filofax under his arm, every item that hung about his person was for sale — with the possible exception of the Sony Walkman that beat pop-music into his eardrums.

One Harvard dealer had his name abbreviated to 'Hendo' because this had a brassy ring to it, in keeping with the tone of his pitching. A direct opposite to Hendo was a dealer in his mid-forties nicknamed Patsy for his softness.

There was a harder dealer than both of these. He had dark skin, a moustache and an aggressive telephone manner. He was nicknamed Colonel Gadaffi, which later became abbreviated to 'The Colonel'. His working briefly for London & Norwich Investment Services Ltd without getting paid a penny, almost knocked the stuffing out of him. He retreated into financial consultancy, and having learned his lesson, became a softer, more caring salesman.

Less energetic was a scruffy, pipe smoking Harvard dealer who had allegedly been a stableboy. He was nicknamed 'Compo', an abbreviation of 'compost heap'.

Another Harvard dealer with a high profile was nicknamed GI Joe, after the American Action Man style doll. This appelation mocked his rigid loyalty to his employer. He always gave the impression of being mentally drained by his work, but plodding on out of a sense of duty.

All dealers are familiar with the client who works in estate agency or computer sales, and who thinks of himself as a real hot businessman. He will ring into his sharedealer daily from his car phone. There is a type of dealer tailor-made for this sort of client. He is perhaps the nearest thing to a yuppie in licensed dealers. One such salesman at Harvard was conveniently called Wheeler.

Wheeler talked fast and furiously to clients. His accent was very

East End. He would introduce himself like this: 'Hallo Guv. This is Wheeler. Your wheeler dealer on the line.' He drove the training manager crazy. 'Don't call clients Guv,' he shouted. But Wheeler's previous experience as a Forex dealer, coupled with his youthful zeal, ensured his success as a share salesman.

More lacklustre but as well remembered was the Harvard dealer who was nicknamed 'Nightmare', due to the fact that he called every stock, from deadend rubbish like Bleasdale Warrants to honourable blue chips like Glaxo 'a nightmare'. For instance, if a client asked him, 'What do you think about Trusthouse Forte?' he'd reply 'Oh that nightmare'.

If Harvard produced a new stock for him to sell, he'd call it: 'Just another nightmare.' If the FT 100 Index was down, he'd tell clients, 'Everything's a nightmare in the market today'. If the market was up, he would groan: 'Everybody's rushing to buy. It's a nightmare.'

'Nightmare' lost several thousand pounds dealing in Sound Diffusion on the account. He went round telling his fellow dealers: 'I'm getting out of this nightmare.' He went off to Saudi Arabia to be an engineer, 'another nightmare'.

One Harvard dealer of Dutch descent was never given a nickname, although he was perhaps the most eccentric of the lot. He spent hours on the telephone to prospective clients, solving tax problems and sorting property deals. In this way he found a few big punters. It was enough for him to live on.

In the evenings, he would drink in the local pubs near to Harvard and, perhaps three times a week, would return to the building late at night. He would say to the security guard something like: 'I've missed the last train. Let me back onto the dealing room. I'll sleep on the floor.'

Once safely there he would drape cloth over the lens of the video camera high in the room corner. His assumption was that the eye of Harvard's camera never sleeps. He would then browse through Harvard's private files.

Then he made a stupid mistake. One morning, going up in the lift with two Harvard directors, he heard them complaining about a missing file, and said: 'Try the top left hand drawer at the back, if you're looking for *that* file.' Shortly afterwards, the dealer was sacked — too much knowledge is not always a good thing.

Dealers' disposable income goes like water on a plethora of pop concerts, football matches, nightclubs and expensive restaurants, which is why they never get the Porsches they aspire to. Again like their clients, they are victims of their own shortsightedness.

Dealers who earn the big money have been known to have it snatched from their grasp. Share salesmen at one notorious bucket shop in Costa Rica offloaded stock onto greedy speculators world-wide, and were highly paid for it, cash in hand.

They were put up in beautiful condominiums provided by the company. All dealers were warned not to go into the nearby city with big money in their pockets. They were told that in the prevailing climate of political unrest, it was possible that they might be searched, and if huge sums of cash were found on them, they would be suspected of being drug dealers.

One day, when they were all at work, the condominiums were raided. Their money was stolen. Who did it? The embittered dealers wondered. It was only after they had quit Costa Rica that they thought of blaming the company they had worked for. But what could they prove?

A surprising number of dealers blow good money on speculative investments or account trades. Like their clients they are natural gamblers, although there have always been a few canny dealers who shove all their money in the building society, and still fewer who make big money from their own share dealing.

One young Harvard dealer of Indian descent who wore plain suits and plain glasses, and looked just like a boring accountant, was given a cash gift by his parents as a start in life. His most sensible move, as average people would see it, was to put it down as deposit on a flat. But this dealer had a more ambitious proposal.

So long as he had a SEAQ screen in front of him, he reckoned he could make real money from the capital. This was why he had come to Harvard Securities in the first place.

This dealer chose his own stocks during the bull market. They were mostly penny punts, including Blacks Leisure, Mersey Docks, Jack Israel, Benjamin Priest, Acsis Jewellery and Borland International. He also went for the occasional blue chip.

Although inexperienced in trading, he had an animal instinct for the market. He knew exactly when to come in and out of stocks. It was a kind of genius. He would in the midst of dealing for clients ring his own broker and pick up, say, 50,000 Blacks Leisure for himself, jotting down the bargain in a little black notebook.

He would come out of stocks often within the account and certainly after only a brief period. He was happy to take lots of small profits, and he never seemed to lose.

He would buy stocks just before they had cash injections. For example he would say of one company: 'I'll bet you a rights issue is coming up' and he would buy big. If a rights issue was in fact due, the price would go up beforehand as it usually does, and he would make a bomb.

This wheeler-dealer gained his information from the tip-sheets, television and newspapers. He was an avid researcher. Furthermore, he made it his business to know which stocks were being ramped in which licensed dealers, so when Dares Estates, for example, was all the rage, he would pick up shares in that, monitoring the price rise on the screens and dumping his shares on the market at a good price before the licensed dealers should dump what remained of their bulk pick-up. He was never, however, involved in insider dealing.

Market-makers at Harvard Securities were always calling him into their back room to ask his opinion. He would feign annoyance beforehand at this, murmuring: 'Not again' and then he would disappear for a long while.

After only a few months, he had made for himself over £40,000. He had gambled and he had won. He promptly bought a flat outright.

At Harvard he was now a guru. When he went into a stock, others followed. Dealers made fortunes on his back.

At the time, brokers were still willing to deal with Harvard, so Harvard dealers could do occasional agency bargains for clients on any listed stock of their choosing.

The master dealer started making his clients real money on agency trades. Harvard Securities offered him a job running its options department, but he turned it down. He ended up working at S.G. Warburgs, his own brokers, who had been impressed with his investment talents.

An insightful few use their earnings to buy first properties in Docklands, Fulham, or other areas up and coming in any property boom at the time. They look to making the fastest possible capital gain. A minority buys a second property, covering the mortgage by renting it out. Such dealers live one day in their London abode, another day back with their parents, and at weekends somewhere esoteric but good for capital gain, like East Anglia.

Any money these thrifty types squander is for prestige reasons, perhaps on portable telephones or on computers for storing stock market data.

Dealers find catharsis in loud unsubtle music, in heckling crowds. It is a hectic relaxation from the hectic dealing room. They seesaw from one crisis to another, and this is their life until they flunk out.

Even dealers who are university graduates are prone to the same. Any interest they may have had in a better sort of culture becomes fogged. Dealers also play football, tennis, etc, and those who play it deviously, unpredictably are likely to do business in that way too.

Dealers lack taste when it comes to choosing restaurants. Trendiness here, as in other spheres of life, is more important than quality. They might eat at a smart new joint in Chelsea, spending collectively hundreds of pounds on meals hardly fit for the dustbin.

If they are trying to impress girlfriends, it is the service that they want to look good. One London & Norwich Investment Services Ltd dealer threatened to beat up another for recommending a restaurant to which he took his girlfriend, only to discover they had to wait forty minutes before being served.

At lunchtime a few dealers will take sandwiches and Perrier water at their desks, but most do not take such dietary precautions.

Many dealers at Harvard Securities used to crowd out a workmen's 'caff', stuffing themselves on fried sausages, eggs, chips, etc, washed down with revolting tea. Some had more in common with the workmen they ate alongside than with their clients, even if they *were* the only people wearing suits in the 'caff'.

Dealers often wear blue pinstripe, or dark formal suits. Some of those who have been in the business for, say, longer than six months may have tailor-made suits, preferably Saville Row and double-breasted; they may of course be slow to pay for these. Shirts are often tailor-made cotton, as manufactured by Pinks.

Dealers sometimes pride themselves on being treated better than their stockbroker counterparts in the Jermyn Street shops. Some flourish their American Express cards under the shop assistants' noses, treating the poor blighters with a curious mixture of disdain and mateyness.

Bright ties are the norm. Bow-ties are not out of question with the spivvy types, especially if they rarely meet clients. Some firms forbid their female dealers to wear trousers, insisting on skirts.

Child labour has flourished in certain firms. Young boys, sons of senior personnel, scurry about, sometimes in school uniform. A runner, briefly working at Harvard Securities, was certainly only a child.

The better the dealer, the more leeway he is granted in what he wears. One whizz-kid always came into work wearing faded jeans and T-shirt, whereas his colleagues wore suits. When a manager objected, his superior said: 'Look at all the money be brings into the firm. He can wear what the fuck he likes.' Dealers who are sacked come back to visit their old firm in similar casual clothes. This smacks of old boys revisiting their former schools.

Earning a high commission, or the ability to do so, commanded more respect, dealer to dealer, than anything. A parable did the rounds amongst top dealers, called 'The Rich Man and The Poor Man'. It was a tale invented by these 'Thatcher's children', citing the difference between, for example, a dealer and a clerk for the same firm. Particular persons were cited.

Another version which developed as a private joke between the dealers at Harvard Securities was 'The Rich Nigger and The Poor Nigger', comparing a black director with a black cleaner. Despite being offensive, this version lingered.

Racism amongst dealers has always been pronounced, whether Irishman against Welshman, Indian against black, white against oriental. A team leader at Harvard Securities (early 1987) would do a quick deal then glance up at an Indian female dealer in his charge: 'How much have you done, Paki?' he would say.

She got her own back when sitting next to a young Jamaican dealer in her next place of employment, Tudorbury Securities (early 1988). One day his files and client cards were spreading onto her desk. 'Keep all this to yourself,' she said, and swept it with her arm into an untidy heap. 'You've messed all this up,' he shouted. 'Serves you right, you nigger,' she retorted. Sadly, these sort of epithets are still being used in and around the City. There is a serious need for a change in attitudes.

Dealers from outside the South East, or of ethnic minority groups, must work twice as hard to command respect. If they are mediocre salesmen, their chances of survival are slim.

One Welsh dealer was obviously enough nicknamed 'Taffy'. Proving a fish out of water, he was sacked. A trainer's last words of wisdom to him were: 'Take your phlegm and bugger off back down the motorway to your farm in Wales.'

The same trainer would likewise rebuke a lazy Indian dealer: 'Come on. You're not eating an Indian curry now.'

A Chinese trainee dealer at Tudorbury Securities called Tang was nicknamed 'Boat Tang' — a reference to the boat people — or 'Tokyo Tang'. Once he lowered his head on the table, slamming down his fists in frustration at his failure to sell stock. A fellow dealer grinned rudely at him: 'That tunnel shit don't work. You tunnelled your way through Vietnam, and all those trenches. But you can't tunnel your way through the City.'

The good news is that coloured dealers, without an accent, are not usually subject to racism from their clients, who cannot see their faces.

There are certain races dealers favour doing business with. Irish punters, most dealers consider, are especially greedy. In most licensed dealing circles, they are 'prime rib'! They settle on time, they buy large, and they don't grumble when they lose. They are often ready to speculate with money they cannot really afford, or with 'the luck of the Irish'.

There is competition as to who will get the Irish punter's money first, the licensed dealer or the bookie! One thing is certain, the greedy hand of the British share salesman is reaching across the waters and seizing on the Irishman's weak points like a limpet.

The astute dealer will feign a strong Irish accent, modelled on that of the weatherman on BBC Television. The dealer sounds over the top, but he seems to take in the Irishmen alright, bellowing down the phone: 'Ha-l-l-o-o-o . . . I have something for y-o-u . . '

Often dealers would change their name for the Irish pitch into, for example, 'Paddy O'Dougall'.

Bona fide Irish dealers could not tolerate seeing their countrymen done down in this way. They would beg, borrow, and maybe try to steal details of Irish clients so as to deal them personally. Their heavy-handed patriotism would thus secure them more business.

Dealers have jumped onto the prestige bandwagon of wearing Rolex watches. Some too have touted fake Rolex watches they have picked up direct from Hong Kong, or else, perhaps, illicitly from a middleman in England.

Obviously, real Rolex watches have more prestige than the fakes, although the two are hardly distinguishable. Gossip has immortalised the case in which a notorious sharedealer bought a £2,000 Rolex watch for £500 from a friend who had stolen it from the jeweller's he worked for. The dealer sold it to another dealer for £700, then claimed £2,000 from his insurance company on grounds that he had lost the watch. Rolex watch wearers are out to impress each other, more than anyone else.

Another dealer successfully put in a false claim with his insurance company for theft of an expensive camera on holiday. Many dealers have since fiddled their insurance companies. It is quite the done thing now.

Even dealers earning £50,000 plus per annum could not resist cheating the system. They would recycle old season tickets for commuting to work, or would otherwise renege on their fares. They would get a kick out of petty crime. Staplers, scissors, files, typing paper, lavatory paper, and up to date financial magazines were always disappearing from licensed dealers' offices.

Something for nothing, never mind the legality of it, proves irresistible to dealers. As the story goes, many shoplift. They know where and when to go; perhaps Chelsea boutiques on Saturday afternoons, or department stores where they're in with the security staff. For instance, two Tudorbury dealers have walked out of pizza restaurants after having eaten, without paying, and one steals make-up and sweets from shops. Most dealers who do this sort of thing are much too wily to get caught.

Dealers will stick in amazingly multiple applications for new issues and will often get away with it. They are more skilled in such fraud than MPs.

Many dealers have contacts who will get them suspiciously cheap stereos, cheap cars. Stocks and shares are only one small part of their trading interests, and often the part they would give up most willingly.

Share salesmen are past masters at running up bills on credit cards, often for account trades that haven't worked out, if their broker threatens to sue them. Most often, however, they will refuse to pay losses, full stop. American Express gold cards are popular as the loans they offer are cheap. However, not all dealers are granted these cards. This is because many have been found not credit-worthy. Some will change accounts from one bank to another quite regularly, moving on to escape repercussions from the last one.

Some dealers like to buy up houses (with dodgy mortgages), repairing and decorating them, for subsequent sale at a good profit. They have no interest, of course, in what they are doing per se.

Dealers unable or unwilling to pay for mortgages, rent a room or live with their parents, in which case they almost invariably fritter their earnings.

As a variation on the theme, many dealers club together and live several under one roof. This way they can party into oblivion on a regular basis together. They can also put up vagrant dealers, one of their rare shows of altruism.

Some, buying property in the East End, for instance, have made considerably less gain than they had expected, because they had to sell out after only a few months, when either they stopped being dealers, or could not keep up payments — references for building societies and banks were often rigged to state a higher income than was actually the case — and this could be counter-productive. Almost all dealers at Harvard Securities would say they were earning £40,000 a year. The majority, due to fines, and quitting after a few months, did not.

Many dealers chain-smoke. Almost all drink heavily. Any who supported movement towards ethical investment, i.e. banning tobacco manufacturers etc., was showing the utmost hypocrisy. A short life and a carefree one, that is theirs. Anyone who advocates otherwise, they designate 'boring'.

To increase plausibility, some dealers have cultivated a yuppie telephone manner. A Tudorbury client once picked up on this, asking a settlements clerk over the phone:

'Is my dealer an 'OK Yah' lady?'

'What do you mean?' asked the clerk.

'Does she go horse-riding in hunter wellies?' asked the client.

The clerk confirmed that perhaps she did. The dealer concerned and her client then had a good laugh about it all.

Sharedealers raise sponsorship for private interests from clients. One Tudorbury dealer was frequently offering dealers 20% of any funds raised from clients to sponsor his car-racing activities.

The more money some dealers make, the more they burn. Imitating his elders and betters, one dealer spent thousands of pounds on a personalised number plate for his shiney black BMW. Nobody could then realise its age.

Another dealer drove a BMW, and mentioned this at a party to a highflying forty year old PA who drove her own Porsche.

'You look very young to be driving a BMW,' she said. The dealer laughed: 'You look very young to be driving a Porsche.'

She smiled, and he quickly made a date with her.

One share salesman had the greatest contempt for Northern clients, even though he had lived in the North of England himself. Most seemed unworldly, as he himself had been until that time, and he called them 'thick'. He was particularly contemptuous of one punter, a Northern businessman, who made a point of paying for shares he had bought from Eyas Securities, even after that firm was suspended from trading.

The White Hart, Southwark. Harvard dealers believed that Tom Wilmot owned this pub as he occasionally made free drinks available to them.

Harvard boss Tom Wilmot once, but not for the first time, threw open the White Hart pub with free drink for all Harvard Securities dealers. The training officer ordered from the stunned barmaid a round of quadruple vodka and tonics, 'and one for yourself . . . '

In the meantime a Harvard dealer had whisked away a trainee's briefcase and had inspected its contents before offering it back to its owner. 'This was getting trampled under, so I rescued it', he told the trainee. He had, of course, been checking his colleague out.

A dealer will occasionally spy on a colleague, then expose him for his own gain. He will more often than not have his paymaster. Many spies and insider journalists in the licensed dealing community have never been uncovered.

Most camouflage their missions brilliantly. Mini taperecorders are hidden in briefcases, and notes are jotted in filofaxes in secret code. Spies are likely to have mediocre dealing records. The last thing they want is a high profile.

Harvard Securities got wind that traitors were making unrecorded outgoing calls on the brown internal phones. One spy was recording vital information this way on an answerphone at his home.

While the Harvard dealing floor was at work one day, a British Telecom engineer toured the desks, ripping out the internal telephone wires. Several dealers had important telephone conversations cut dead.

Spying can pay better than sharedealing. Licensed dealers try to keep their staff too busy to think of it, even when business is going through a slack period.

The wrong people get suspected of stabbing their firms in the back. One female dealer at Tudorbury Securities came onto the dealing floor wearing new mirrored sunglasses. 'Caper . . . caper,' she murmured.

'Miami Vice,' screeched her colleagues.

The dealer, long subject to witch hunts as she wouldn't sleep around, now came under fresh scrutiny. When she was about to go home that night, a manager stared at her bag. 'How many of our leads have you got in there?' he said.

She shook her head. 'I bring clients into Tudorbury. I don't take them away,' she said.

He grinned: 'How would you like a poke with my rod?'

She laughed and said nothing. She wanted to keep her job.

To keep their sanity, Tudorbury dealers had formed a close knit group. Some on cocaine, they were sustaining their high with alcohol. All day they were lounging about. Their sweet youthful faces seemed to say that they wouldn't hurt a fly.

They developed their own patois.

New catchphrases originating from popular British TV shows were introduced onto Tudorbury's dealing floor. 'Hallo Peeps . . . Goodbye Peeps' was commonplace. A 'Woody Woodpecker' laugh tailed every sale. They constantly chanted 'Caper . . . caper . . . ' This was their celebratory phrase for anything that dispelled the monotony. If someone made a sale, they shouted 'Caper' — it was getting to be a rare event. If a dealer came into work late, it was 'Caper'. When a fight broke out, they chanted: 'Ca-per, Ca-per.'

Recently, one of the group brought in some new white T-shirts. On their fronts was printed: 'What's your caper?' On the backs, under 'Caper Crew SW1' were printed these options: 'Raper Caper — to have sex. News Caper — 'The Sun'. Kipper Caper — unwashed. Beard Caper — to be offensive (referring to a dealer's name). Caperettes — Bimbos.' Below was a black circular logo for 'Caper Merchandise Inc'.

Dealers purchased these T-shirts for £15 each, and for a while afterwards actually wore them.

By way of comparison, Tudorbury Group ties were next made available to the dealers. They were just another sweetener. Gold stripes indicated senior dealer status. All dealers were keen to get their ties. The struggle to get something for nothing then proved to be an end in itself. Nobody ever wore them.

One dealer at Tudorbury Securities had a life chockful of impermanent luxuries. It was like a fluctuating dream. He would live for the present. When his salary cheque came in, he would relate that he had booked himself a room in a 4-star hotel for the next couple of weeks. He might then squander what was left of his money in style on rounds of booze for the other dealers, on 'tarts' to fill his lonely nights, and on 'sniff' (i.e. cocaine).

Although he treated his earnings thus like pocket-money, this was adult behaviour. His spurts of lavish living gave his vision the breadth and assumptions of a wealthy man. This enabled him to address wealthy clients like an equal, and to prise *incredible* sums of money from them, the likes of which no other dealer could match.

The other side of the coin was when he was broke. He might then sleep rough at railway stations, or cadge lodgings with his friends. His mother's house, off the beaten track, outside London, was a last resort.

He obtained permission from BOM Holdings director Michael Lucas, who was on Tudorbury's premises, to borrow his Mercedes with chauffeur so he could get to his bank in style.

That afternoon, he arrived in the splendid Mercedes with its personalised number plate, outside Barclays Bank in Old Broad Street, the City of London. This branch, unlike most, closes early at 3 p.m.

The chauffeur opened the Mercedes' door. The doorman at the bank greeted him as if he was royalty. Even though the branch had been closed for thirty-five minutes, banking privileges were extended to him.

As the dealer gruffly reconstructed it to his colleagues on the dealing floor: 'I walked into the bank. Attention all round from the girls . . . ' He had certainly arrived.

As he was ushered from the bank, back into the Mercedes, he glanced up the street. Approaching the bank was John Harris, director of Harvard Securities and this dealer's one time boss.

The Tudorbury sharedealer, this man who could get clients to part with perhaps £100,000 on the basis of a two minute telephone call, smiled as he caught John Harris's eye. The Harvard director stared at him. The dealer winked at the chauffeur: 'Put your cap on.' As the chauffeur complied, and started the engine, this dealer, in the back seat, picked up the mobile phone, pretending he was talking business.

As the car carried him away, he lowered the electronically controlled window, and shouted out 'hallo Chopper' (John Harris's nickname).

. . . 'Guess who I saw next,' he explained to the dealers back on the floor: 'Chopper Harris'.

This was greeted with a gale of laughter.

There was a small number of sharedealers in various firms who plied a second trade as drug dealers. They have been known to deal from BMWs on portable phones. To impede access to their equally shady clientele, these entrepreneurs threatened use of hired thugs to beat up any serious competitors. Conducting operations from telephones on their dealing floors, they used code phrases in their conversations, such as: 'I need a good Columbian duster (Cocaine).' But everyone knew what they were about.

Marijuana and cocaine were commonplace, while LSD was seen as wild, fit only for a one-off experiment, or for weirdos.

Cocaine, the prestige drug here as in other City environments, was the most sought after. Just as a film-star might snort the stuff, so might a top dealer, claiming that it stimulates him. The drug was made freely available at parties where occasionally, after the American tradition, coke-spoons are offered round for free, to be hung round the neck. But dealers did not bother with such trappings as cocaine corners, snorting devices, etc.

Money was needed to finance the cocaine habits of a select number of dealers. Cocaine was costing between £70 and £100 a gramme. In an extreme case, a gramme might last a dealer one day. On the basis of a seven day week, this would mean £490-£700 spent on cocaine before the more routine expenses. Furthermore, dealers needed increasingly more to get the same kick.

It is perhaps because of this costliness, and the need for a regular supplier, that cocaine snorting has become an essential habit of the up and coming shares or futures salesman. He pretends that this is his glamorous escape route from pressure, and gets a kick out of knowing that it exerts a more dangerous pressure in itself.

Cocaine intake comes to replace the grind of share-dealing, for the dealer going through a barren patch at work, or who is un-employed. The more hardworking is the dealer, the more intensely he might snort the stuff. What might be the consequences?

Some dealers in their teens or early twenties look, speak and walk around stooped, moping and almost wizened like old men. The area between their nostrils gets eaten away. Severe colds and nose bleeds come too.

Many would be well advised to cut down before they wreck them-selves. If they needed less money to indulge their drug habits, they would be less prone to hard sell clients.

The sensible dealers, and sometimes their directors too, approach private hospitals for help in fighting the addiction. One institution that has served the City in this way is Charter Clinic, whose director

Tony McLellan declared in an interview with the magazine *Time Out:* 'This place is not cheap. We are a profit-making organisation and can't take the stereotype drug addict — the young homeless unemployed. Many of our enquiries come direct from City employers who can't afford to lose key personnel. They see the problem as an illness rather than a criminal act and come to us rather than go to the police.'

A police drugs hot-line installed due to reports of post Big Bang drug abuse found few callers. Amongst certain dealers this was rechristened, 'Grassline'. The public has concluded from this line's unpopularity that the drugs problem for the post Big Bang high-fliers has been exaggerated, but nothing could be further from the truth.

Of course every cloud has its silver lining. Dealers with a cocaine problem find they pitch clients in a less patient, less diplomatic, less meticulous way. They become what in the jargon would be described as more bullish — the dealing managers often applaud this and don't look too deep into the causes. The reason for this is that they are sometimes on cocaine as well.

One dealer who was so thin that his stomach seemed to meet his spinal column, confided his cocaine problem in his training manager: 'This makes me erratic, so don't sack me. I'm fighting it,' he said.

The training manager seemed most interested to hear about this. He subsequently became quite tolerant when the dealer came late into work, with a fit of the shakes. He would dress in scruffy clothes, not City type suits.

In his condition he demanded immunity from regulations appertaining to such matters. To some extent he got it. Drug users have prestige in this industry.

His mind clouded, he had littler tolerance for the intricacies of profit figures, and even for the crudest details of the sales pitch. His method was direct and effective, his bluntness maniacal.

When selling shares in XYZ Investments for instance, he would ring clients and scream down the phone: 'Buy Mr P.'

'Where's the company quoted?' a client might ask. 'Not quoted anywhere,' the dealer would reply. 'Mr P is chairman of XYZ Investments. But you're not buying XYZ. You're buying Mr P . . . '

This dealer, increasingly struck for money, and increasingly delirious on the phone, left his company.

Later, he met up with some ex-colleagues who were still dealers there, one evening at a Thames wine bar. He got blind drunk. Walking back with them near his old firm's offices, he stopped in front of them. He scaled the wall, landing on a high up window ledge, where he edged himself to face the road below him, like a stunt artist.

'Is it a bird? Is it a plane? No, it's Superman!' he screamed.

The other dealers were roaring with laughter, but at him rather than with him. They eventually had to call the security guard after he had pleaded for long minutes, and they jeered at him because he did not have the guts to climb down again.

The security guard opened the window for him, letting him back down through the building he was already nostalgic for. What easier way would he ever find again to finance his drug habit than by hard selling OTC shares?

Securities dealers, being rebels, may have tales to tell of how they ran away from school. Their success in their professional lives may be complemented by their failures as school children. A significant number of them have been up against authority for as long as they have lived.

Consequently, dealers and the police are often temperamentally at odds with each other. Many dealers have had their driving licenses endorsed for reckless speeding, or else for drinking and driving. One dealer, stopped for speeding, gave police the name of an ex-Sheridan securities dealer who had died of an overdose. He was later to claim that he got off scot free. Some dealers have spent nights in police cells for being drunk and disorderly, or for urinating in the street, or similar petty offences. Most see the law as fair game, just as they seek out loopholes in the financial legislature. To this extent, for starters, they are not yuppies, or if so they are yuppies gone wrong.

Dealers rarely or never indulge in the traditional yuppie activities such as hunting on Sundays, or sightseeing weekends in New York. Their leisure activities are more dissipated than that. Their idea of keeping fit is the odd game of football or squash, worlds away from the routine work-outs of the dedicated. Likewise, idiosyncratic outlets such as war-games, and luncheons at 'School Dinners' are the preserve of real City people, and seem pretentious to many bucket shop merchants.

In fact it is true to say that dealers in futures and shares from the less salubrious establishments do not have the social decorum common to people on their income level working in the financial services industry.

Typical oafishness was demonstrated during Harvard's staff meeting at the Inn on the Park, Park Lane, towards the end of July 1987. The purpose of this was for an announcement about Harvard's takeover. All staff had to attend. Coaches of the Pennant Group (in whose shares Harvard made a market) ushered them to the posh hotel where they made their way to a ballroom.

The atmosphere inside was tastefully opulent. Flower arrangements were precise and colourful. Waiters lavished on the guests exotic food, champagne and every variety of expensive wine, in a banquet to which most dealers had not seen the parallel. Many lapped it all up as if it was their natural due, making sure to get drunk en route.

The food was too delicate for some of their tastes, and indeed one dealer remarked to a neighbour: 'I prefer fish and chips.' But the more discerning were appreciative. It wasn't every day that they could stuff themselves on decent food. The expensive restaurants some frequented were put to shame here. The waiters were nearly mobbed by a vociferous minority who had not eaten all day in preparation for this do.

As the evening progressed, the waiters became increasingly less respectful. Disgust flashed across their faces on no few occasions. 'Who are these animals?' one said. Their defensive attitude did little to endear them to young men who might accurately be described as amongst the toughest sharp practitioners in the fringe City. The dealers went on the offensive.

One after another, they ordered beer. The waiters were sweating as they replied: 'We don't serve beer in this sort of establishment, sir.'

These were the lucky waiters. Others were subjected to the Harvard style hard sell. One top dealer stopped a waiter in his tracks just as the poor man was trying to take a tray back from the ballroom to the kitchens.

The dealer undid his tie. His jacket was already off. He pushed back his cuffs. His face took on a faintly menacing look. Drink had brought out his true nature. He might have been on the Harvard dealing floor at that moment. A spasm of fear crossed the waiter's face, but he didn't move away. His safest move was obviously hear the young rogue out.

The dealer's chest swelled. 'We're Harvard Securities plc. The UK's largest market-maker on OTC shares. Have you heard of us?' he boomed. The waiter mumbled something non-commital. Spurred on by his reticence, the dealer pressed on. 'Do you know what OTC shares are? You could make money investing with us. You'll end up owning this hotel, not just working in it.'

By the time the waiter had escaped, some dealers were riotous. Their critical faculties, such as they were, had become dulled.

Tom Wilmot then made the announcement they had all been waiting for. The announcement was that there was no announcement. An eleventh hour bidder for Harvard had come on the scene, but no more would be revealed for a fortnight. Until then, 'Enjoy yourselves . . .'

Tom Wilmot then turned the evening over to one of his favourite dealers, the ex-taxi driver mentioned earlier, who gave comic impersonations of Ali Akbar, an imaginary Arab. The comedy fell flat. Some dealers, disillusioned with the lack of concrete news on any takeover of Harvard Securities, determined to cut their losses and 'get well pissed'. They plucked at the flower arrangements and dismantled them. Some girls put carnations in the boys' lapels. Everybody was behaving as if they were in the dealing room on a Friday afternoon.

At around 7 p.m. dealers staggered down the winding staircase and out. They were chanting 'Here we go, here we go'. The hotel residents stared at them in horror.

Some twenty Harvard dealers ended up at a trendy local wine bar, where they got still merrier. Here, a dealer called a Harvard secretary a 'tart', after she had failed to respond to his somewhat importunate advances. Another dealer, acting on her behalf, hit him. A fight broke out, and all the dealers were promptly turned out.

On the dealing floor, as well as socially, dealers, like stockbrokers, offer a good line in dirty jokes. Telling them is a good excuse for not working, since team leaders, managers, even directors, join in and stop yelling at them to carry on raking in clients' monies. The racist jokes unfortunately prove the most popular. If dealers worked instead of messing around like this, then they could earn fantastic incomes, even on the average commission structures for these firms. But whether in work or in play, their moral compromises are marked, and become more so in their accumulation.

Language used by dealers is riddled with cliches. When they are trying the 'friendly' approach on clients, the streetwise lapse into some of the colloquial language they use amongst themselves. They might say, 'Come into this one, Sir, it'll fly.' Or, 'The shares have done a dive, Sir, they'll soon be back on top.' They might almost be traders at a fruit and veg stall. Judging from their level of literacy, it is a good thing some dealers don't have to write to their clients.

To each other, dealers are often still more outspoken: 'Fuck(ing)', 'crap', 'shit', 'prick', and other such words punctuate their conversation as naturally as breathing. Clients who pay late are 'cunts'. Dealers who successfully wheedle huge sums of money out of their clients become enviously tagged 'moneyfuckers'. OTC stocks that are unlikely to perform may be termed 'tinkers', a word that was introduced to many by a Harvard Securities director.

Directors of some licensed dealers will swear as much as their employees, sometimes by way of motivating them. The pace of work on the dealing floor permits little in the way of time or of opportunity for more subtle communication; nor would most dealers exactly respond to it.

Dealing floors are sometimes too accessible, and the staff at a firm like Harvard Securities has turned over too rapidly for easy identification of individuals.

At various firms, thieves have plundered dealing rooms for wallets and handbags, and if spotted have been mistaken for dealers. It has been suspected but never proved that some may have indeed been ex-dealers, taking a belated vengeance. It seems that leads too may have gone missing by this route. If the thieves have accomplices still employed by the firm, they are at an obvious advantage.

Motivation to earn money, stimulated by licensed dealers, makes dealers amoral. Dealers are being ruined, as well as their clients.

Some would argue that the dealer's talent at selling, though essential, is useless without a lot of hard work, and more importantly than anything, without a certain looseness of moral vision. This is why, the argument continues, many dealers, like terrorists, can usually only do their dirty jobs when they are young; too young to appreciate the effects of ruining people.

One wealthy dealer is almost totally unable to close a sale on the telephone, and yet she is retained by her firm on a special remuneration arrangement, because she has clients in high places who happen to be her friends, and who will deal big, as well as being helpful in various little ways to the directors of her firm.

Individuals who are useful in a licensed dealers may be accommodated in this way. The structure remains fluid as it has to be for survival. No rules are inviolable, least of all the written ones.

Older dealers too have their uses, even though at Harvard they were sneered at by younger men for their inability to be so bullish, so conniving.

But at the end of the day, the elders had a charm and flair that the youths could not cultivate. Their jokes about life were more cut-throat. They could generally make young dealers who were posing, look very green.

As one older Indian dealer would say while he scrutinised the young ones severely over the top of his bifocals; 'You kids don't know what life is about. You'll be on the dole queue before my pension comes up.'

He would then get back on the phone. In a bear market he, like the other older dealers, retained consistent levels of business, whereas the younger ones were floundering. He would cultivate an elderly statesman image with his clients, and they found solace in his maturity.

For some reason, his clients would ask him: 'Can you guarantee the share price will go up?'

'Sir,' he would reply, 'Can you guarantee that the chair you sit in will hold you up? . . . There are only two guarantees in life: death and higher taxes. Although I can't guarantee what the price will do, coming into this one is guarantee enough . . . '

After a deal was done, he would put the phone down and write out the bargain slip, smirking. He would then snigger and say: 'It's guarantee enough that you'll be floating down the Thames.'

Another older dealer was a small black American. He was slim, mentally and physically active, and very fit. About forty years old, he could have passed for twenty-five or twenty-six, in casual clothes. In a dark suit, with a little gold jewellery, he was smart and business-like. He rose to power at Harvard quickly.

What a powerhouse of a salesman he proved himself. If a client prevaricated, this is what he would say: 'Can't you make a decision on your own? Are you a man or a mouse? You listen to me. You get out your cheque book right now and you write me a cheque for £4,000, while I wait on the line . . . Fine, now you get that out to me by this afternoon's post . . . ' His techniques worked like a dream. He was brilliant; there was no other word for it.

Although a kindly man, he became increasingly hard and professional after he was elevated into a market-making position.

There was a way to crack his defences. A female dealer who happened to be also an American, was talking business with him, when she blurted out: 'Hey, I miss the good old Yankee food. You remember Denny's in the States? Their Grandslam breakfast?'

Harvard's top market-maker licked his lips: 'Mmmnn, those hash brown potatoes, those mouth-watering biscuits . . . '

'And chocolate chip cookies,' she said.

'I just love dipping those cookies in coffee,' he replied. 'Why can't you get a decent cup of coffee in England?'

'And Golden Bird fried chicken in Los Angeles,' she continued.

The newly appointed director of Harvard picked up a book and made as if he was aiming to fling it at her: 'You get the hell out of this market-making room before I kill you,' he said.

Dealers transmit their enthusiasm for money to their clients. Some quote famous people on the subject of money, for instance Jimmy Saville who called it the 'lubrication of life', or Howard Abraham who said: 'I'm so happy to be rich, I'm willing to take the con-sequences.' One dealer at Harvard Securities regularly quoted Oscar Wilde, and nobody else, although he was unacquainted at first hand with his works. Clients too like being quoted at. It makes their dealer appear more erudite and some will try to quote back at him, e.g.: 'Up to a point, Lord Copper,' when they have heard out a eulogy of some shares.

Some dealers skilfully present punters with images of quick easy wealth. The dupes become fired with greed. They simply must have the shares. If the price goes up around 1p — as invariably happened with particular OTC shares after a sales campaign in them at Harvard, the client will feel he is walking on air, even though the likely big spread (i.e. difference between buying and selling prices) will not enable him to realise a gain. The dealer may not explain this, but might say something like, 'At this rate, you'll be a millionaire.' Any small loss makes less impact on the client. He doesn't want to believe it, so he doesn't really.

An especially dedicated type of dealer will give clients his private telephone number, will speak with them from his home. This might enable him to do considerably more business, although it entails a sacrifice of privacy that increasingly few are prepared to make.

It must be said that if a dealer lives with his parents, and they answer phone calls, clients may catch on, and, if so, will not be impressed. The dealer's image becomes deflated. It's as if the client has been trading on the recommendations of a mere child, all along.

Generally, few clients realise quite how young their dealers are. An authoritative voice on the telephone is to a large extent ageless. It proves the most lucrative way when youth and inexperience remain a well-guarded secret.

For this reason too, many licensed dealers don't generally encourage clients to visit. Dealers barely free of their mothers' apron strings, operating with minimal equipment from dingy offices, are not unknown and are not a sight to inspire confidence.

However a client's ego receives a tremendous boost when he is shown round one of the better dealing rooms, and is introduced to the firm's directors.

Visiting clients often dress casually, perhaps in tweed jacket and corduroys. Many aim to appear the laid-back, affluent businessmen they aspire to be. However, if they aren't, potentially at least, large clients, they may not be allowed to visit.

Clients are liable to panic sometimes if their dealer leaves the firm. He will quite likely have moved to another licensed dealer, in which case he will possibly contact the client afresh. They may continue their business relationship, but new difficulties will doubtless arise. The client may still have some money tied up in OTC stock, in which the dealer's original firm is the sole market-maker.

It is convenient if an ally remains in the old, now rival camp, to whom the dealer can refer the client for the purposes of selling his OTC stock. Most dealers at his old firm, his previous friends, are likely to be saying treacherous things about him to clients and indeed the firm may, arguably out of sheer spite threaten him with legal action on grounds such as debts or removal of client records. The better the dealer, the more he is at risk.

Some dealers leave and take masses of clients with them, not all their own. If they take dealers as well, they are the pied pipers of the licensed dealing world, and the curse of their erstwhile workmates whom they may still meet in the evenings to swap gossip over a pint.

It is not advisable for the dealer who moves on to let his old firm know where he has gone immediately. One of the pied pipers described above, upon leaving his old firm, had a friend send them a postcard from Italy, where this maverick was pretending he had gone on holiday. In reality he had started up in a new firm, which then became seriously considered by his former colleagues, with regard to their own future employment.

A dealer's relationship with his client is a very personal phenomenon. Many clients will be happy to sustain an interesting relationship which keeps them vaguely in touch with the market, even if it doesn't make them money. Perhaps they have stockbrokers who make them enough to compensate. Perhaps they are well loaded already, and simply don't care how their speculative investments turn out.

Share salesmen from time to time strike up deals with clients, for example: 'I'll buy a crate of wine off you, if you buy shares off me.'

The most dedicated dealer of all goes so far as to invite clients round to his house, cementing a relationship that may last for decades. If, in later years, he sells insurance, or unit trusts, or even kitchens, he will doubtless hold onto some of his original clients. He may put to good use his sometimes intimate knowledge of their personal finances, jobs and other details.

The client under such circumstances may feel flattered by the dealer's apparent deep interest in him. Before he knows what he's doing, he may find himself in the dealer's power, manipulated. He may be persuaded to invest in property syndicates, unquoted stocks, investment holding vehicles, indeed anything that appears remotely plausible and brings a fat commission to the salesman's pocket.

Certainly the salesman himself would avoid many of the investment propositions he offers. He may sometimes lose money on his own investments, but they are at least Stock Exchange listed stocks, or investments with an otherwise limited downslide potential: a calculated risk. He takes full advantage of the little he does know about his professional field, and he hedges his bets. If he sometimes blows his earnings, he at least enjoys the use of them.

If he feels tempted to go to work in a more respectable field, he need only, to be cured, listen to his colleagues, his superiors, the colourful two-faced bastards that flit in and out of the twilight world he has made his own: 'Don't be stupid. The most you'll earn in a normal job is fifteen grand a year, perhaps twenty grand in the City. Think of the money here . . . '

Indeed, one dealer of a London-based dealer in American OTC stocks was reputed to earn £500,000 in a particularly good year. Quite a few dealers have earned well over the £100,000 per annum level. It is no wonder that the successful ones develop excessive self confidence and cling sycophantically to their positions. Nonetheless, many change careers, and a few even do so successfully.

Many salesmen are protected from worry about the future or about regulations by their own ignorance. When it comes down to it, they don't know too much about their field, nor do they care. Keeping thoroughly up-to-date with developments would be too much like hard work. It would entail reading, something to which these fast-talkers, these smoothies, are often allergic. Even the graduates, in this respect, become like the rest. Developments in screen technology, and computerised print-outs are a blessing to many licensed dealers. So is public ignorance.

In many firms, the computer is becoming a convenient scapegoat for errors in client details and in dealing records. In truth, the faults are usually traceable to specific dealers or administrative staff.

One problem is that many dealers can't spell. In addition, some are developing esoteric forms of shorthand, comprehensible only to themselves or to their small group. Here is a tactic that can adeptly protect the confidentiality of client records or leads. Any dealer who inherits or steals them cannot read the scrawl. All this is proving a growth area which will later perhaps assist in the licensed dealing community's self-preservation.

A high proportion of top dealers have done something artistic beforehand. One was a freelance artist, another a photographer. Several dealers have been actors. One was a circus magician's assistant, another a copywriter. No ex-journalist has, to the author's knowledge, been employed as a dealer, perhaps for obvious reasons.

Evidence is undeniable of a correlation between flair for pro-fessional make-believe such as acting, and flair for selling shares. Two sides of the same coin, perhaps?

It is no wonder then that dealers are talented mimics, a natural offshoot of their flair for self-expression and for directed hysteria. They can thus help each other in extraordinary ways.

One dealer at London & Norwich Investment Services was quarrelling with his insurance broker, mainly because he could never get through to him on the telephone. His colleague promptly rang the company, pretending he was a solicitor acting on his client's complaints: 'This is David Chaseham Associates . . . Your manager's busy is he? . . . Just tell him if he doesn't come to the phone he'll be facing legal action . . . I think you'll find he'll speak to me.' This and even heavier stuff that followed was delivered in the ponderous tones of the stereotype legal eagle, and the whole deceit worked like a charm.

Dealers also enjoy baiting employers who have advertised sales vacancies. Obviously they refrain if they are personally interested in pursuing the vacancy, that is, in the unlikely event of it paying more than they earn.

Salaried sales vacancies are most likely to offer first year earnings of around £15,000, which successful dealers in shares and futures find derisory.

Commission only sales work sometimes falls target to dealers' ridicule too. Recently, a dealer made an obscene phone call to a manager of a large insurance group, with a reputation for nurturing the hardsell. The call was in revenge for the manner in which that person had once bullied a colleague during a job interview with that insurance group, telling him: 'You're nothing, because you earn so little. You're one of the great unwashed masses, whom I enjoy splashing with mud as I drive to work.'

This arrogance and obsession with money may be shared by employees of licensed dealers too, but is not displayed by them so openly. A good dealer is likely to be considered charming.

Two sorts of charm prevail, side by side. The English Public School, or pseudo-Public School type of charm comes easiest but to a few dealers. This serves to woo the posh clients, who don't necessarily have the most money. The wide-boy charm comes easiest to most dealers, and accommodates clients who blossom on a matey, familiar approach. The dealer will often then present a self-advertisement that fascinates his clients; he will be the player of piped music that entrances the snake. 'I'm an East End boy myself, so believe me, I know what's what. I've experienced the sharp end of life at first hand . . . ' Of course, he must be careful not to sound boastful about this to a self-made East End client who might retaliate either with words or with a silence to the effect: 'So what? You're not the only one.'

The streetwise cater for their minute-by-minute erotic requirements by propping photographs of nude women on their dealing desks. In the male lavatories, similar photographs are displayed on the walls, and stay fixed there for months.

Dealers also show a more practical interest in sex. For sharedealers, sex is a V-sign in the face of convention, an adolescent reaction fixated in early adulthood. They are thinking about sex even when at work. This adds a curious illusion of concern to their sales pitches. Their words gush out, hot and caressing, a thrill for lonesome or bored clients, indeed sometimes a need. Likewise for the dealers. One female dealer admits that she finds opening up new clients 'orgasmic'.

Several dealers have made a market on the side in sex devices such as vibrators and aphrodisiacal aids — probably manufactured in Hong Kong, and with luck, not second hand!

Harvard dealers, male and female, were always arranging strippograms and trainees were usually asked to contribute to the cost of sending for one. The good dirty fun was not always enough. One dealer, whose birthday was being celebrated with a strippogram on the Harvard dealing floor, grabbed the huge-busted nude girl who stood before him, and amorously pressed against her, causing almost everybody in the room to shriek with laughter, and to call out encouraging remarks. Meanwhile, some dealers were talking on the telephone to their clients.

If an unexpected female turns up at a licensed dealer, one of the lads will often shout out, 'Are you the strippogram?' It never fails to embarrass the victim.

Female dealers are usually flirtatious, and ask for what harassment they get. One lady dealer at Harvard who was known to be a bit of a tease, dared a male dealer to expose himself. He promptly unzipped his flies and pulled down the front of his pants . . .in the dealing room. She shrieked and shuddered, exclaiming to all and sundry what he had done.

Another girl at Harvard audaciously went into the men's loos, on the understanding that a dealer kept guard outside. Unfortunately, her friend became embarrassed waiting for her and left. Male dealers came in after her and crowded out the urinals. She came out of a cubicle and fled the whole convenience, shrieking that several boys were in there brandishing their 'huge dicks' at her.

Another intrepid saleswoman at a licensed dealer touched almost everybody she talked with. During one sweltering hot afternoon on a hectic dealing floor, she went up to a young novice male dealer. She pointed two fingers at him, as if a gun. Sweat pricked her forehead and she was breathing hard. 'This is a stick up,' she snapped. 'Pull down your trousers . . . '

Powered on by anticipation, the young male dealer did a very good afternoon's work.

Some female dealers specialise in massage. One Harvard training officer, after coming in late every morning and yelling at the trainees: 'Get on the fucking phone,' would look at his regular masseuse, who at the time was a trainee as well. 'Ooh ah,' he would say, wriggling his shoulders.

Recognising his signal, she would come over and massage him. He would sigh and pant as her fingers traced his neck and shoulders, his back. She worked to relax him. He repaid her by making sure she was properly supplied with leads.

Another manager begged her to massage him. She made excuses, saying jokingly that the one she already attended to was the only man for her. She knew that he was looking for sexual stimulation, not relaxation.

Female dealers don't necessarily need the men. At another dealer, one female dealer used to vanish from the dealing floor when pressure was at its hottest, as if she was going to the loo. Once in the corridor, she would thrust her hand into her blouse and would massage her own nipples until they were as hard as acorns.

Once a male dealer caught her in the act. 'Why don't you let me do that for you?' he inquired.

Tudorbury dealers find a little light relief on the dealing floor.

She grinned. 'Last night, my boyfriend caressed me like the Wild Man of Borneo. The breeze from the windows in the dealing room makes my nipples itch. I just had to rub them. But if you're willing to do my dirty work, perhaps we can come to some arrangement . . . '

Female breasts are a distraction on dealing floors too. A director of Tudorbury Securities stood before a female dealer on the floor. 'I can see her pretty face, but I can't see her nipples,' he announced, then smiled at her: 'Flop your tits over the top of the desk so I can see them.'

She laughed: 'They're not large enough.'

A male dealer seated in front of her, added in a rasping tone: 'Let me be the judge of that.'

Another dealer growled: 'Take 'em out.'

The director leered at her: 'I think we should keep an electric dildo on your desk.'

'I either want the real thing, or nothing,' she said.

Dealers are more motivated to take personal calls than calls from clients -- likely sellers. For instance, one dealer at Tudorbury Securities a husky, macho fellow, whom for the purpose of this book we shall call Robert, was sitting guzzling a McDonald's hamburger, with his feet up, at lunchtime. The telephone rang.

'A call for you, Robert,' a dealer shouted.

Robert grunted: 'Tell 'em I'm out to lunch.'

'It's . . . ' he said.

Robert turned: 'That's last night's pick up, calling in for a bit of pussy. Gimme the phone.'

Women who ring into the dealing room may stay chatting with the dealers for quite a while. As one Tudorbury salesman put it: 'Telephone sex in its various forms has become quite the norm in this industry.'

In the meantime a queue of clients might be waiting to get through to the dealing floor.

Some female dealers cannot take the strain and so leave after only a few weeks. One girl decided to leave her firm in style, and so she had sex with one of the top dealers mere hours before her planned departure.

The Sun newspaper had become the oracle of the dealing rooms at most licensed dealers and the Page Three girl its high priestess. Dealers would pour over the latest dishy model, assessing her statistics greedily, fingers tracing bodily contours. They were almost making love to a newspaper photograph.

Early one morning on the dealing floor, a Tudorbury director approached a female dealer: 'Did you buy *The Sun* today?' he asked.

'No. I don't read *The Sun*,' she replied.

'Oh, I must have it,' he moaned.

Tudorbury dealers' new name for *The Sun* at one stage was 'Currant Bun', i.e. making a veiled reference to the nipples of the Page 3 nude. They would ask: 'Has anybody got today's currant bun?'

As further evidence of their outlook on life, dealers at certain firms would boast how they often took their copies of *The Sun* to the men's lavatories where, bolting themselves in the cubicles, they would jerk themselves off over the pictures.

As they were also used for drug taking, the men's loos became a haven of illicit pleasures.

Occasionally, a dealer would remain a non-smoker, a non-drug user, a sexual monogamist, or even — and it was not unknown — a virgin.

Other dealers would attempt to make a man out of him. If they failed, they would actually show some guarded respect. One commented on a young dealer's abstemious qualities as follows: 'You have no vices. You don't even smoke. And I've never heard you swear. I wish I was like you. I'd live longer. But you must have a dull life . . . '

Dealers have organised parties which they afterwards claim turned virtually into orgies. A good many dealers wax lyrical about bizarre sex, bondage, whippings, enemas, and such other ramifications as seasoned London prostitutes practise all day. It is not unknown for male dealers to present their bottoms to female dealers on the dealing floor, for the purposes of having them beaten.

These are tastes that dealers share (so some psychiatric opinion would have it) with other professionals who live on their wits, such as comedians.

Dealers have been known to boast how they would experiment and practice with each other.

Three salesmen from a now defunct dealer claimed they went for a 'piss-up' in celebration of some big business they had cleared, taking with them a dealer of a firm where they had all previously worked. They were on a fact-finding mission, they said.

Their story was as follows: they got the dealer so drunk that he could hardly stagger out of the wine bar without falling down, and then they whisked him in a taxi back to a luxury flat which one of them was leasing. Here they laid him out on the settee, and the owner of the flat hypnotised him.

The hypnotist had taken courses in his art, and had a natural flair for it. In a matter of minutes, he had his victim entranced. The dealers then asked him questions which would provide information helpful to their survival as share salesmen:

What did you sell today? Who is the dealing director having an affair with at the moment? Which firm would *you* like to work for?

As the story went, the three then slipped off the dealer's trousers and underpants, proceeding to stimulate him with a vibrator until he awoke from his trance and screamed.

'That's enough,' shouted one of the dealers. 'We'll put him on the night train, and he'll wake up in the middle of nowhere.

This dealer was not in fact the only one to have been carried out of his way by night-trains. Another dealer from time to time drinks too much, goes to sleep on his train home, and wakes up at some strange station in the early hours of the morning.

Sharedealers' continental trips may, of course, be no respite from decadence. Two ex-Public School dealers at Tudorbury Securities came back from a holiday on the Greek Islands with stories of how they had flogged each other naked in their hotel bedroom. They produced photographs which they claimed proved it.

The female dealers who claim to participate in the spirit of this sort of thing, are proving in this as in other ways how tough they are. Some of them are married, and a stable marriage doubtless gives them the strength to put up with it.

When the male dealers crack sexy jokes before the female ones, they are really making veiled advances. At Tudorbury Securities, one male dealer pinched a younger male dealer's nipples until the victim screamed 'Ouch'. The aggressor then looked at a female dealer sitting on their table, and sniggered: 'Perhaps I should pinch your nipples. I might find it more fulfilling.'

Even the real hardnut females can feel isolated in so masculine an atmosphere. One lady dealer at Harvard Securities was once extremely upset 'Everybody keeps touching me, and teasing me,' she said. Six dealers have asked me today whether I'm wearing any knickers. I asked the last one if his prick was as big as his mouth, and that shut him up.'

She rapidly gained confidence. Next a Harvard dealer asked her sweetly: 'Do you want a fuck?'

Equally sweetly, she replied: 'Do you want a kick in the balls?'

Female office staff at certain dealers claim they carry around pocket spongebags, so as to spend the night with whomsoever they fancy, but the AIDS scare is slowly killing such enterprise off.

At certain firms, a few female dealers greedy for money, have resorted to prostitution — preferably with male dealers whom they know. These latter studs would think nothing of spending £150, perhaps half a day's earnings, on a night of pleasures and passion. A generous dollop of sex smooths over the rough edges of the their shares or futures selling.

Some female dealers are not just promiscuous but go, as it were, public. Some dealers tell the story of how they all went to a posh restaurant one night. After the meal, the drinks continued to flow. The dealers were singing: 'Bottle of wine, fruit of the vine, when will you let me get sober? Let me alone, let me go home, please give me time to pass over.'

The male dealers were inspired into stripping to their waists. Little did they know how much they were exciting a buxom female dealer who jumped onto the table. Some called her a slag, but by God she knew how to use body language. The dealers roared encouragement as she danced a drunken little jig.

Waiters stopped in their tracks and other diners stared as she unbuttoned her blouse, flinging it onto the floor. Contorting her body, she unstrapped her bra. The strip-tease was rhythmic and classy. The dealers became riotous.

Her current dealer boyfriend, who was there, pretended to enjoy the spectacle, although the strain showed in his face. He maintained to his fellow dealers: 'She's fucked many men but I'm not bothered. I've fucked a damned sight more women.'

The more conventional girls quit this profession. All female dealers who remain, bitch in the lavatories at odd moments throughout the day. In the dealing room, they vent their frustrations on the female trainees. One female business manager at Harvard rebuked a trainee severely for wearing unbusinesslike 60s style long skirt and blouse. Masculine women have reduced less masculine women to tears.

Less masculine men are protected from such harpies by the predominance of men generally. Here is an archetypal male chauvinist world. It is not unlike the boys' school where the author taught, prior to becoming a dealer, in which a few girls, conspicuous in the sixth form, were sex objects pure and simple to the rest of the school. A certain sort of girl revels in the lack of feminine competition.

This kind of community also provides a playground for social misfits. Dealers are all in it together and their individual pasts may be held over their heads.

When it comes to the real thing, homosexuality is glossed over in licensed dealing circles.

Gays in these circles hide the proverbial powder-puff to survive. The environment caters for the womaniser, and not for the girl's blouse. The gay men usually flaunt girlfriends to cover up, and will not have steady male partners.

The body of the gay dealer is not stereotyped. He may be tall or short, fat or thin. One thing though is for sure. The appearance of being straight will override his homosexual tendencies by a mile.

Lesbian dealers may be ruthless with their male colleagues. One female dealer was a lesbian, and this was an open secret.

She mixed not just with dealers but with transvestites and butch lesbians, while she herself maintained her sleek feminine figure, largely by what some would term neurotic dieting.

Male dealers, upon seeing her for the first time, would drool over her, captivated by her teasing personality. As it transpired, she was just leading them up the garden path.

She slept with one male dealer who had fallen in love with her, but once she had all his leads, that was where the relationship ended.

All the while, she had allegedly been wooing glamorous women in the London clubs. Her male victim lapsed into a depression. Never had he suffered such an anticlimax.

One flamboyant Harvard manager had a meaty suggestion to put hairs on the male dealers' chests, one he had recently followed himself.

When a green dealer expressed his desire to take holiday time, the manager would blurt out: 'Go to Bangkok. You can have any fucking thing done to you, when you want, and where you want.'

He would then quietly take a seat next to the dealer in question and distract him from his work by telling him of the sexual extravaganzas practiced there. Too bad if the dealer got sacked due to poor sales figures as a result of this.

Among the exotic Bangkok delights he would relate were long and savage whipping sessions, steamy massages, and sandwiching often by young girls clad with dildos. It was a young sharedealer's dream, and the manager's advice to go out there was not wholly ignored.

Generally, many heterosexual dealers are willing to deviate. They are game for a little sexual horseplay, particularly after a bit of Columbian stimulation (i.e. taking drugs).

Dealers at one licensed dealer found it stimulating to slap unsuspecting colleagues on the back with a thick plastic ruler, perhaps while they were busy pitching clients on the telephone.

One black dealer, when subjected to the treatment roared out: 'For fuck's sake,' while his persecutor growled; 'I'm teaching you a lesson.'

This little incident epitomised the relationship between the novice dealer and his elder and better. The teasing is in different ways exciting for each of them.

Physical stimulation is not always so mild. Le Vice Anglais is an old favourite. Certain dealers, of no specific firm, will pay enormous sums of money to prostitutes for the privilege of getting the living daylights thrashed out of them. They are perhaps compulsively recreating old Public School terrorist regimes.

One male dealer has boasted of his sessions with his self-styled mistress who keeps giving him however many strokes of the cane show up on the continued throws of a dice.

'Bottom marks for naughty boys' is the sort of advert this revered lady has placed — on illicit labels stuck inside telephone boxes, and on cards in shady newsagents' windows.

She does it two way. Indeed, just as some dealers perversely crave to be thrashed, so they want to uphold the high standard of the golden rule, 'Do unto others as you would have them do unto you.'

Nor are the female dealers exactly innocent. One female dealer of a firm the author will not identify claims she found her entrance into the sharedealing world very stressful. The reaction she says she was driven to is an extreme example of the sort of bizarre sexual antics with which some dealers are preoccupied. Here is her account of what she jokingly calls her own 'Big Bang' experience:

'I would leave the dealing floor in a rush of hot fury. The shouts of 10,000 shares, 50,000 shares, 100,000 shares often brought me to the brink of orgasm. I made up my mind this was it.

'I put an advert in a contact magazine, and screened my 'Lord and Master' carefully. By a stroke of luck, the right one turned up.

'What attracted me was where he lived, in a cottage in a small quaint hamlet, miles from the City. He was a little timid at first, but expressed willing to have a go.

'I arrived at the local station, while he was driving me to his place, he stopped by the roadside and made me give him a blow job. I was pleased to discover his cock went along with his beauty.

'He unmasked me in what he jokingly called his torture chamber. I found myself in a largish bedroom, where he quickly lit a real log fire. He laid me spreadeagled on the four poster bed, tying my ankles and wrists to the frame. Next he gagged me, I felt like one of those victims in the continental movies.

'Hearing my muffled screams, he raised the whip, cracking it lightly but firmly over my nipples and across my waist. He then fell on me and fucked me, and I had no control at all.

Female dealers and office staff are not above dressing in black leather. Some male dealers claim this turns them on, likewise giving the thumbs up to rubberwear and heels.

A catalogue of leather and rubber wear, passed around Tudorbury's dealing room in 1988 reduced some of the men to a jelly-like state.

The few women present may have been turned on not so much by the pictures as by the turmoil of so many males on heat.

Sex is on many dealers' minds, minute by minute, morning noon and night. Here are Casanovas in the making, here are so many spoilt seducers and whorish spirits.

They work in a glossy fake industry where sex is on tap and where marriage has little meaning. Many dealers rate each other on a 'fuckability' scale, one to ten. They develop bedroom eyes after they have been in the business only a few weeks.

'Here a fuck, there a fuck, everywhere a fuck fuck' is some dealers' way of life. Not content just with the real thing, dealers have been known to patronise live sex shows on the continent, applauding the stage girls who stuff bananas into their vaginas and men in gorilla suits who squirt water from the artificial penises, all over the audience.

Hard pornography rules OK in the dealing room too. At Tudorbury Securities organisation appeared underway for a secret pornographic video retailing scheme, not condoned by the directors. An eye opening catalogue was shown surreptitiously to dealers. It was open for them to club together and buy these red hot films at a discount.

The films were individually priced from £10 - £50, and the company was operated by a Tudorbury dealer's brother from a mail order address.

Videos on offer from this catalogue bore zippy names like: *Rubber Party, Born to Raise Hell, Animal Tricks,* and *Oh Shit 2.* Such names fronted films catering for revolting sexual deviations, including: bondage, bestiality, sexual torture, and even excretory perversions.

It is something creative in the dealer's temperament that makes him even hear of such sordid stuff? Is it, once more, the attraction of the forbidden, albeit in an unpalatable form? Certainly, the dealing-rooms seem alert to suggestions of bizarre sex that the author cannot stomach.

At times, racing becomes a familiar pastime on the floor of most licensed dealers. Many dealers know more about horse racing than about stocks and shares. They equate buying shares with placing bets. Serious investment is outlawed from their scheme of things.

The dealing screens of Harvard Securities were periodically converted to TV screens. Dealers watched horse racing and other sports during working hours on the box. Some found this more stimulating than sharedealing. They periodically had a whip round, placing bets during working hours. They occasionally made money this way.

A few dealers in various licensed dealers would get racing tips from clients in exchange for share tips. The racing tips could, of course, be bad, maybe tokening revenge on the clients' part for poor share recommendations. Dealers at one firm lost money on a client's tip for the Epsom Derby, and from then on determined to 'fuck' that client.

The races could interrupt the whole of Tudorbury's dealing routine. While the Royal Ascot races were being shown on TV, Tudorbury's lady credit control manager burst onto the dealing floor. She turned the screen onto the appropriate TV channel, so that the race was being shown.

This meant dealers couldn't get prices for their clients, but most didn't seem to care. Any break was welcome to them, and besides they had placed their own bets on this race.

'Is that my horse, love?' the credit control manager kept burbling. 'Where's my horse, love? I've put £10 on this horse . . . '

One of the dealers stood up. On the TV screen, the horses were filmed moving into the starting block. The beast in question was bucking. 'There's your horse, woman.' he growled, 'Kicking up its balls.'

Male and female dealers alike tend to be adventurous extroverts, not just in business or sexual terms. They are go-ahead, and might suddenly decide to organise a trip round the world, or an expedition to hunt down the Loch Ness Monster.

A few dealers have even investigated certain weird occult movements. One female dealer was called a witch on the dealing floor. She professed to communicate with spirits, and her flat was chockful of textbooks treating modern day magic. She was also an amateur astrologer.

Both seriously, and tongue in cheek, dealers have investigated cults such as the Scientologists and the Moonies. Some are fascinated by the mind control used by these organisations in recruitment and in training.

One dealer recently did a free written personality test in the Scientologists' recruitment centre on Tottenham Court Road in London's West End. A counsellor then saw him in private, told him his life was a mess. He continued: 'It's in your interest to sign up with us right now for counselling sessions. It'll cost you £30, so please make out a cheque now.' Ex-dealers occasionally join such movements, where they doubtless find every opportunity to apply the hard sell techniques they have learnt.

On a lighter note, one dealer gave up smoking after a hypnotism course, although he cynically denied its effectiveness. One thing was certain, something had helped him to give up.

Much of salesmen's textbook wisdom is not applicable to the work of some licensed dealers. A share salesman's major problem is not usually getting past secretaries on the phone, as it might be if they were selling advertising space. Nor are they at cut-throat competition with salesmen of other licensed dealers. Photocopier or advertising space salesmen wouldn't necessarily be able to do the sharedealer's job, nor share salesmen theirs.

People associated, deeply or peripherally, with licensed dealers often lead exciting lives. Many make more enemies than friends. Many have lost countless people thousands, even tens of thousands, of pounds.

After the Stock Market Crash, one Florida based sharedealer was confronted by a frustrated client who riddled his body with bullets. He died instantly.

One fraudster, Guy La March, who sold securities from Amsterdam offices to gullible investors worldwide, was killed by a gunman in 1987.

Nor do top financial journalists always escape the flak. Michael Walters, Deputy City Editor of the *Daily Mail*, once claimed he had been threatened with his life, due to his writings about the licensed dealing community. It is hardly surprising then that newspapers running stories on licensed dealers sometimes choose to omit a by-line, so that the writer's identity, publicly at least is safeguarded.

Unexplained deaths can look suspicious. Several decades ago, the flamboyant financier Alfred Loewenstein, who had offered the public a number of dubious yet attractive sounding investment propositions, supposedly fell to his death from a plane over the English Channel. There was never an official investigation. How did he really die?

Threats to break noses and ribs have been made by one dealer to another. Ambushes have been known to be laid, and vows of vengeance taken. Names, addresses and telephone numbers have been sneaked out of firms' files. Confidentiality is fallible alright. Dealers break the moral as well as the legal rules. The laws of the jungle prevail, and self interest rules OK. This continues when dealers go abroad. At 5 a.m. in Amsterdam's red light district, one dealer, reputedly high on hash, got beaten up badly by some locals. This was allegedly a put-up job. Even directors of licensed dealers threaten their employees, not to mention their enemies. This sets standards for their underlings.

Dealers wanting to harass one of their flock, or even a disagreeable client, may choose to ring the poor victim up at all hours of the night, maybe pretending to be an Irishman who's dialled the wrong number, or else making obscene comments, or even just breathing in a hard, sexual way.

Often enough a dealer will suspect his colleagues are getting at him, but has no means of proving it. He may be right or he may be wrong; paranoia is rife.

The naive clients, and often indeed the more aware ones, do not appreciate the deep rooted criminal mentality of certain dealers. Their incestuous links with companies whose shares they promote, in addition to their shady connections with convicted fraudsters and other dubious characters, indicate their pathological ruthlessness.

Prospectuses of unlisted companies can often scare potential investors off with ambiguous clauses and waffle, with warnings of risks, and lack of hard figures. But many investors won't receive a prospectus, and if they do, won't bother to read it. Advice printed on blurb that if a client is in doubt he should contact a financial adviser is ironic, as it is supposedly a financial adviser who sent it to him in the first place.

Literature offered by licensed dealers to inform of their services sometimes tends to be plausible and flashy, appearing comprehensible to the ignorant public and so luring it. The sedate grey and white pamphlets preferred by the City's top legal and accountancy firms are not licensed dealers' cups of tea at all.

Licensed dealers offer an apparently impartial service. Investors could hardly fail to have been soothed with these statements from the brochure of the now defunct Afcor Investments: 'The aim is to profitably enhance the individual's share portfolio in the medium-term with a service which is both personal and substantive.

'Firstly, a Dealing Executive reviews the investment objectives of each individual client with a view to specific share selection and spread.

'A realistic target is set, a suitable plan is implemented and then maintained — with each client being regularly up-dated on market situations and viewpoints.'

Sadly, many dealers in the business generally have neither the ability nor the will to fulfil such promises. Arguably too, they have insufficient backing. Sitting at desks, browsing through their expensive Filofaxes, the thoughts of most dealers tend in one direction: themselves and their money, however cleverly they may conceal this.

It is the same self interest that turns dealers into roadhogs when driving to and from work. They weave through traffic in sports cars like Grand Prix drivers, honking throughout Central London jams like bleating sheep.

On the Underground, dealers make reckless dashes for available seats, and when the trains are overcrowded, they shove like football hooligans, getting their own seats and squeezing out the less competitive. They must be seen as winners in the little things, as well as in the big.

Conceited though good dealers are, they suffer from inferiority complexes. Like many lesser lights, they stand in awe of professional people: doctors and dentists certainly, but particularly lawyers and accountants. Here are people who seem to really know something beyond how to bluff, and who have social prestige too, even if their incomes are not exactly startling.

Good dealers even more than the bad ones get worried about the future. It's all very well earning good money and living it right up while they're in their early twenties, but what are they to do afterwards? Where does it all lead?

Upright City firms don't rate the experience of the bucket shop salesmen, and won't offer them jobs at anything like the salaries they've been used to.

Unless they happen to be economics or business studies graduates, or to have an alternative good career behind them, dealers are probably unqualified to do much else. If they have passed the Licensed Representatives' and Traders' exam, they can move to any stockbroker who will have them, but must compete with candidates who have worked in Stock Exchange member firms.

Even if a dealer bluffs his way into a real stockbroker, he may find the soft sell, sophisticated approach there too subtle for him. One dealer who moved from Harvard to a respectable member firm, left after a short period, partly because the long hours and quiet, serious working atmosphere were beginning to drive him crazy.

In the end, most dealers settle for living for the day. However, if they run a business on the side, they are aware that it could be developed in the years to come.

The Bohemian streak in dealers bobs up and down like a yo-yo. For two pins, they would quit their desks and dealing room, they sometimes do. Besides money, the one thing that makes their difficult work tolerable is the whole glorious unpredictability of it all.

They develop naturally into flies on the walls of the establishment, and gain a sort of bitter satisfaction from this role. Their senses of humour become rumbustious.

This is why top dogs in licensed dealers have a talent for playing the court jester. They are expert at making themselves liked. Dealers warm to their wittiness and they learn to emulate it.

The salesman of shares or futures is nothing if not charming. Without a natural inclination in that direction he is lost.

Recently, licensed dealers have been presenting a lower profile to the public, as indeed they have been threatened with extinction. No longer do their directors prance up and down outside share shop queues bearing sandwich boards. It has been several years, to the best of the author's knowledge, since a plane was seen flying a licensed dealer's flag over the City.

Dealers still unpop their champagne bottles and dance their nights away in West End clubs. Following one party, a dealer went down with a stomach bug, due to something nasty in the food. Who might have been responsible?

Some dealers who are paid cash by their firms without tax and National Insurance deductions, end up having problems with the Inland Revenue. They may eventually pay their full tax contribution, or make tax-deductible claims by going self-employed, but they will first spend many happy months plotting to open secret Swiss bank accounts, in which to stash their earnings tax-free. Some even nip over to Geneva to sort facilities out.

Tax, as part of the establishment, in some firms, goes emotionally by the board. Dealers are celebrating not their contribution to society, but their exploitation of it. Herein lies the glory that is their own.

Chapter Six

RULES ARE MADE TO BE BROKEN

Traditionally, the bucket shop has survived because, although it is the antithesis of bureaucracy itself, it understands the bureaucratic system it is up against. It knows to ask for *evidence*. It knows how effective legal action on the one hand, and charming hospitality on the other hand, can be. It knows that letters of complaint must be *answered*, that the fighter goes down last.

All this is called 'knowing your enemy' which is more important to the bucket shops than 'knowing your client'. Will their skills handle the new legislation?

In the first half of 1988, the UK pirates had made the last moves to hard sell the naive investor, ripping him off for every pound they could. Many unsavoury practitioners had been working overtime until their cut off point, the refusal of authorisation. To carry on after this would be a criminal offence under Section Three of the Financial Services Act (1986).

Share-pushers on the Continent are still laughing up their sleeves, as they are unaffected by the UK based legislation. Some naturally continue to play the buccaneer.

The date of full implementation of the Financial Services Act (1986) — 29th April 1988 (A-Day) has now passed. Why has change taken so long?

It is clear that since P-Day (27th February 1988) when all applications for authorisation had to be lodged with the appropriate body, investigatory boards have been overworked, and unable to process these in good time.

As a result, firms have been operating under interim authorisation which ought to be closed down. Investors even late into 1988 have been suffering. But the delays have an earlier foundation.

Parliament had been delaying legislation by continually making amendments to the rules.

The Securities and Investments Board (SIB), the new City watchdog, was impeded from functioning until various pernickety points had been cleared with bodies such as the Office of Fair Trading.

The institutions were concerned to protect their own interests. If anyone had to lose out, they preferred it should be the private investor. The Life Assurance Industry, for instance, represented by the Life Assurance & Unit Trust Regulatory Organisation (LAUTRO), got into dispute with the SIB over its rule book.

In 1988 the SIB took the bull by the horns. It closed down firms like Barlow Clowes and DPR Futures, where the Department of Trade and Industry (DTI) as was explained earlier, had failed. Even a few established stockbrokers had to fight to achieve membership of The Securities Association (TSA). Unsuitable individuals as well as firms were faced with the prospect of being weeded out. Contrary to what cynics had predicted, the new legislation was starting to bite. All the delay had been ostensibly to one end, viz so the legislature's teeth could bite the harder.

Under the new legislation, there is an umbrella compensation scheme. Stockbrokers have objected to abolition of the previous Stock Exchange compensation scheme which was cheaper, and exclusive to them. Now everybody chips in when a firm goes under. Stockbrokers will be supporting crashed FIMBRA financial advisory firms, which some would rather keep at arm's length.

Likewise, many building societies objected to being forced into the Financial Intermediaries, Managers & Brokers Association (FIMBRA). As John Spalding said on behalf of the Halifax (February 1987): 'There are grave disadvantages. We would be expected to finance compensation for a motley crew.'

Under the old legislation, if his dealer went into liquidation, how did the private investor fare?

Reasonably enough if he dealt through a stockbroker. The Stock Exchange's compensation scheme allowed him a refund of any sum up to £250,000 he had lost through a member firm's incompetence or fraud.

The Exchange's surveillance department had the task of making sure that the fund was not drawn on too frequently. Obviously, anyone who invested stupidly would not be compensated for that alone.

Those who had invested with a crashed licensed dealer were not so lucky. When, for instance, McDonald Wheeler Fund Management went under, there was no compensation scheme available. As in many similar cases, investors lost most or all of their money.

This disastrous state of affairs has been rectified. Through the SIB, under the Financial Services Act (1986), FIMBRA offers investors compensation on all losses up to £30,000, and 90% of the next £20,000, although nothing above it. This is the umbrella compensation scheme in action.

Clients of a FIMBRA firm may still be subjected to high pressure selling of certain stocks. Illicitly now, they may not be told of their highly speculative nature, or that they are owned by the licensed dealers themselves.

Indeed salesmen have sometimes not known or cared about such details, which don't, after all, affect their own commissions earned.

Dealers of (FIMBRA authorised) London & Norwich Investment Services Ltd had no idea, until the national press enlightened them, that Pattinson Hayton, London & Norwich Services Ltd's affable managing director, also had a majority shareholding in Silverton Industries, the sole stock they were recommending to their clients.

Some wondered why FIMBRA had not closed down London & Norwich Investment Services Ltd earlier. The fact is that FIMBRA had not at that stage quite obtained recognition as a self-regulatory organisation (SRO) and so could have been open to defamation suits if it closed down a member firm.

Notwithstanding threats of defamation action, FIMBRA had successfully closed down Financial Management Services, active at the time of the British Gas flotation. Also petitions to wind up FIMBRA filed in Scotland and England by directors of the crashed Walter L Jacob & Co have been dismissed.

Nonetheless, people in the industry treated FIMBRA like a joke, even as the new legislation was being put through.

Here follows the procedure Eyas Securities adopted when FIMBRA visited:

Dealers, as yet unlicensed, were forbidden to show up on the premises for the entire week. They had already started selling shares in Crane Holdings, and if FIMBRA caught them at it, Eyas could lose its membership.

A newly employed dealer was told to start a week later than scheduled: 'Wait till FIMBRA has gone. You can then start dealing your clients straightaway,' said a director.

Eyas Securities was particularly concealing its employment of ex-Sheridan Securities dealers who knew how to bring in big business quickly. Once these characters had lodged applications with FIMBRA, a backlash might occur. Eyas, to save its bacon, might have to sack them, meaning suicidal loss of revenue.

Because it has proved itself so often ineffectual, and because also it is the main regulatory body for licensed dealers and similar bucket shops, FIMBRA has always had many applications pending, and has been embarrassingly short of resources. The organisation takes an average of four months to decide on membership. It takes still longer if it has incidents like client complaints to consider.

Under the old legislation, FIMBRA was able to ask a member firm for information, and arrange that an auditor should check the books, but if the firm refused to cooperate, action was seriously delayed.

The Department of Trade & Industry (DTI) was able to listen to a FIMBRA complaint, and given sufficient evidence, had authorisation to enter and search a firm's office. If ordered to leave, the Department had to do so, and would probably have applied then for a warrant for a police search party.

All this took time, while investors were left stranded, hoping against hope, often against the odds, that they had not lost all their money.

The DTI has appeared far slower to act than FIMBRA. In July 1988, it was subject to criticism for not acting more swiftly on complaints about Harvard Securities. The DTI's evident preknowledge of certain problems in securities dealers has not always prevented its reissuing of licenses or allowing them to continue trading.

A source of compensation has always been desperately sought after.

The Bank of England effectively indemnified its former employees who had invested through the crashed Norton Warburg, for up to 90% of monies lost. The Bank felt responsible because it had permitted Norton Warburg to discuss investment with them. Other disgruntled clients felt that the very fact the bank had allowed Norton Warburg access to its own employees had served as a model for outside investors. Should the bank not then offer compensation to all investors with Norton Warburg?

Norton Warburg's client funds had been mixed with company accounts. In 1982, the liquidators had contemplated legal action against Lloyds Bank on this basis.

Lloyds Bank responded as follows: 'We had no fiduciary responsibility. We were not acting on behalf of Norton Warburg's clients, only on behalf of the company.' A major bank was to mount a similar defence seven years later upon similar allegations following the collapse of the Barlow Clowes Empire.

Under the Financial Services Act (1986) not just is there a clearly defined compensation scheme available, but the authorities are in a position to suspend dealings at once.

FIMBRA was once known as National Association of Securities Dealers & Investment Managers (NASDIM). NASDIM was, up to 1979, called the Association of Licensed Dealers in Securities (ALDS) and catered then for a smaller membership.

In November 1983, the Department of Trade & Industry recognised NASDIM as a self regulatory body under The Prevention of Fraud (Investments) Act, which meant that NASDIM members were exempted from the need to apply annually to the DTI to deal in securities. NASDIM reacted responsibly, banishing five members for breach of its 'modular rule book', and turning away sixty aspiring members.

In August 1984, NASDIM declared an increase in membership by 45% to four hundred and twenty seven. On 1st October 1984, a range of insurance policies, including an impressive form of professional indemnity cover, arrived to protect clients who bought shares through NASDIM members.

NASDIM found a minor competitor in the self regulatory body called The British Institute of Dealers in Securities (BIDS) of which Harvard Securities was a member. The over-the-counter (OTC) dealers set up BIDS in 1983. Unlike NASDIM/FIMBRA, BIDS neither achieved recognition from the Department of Trade & Industry, nor was it to be an SRO under the Financial Services Act (1986)

BIDS stipulated the formation of a disciplinary committee, and a minimum value of shares in which market-makers should make a market. Furthermore, BIDS primary market-makers were obliged to try to find a further two market-makers in each share in which they made a market.

There was a BIDS compensation scheme serving as a pledge, should a BIDS member firm go bust. Clients paid 30 pence levy on bargains up to £1,500 and 65 pence for bargains above this level. In practice, clients have often not realised what they're paying for. The levy was too small for clients to resent paying it, and perhaps for this reason was relatively immune from criticism.

Internal splits were rife. At the beginning of July 1985, the now defunct Afcor Investments served notice to resign from BIDS. BIDS claimed Afcor had been suspended, and owed their contribution to the levy on share dealings which went to the BIDS compensation fund. Afcor offered instead to pay into a solicitor's account to meet any compensation scheme from clients.

Such an incident was symptomatic of unrest developing between OTC dealers which was threatening their unity, something so necessary when they came under attack.

Under the auspices of BIDS, competing OTC dealers had appointed an OTC Practitioners' Committee to explore alternatives to the new-fangled Stock Exchange Third Market, before it had even got off the ground. Ironically, OTC dealers had been amongst the two hundred parties consulted with regard to the Stock Exchange's proposals for its third tier market. This had kept them nicely in touch.

At one stage, the OTC dealers appeared to be getting support for an organised alternative to the Stock Exchange Third Market, called The London Securities Exchange.

Prospective members would be asked to contribute a total of £300,000, to cover start-up costs, mainly for setting up an electronic market place. The fact that money was involved showed that they were serious.

A meeting of the Practitioners' Committee was attended by a representative of the Securities and Investments Board (SIB), whose approval would be needed if the new Exchange was to qualify as a Recognised Investment Exchange (RIE) under the Financial Services Act (1986).

OTC Information, the organisation with responsibility for the market's dealing and settlement systems, then collapsed at what could hardly have been a worse moment.

Most licensed dealers started seeking Stock Exchange membership, recognising the official force of the proposed Stock Exchange Third Market. The Exchange had insisted that members of the Third Market must also be Stock Exchange members. Tom Wilmot, chairman of Harvard Securities, described the proposals as impractical, because stockbrokers were not going to want to sponsor small issues.

His argument was that a sponsor getting a quotation for a third market company would work harder than if he was doing the same for a blue chip, but he would be less well rewarded.

While recognising the necessity for collective action on the part of OTC traders, Tony Prior, chairman of the OTC Practitioners' Committee (and of the now defunct Prior Harwin), pointed out further defects in the Stock Exchange's proposals. OTC-traded overseas stocks were not covered. Also, property and financial service companies which did not satisfy regulations would run into difficulties.

According to the Stock Exchange, the new Third Market would offer to the public for the first time, access to a disciplined, regulated market, 'dedicated to small young companies'. The entire manoeuvre was obviously part of Sir Nicholas Goodison's policy to bridge the gap between the City and Industry.

To this end, the Exchange waived its own listing fees for new entrants to the market, and tried to persuade sponsors to cut their own costs, so that a young company could bring its shares to the market cheaply. The idea was to keep the cost of obtaining a quote down to the £10,000 level.

Harvard Securities applied to become a sponsor for the third market towards the end of 1986. Meanwhile, its application for Stock Exchange membership had been pending for nine months. Harvard dealers were told that the company would 'definitely be getting Stock Exchange membership in three weeks' time'.

After the event failed to materialise, dealers were frequently reassured that delays were only temporary. Most dealers passed on this soothing message to their clients, with relief.

A rumour circulated Harvard's elite dealing room that the Stock Exchange had sent in a file of complaints, about Harvard over the years for the firm's comments, and that Harvard had commented on every one.

Harvard's reputation in the City was such that many neither wanted nor expected the veteran licensed dealer to enter the Exchange's charmed circle. Many embittered Harvard clients would have done all they could to prevent it too — as is apparent not just from their telephone conversations with dealers, but from their written complaints to the national press, to the Stock Exchange and to Harvard itself.

Newspapers occasionally presented a case for Harvard, and for the frustrated Tom Wilmot, who had even threatened to sue the Stock Exchange if it did not come to a conclusion soon. In the *Sunday Express,* Patrick Lay offered this opinion: 'If Mr Wilmot, or Harvard, either or both, has been blackballed, then it would be courteous of Stock Exchange Chairman Sir Nicholas Goodison to pass on the news and the reasons why, without any further delay.'

Anthony Hilton, City Editor of the London Evening *Standard,* argued that Harvard would never have found a gap to fill if the Exchange had been more responsive in the past to the capital raising needs of small companies. He claimed further that the third market, which had been set up to 'upstage' the OTC, would be more likely to succeed with Harvard's help. His argument could be construed as generous, given the apparent incompatibility of Harvard's business principles with those of the Stock Exchange.

Tom Wilmot, in his book *Inside The Over the Counter Market,* has written: 'The OTC is never likely to become part of the Establishment, and, indeed, it should never attempt to do so. It's function is to compete, not to cooperate.' It is arguably this attitude which characterised his earlier dealings with the Exchange.

Following investigation in 1979, the Stock Exchange Council concluded that Harvard Securities was 'not a party to the creation of a false market'. The Council, however, announced that it intended to monitor Harvard's dealings, and that it had issued instructions for all deals carried out by member firms on behalf of Harvard to be reported to it.

This was the first time that the Stock Exchange had ever passed comment on a licensed dealer's affairs, an indication of how seriously the institution took Harvard's practices. What was wrong?

The Council pointed out that Harvard had informed the Investigative Committee that their usual practice, after purchasing a block of shares, was to try to 'substantiate the market price' before selling the shares to their clients, by purchases in the market through the same broker, or a different broker. The Council found this 'undesirable'.

The Council also found that part of the stamp duty paid to Harvard's clients had apparently not been paid to the Inland Revenue in October 1977, and there were 'two series of similar underpayments' in December 1977 and March 1978'. The Committee to the Inland Revenue had reported these cases, and Harvard had said that the failure to pay was due to human error on the part of both themselves and their brokers.

Shortly after all this, Harvard Securities was excluded from a list of outside firms entitled to certain discounts on dealing costs in sizable lines of stock. Harvard Securities estimated this could be costing them £160,000 a year. In 1980, they issued a writ against the Stock Exchange Council, claiming damages of up to £2 million.

A year later, Tom Wilmot was saying there seemed to be scope for agreement. He had perhaps an ally in the Office of Fair Trading which objected to the Stock Exchange's minimum commission structure, and the separation of broker/jobber functions. No wonder Harvard had made it clear that they were prepared to give the Office of Fair Trading what help they could.

While the Stock Exchange was delaying giving a yea or nay to Harvard Securities as to their membership, dealers were optimistic, perhaps too much so, with their clients. 'We're definitely getting Stock Exchange membership,' they continued to tell them.

Ironically, one of these dealers was apparently the godson of Sir Nicholas Goodison, the then chairman of the Stock Exchange, who of course could have disabused him, if he had been asked.

Around mid-July 1987, after waiting twelve months, Harvard had its application for Stock Exchange membership rejected. Dealers promptly glossed over this to their clients: 'We're being taken over anyway,' they said, or 'The Stock Exchange is reconsidering its decision.'

This rejection followed a DTI investigation into Harvard, after the near collapse of two other companies in whose shares the firm had dealt. According to Tom Vallance, Harvard's compliance officer, the DTI had kept the Exchange informed about the purpose of the inquiry, and its progress.

Even while Harvard had been putting on a virtuous front to the Stock Exchange, refunding some plaintive investors and giving money to charity, they were employing the tactics of warfare. A Harvard employee once said to the entire dealing floor: 'Ring up this dealer who's left, and hassle him at his stockbroking firm. Here's his number . . . '

One dealer at Harvard had declared: 'Our directors imagine they can pull the wool over everybody's eyes, but they underestimate people. Not everybody is as stupid as the Harvard clients . . . ' Dealers there were constantly being issued with the ultimatum: 'Do what you're told or get out.'

When the commissions due to Harvard dealers were cut drastically in early 1987, there was an uproar. The director who was informing the dealers of this told one complainant: 'Some of us have put a lot of money into this company, and if you don't like the way we do things you can piss off.' To another protestor he said, 'Well you're hardly one of the best dealers . . . ', and to another: 'What do you know about dealing? Have you ever worked through a bear market?' Of course his own job was on the line, so the rumour went.

It was at this stage that almost every dealer made up his or her mind to leave Harvard. Harvard was also cutting dealers' salary cheques on grounds of overtrading. This added insult to injury. Meanwhile, believe it or not, dealers were being pressed to buy Harvard's own shares.

Some dealers now started taking more time off than ever, although being the casual characters they were, they did not always put it to constructive use. Meanwhile, Harvard started looking for a buyer. Dealers found out from the newspapers, rather than from Harvard, that Tom Wilmot was negotiating to sell his 37% stake in Harvard to a consortium of top businessmen, including British Car Auctions chairman, David Wickens, and his new boss, Michael Ashcroft, of the Hawley Group. The newspapers were a source some dealers considered more reliable than their own firm.

Sadly, the proposed deal proved abortive, although Wickens already had 6% of Harvard. Other takeover whispers flourished, and Harvard's own shares, suspended at 45p in July, started being traded again, on the matched bargain basis which takes three months or so for conclusion and settlement.

Despite its reputation, Harvard was not an unattractive takeover proposition. The firm's market capitalisation of £13¼ million was justified by assets.

Harvard Securities was entitled to various appeals against the Stock Exchange's decision to refuse them membership, and could perhaps even have taken their old rival to court. FIMBRA were sitting on Harvard's membership. Under the Financial Services Act (1986) Harvard needed to have authorisation if they were to trade in securities at all.

When did the need for greater investor protection afforded by the new Act first become apparent?

The antediluvian Prevention of Fraud (Investment) Act 1958 had too many loopholes. Perhaps the most important part of the Act to licensed dealers was Section Thirteen, which made it an offence for any person 'who, by any statement, promise, or forecast which he knows to be misleading, false or deceptive, or by any dishonest concealment of material facts, or by the reckless making (dishonestly or otherwise) of any statement, promise or forecast which is misleading, false or deceptive, induces or attempts to induce another person to acquire, dispose of or subscribe to securities.'

No less relevant was Rule Ten of the Licensed Dealers (Conduct of Business) Rules 1983: 'a licensed dealer shall not make a recommendation to a client to acquire, dispose of or retain any investment unless he has an adequate and reasonable basis for that recommendation.'

Restrictive as it may sound, this legislation did not seem to provide the protection it promised. Harvard Securities operated on the underlying principal that individual dealers could rely on the fact that recommendations were made by Harvard only after proper investigation.

This seemed to propose that individual dealers were to some extent exempted from personal responsibility.

In all firms, dealers were supposed to have regard to the suitability of investments for the clients. In practice, this was not always a priority.

Share salesmen at various licensed dealers, have traditionally been taught that they can make any claim for stock, provided they qualify it with a measure of uncertainty. 'Could' or 'should move up' were fine. However, phrases such as 'I guarantee', 'definitely', 'certainly' or similar were technically taboo.

If dealers implied false prospects for stocks, they got away with it at some licensed dealers who were delighted to get the stock off their books. It was the client who would bear the brunt of such tactics.

The skilled share salesman developed his presentation into a fine art. 'I can virtually guarantee the price will shoot up,' he would say. Or, 'It won't double, but it should rise by at least 50%.' Otherwise, 'You should do exceptionally well on this one. I can think of no better investment for you at the moment.'

Clients fell for this, then came back to the dealer, peeved at the share's subsequent poor performance. 'But you said it would go up . . .'

'I never said so for definite,' the salesman could then rejoinder. If, as at Harvard, the original conversation had been recorded, it could be checked in case of dispute. The canny dealer would cover himself every time.

Dealers had to beware of clients taking their own revenge. A dealer at one of the smaller firms was cornered by a hit-man one night: 'Unless you pay back the £20,000 you cheated my Arab client out of, in cash within one hour, you're dead,' he said. All of a sweat, the dealer obtained the money as a loan, and counted out the notes before him. He knew when he was beaten.

The more seasoned client would write down exactly what the dealer told him, for reference should the dealer's rosy prediction not transpire. He would also ask at exactly what price he could sell back the stock he was buying, and in what quantity. If, for instance, he had bought 50,000 shares in Bleasdale Computers at 6p each, he would have been able to sell shares back at 4p each, but in quantities of only up to 10,000 at a time.

If he sold back more than that number at any given time, he was quoted an inferior price. It was, of course, open to the client to sell back in blocks of 10,000 shares, on five separate occasions until the whole lot had gone, but he would have paid a £12 (later £18) administration charge on every single deal. The client would rarely win, whatever way he sold back OTC stock.

There has unfortunately been no legal requirement for dealers to explain this sort of restriction, and unwary clients have lost significant sums of money through not asking enough questions.

If clients knew the bid prices alone of some stocks, that is the price at which they could later sell back, they would perhaps be loathe to pay for their purchases in the first place. Discovery of bid prices is indeed why some clients cancelled purchases.

The more astute investor in OTC shares may have noticed that many dealing spreads have narrowed in percentage terms, with the raising of the share prices. For this reason, he may only buy OTC stocks with relatively high prices. Many investors have always found the stocks priced at literally a few pennies the most irresistible, especially when they are specifically 'recommended' by the apparently impartial dealers.

Clients wanting to sell back OTC stocks at one licensed dealer found other problems. They sometimes had to ring for fifteen minutes or so before the phone was answered. Their dealer would usually do his utmost to persuade punters to keep shares, and then might deliberately avoid selling him out, only without breaking any regulations. For instance, the line sometimes got cut off 'accidentally'.

A client, in selling back, was forced to trick his dealer into believing his intentions were different. One dealer rang a client who had bought 10,000 shares at around 65p each. The share price had now reached around the £1.20 level. The dealer suggested that he should double his stake as the share price would probably double (something which did in this case happen).

The client said he might do this, and could the dealer quote the spread again. '£1.10 bid, £1.20 offer' was the dealer's reply. 'In sizes of 10,000 isn't it?' the client added casually, and the dealer said: 'Yes.' The client promptly said: 'Sell the lot.'

The dealer's reaction was to slam down the phone. Although in this case the dealer was made to take back the stock, he was in a dealing firm which often refused to take stock back onto its books. The dealing manager would sometimes say: 'No OTC is to come back this week.'

As dealers who did take back OTC stock on Harvard's books were penalised (as explained in chapter 1), this meant that they would find any reason to persuade clients to 'hang on', and most clients found OTC stock extremely difficult to sell. Most were naive enough to believe that the dealers were advising against selling back in good faith.

Rule Eleven of the Licensed Dealers (Conduct of Business) Rules 1983 prohibited 'cold-calling' — making unsolicited phone calls with the aim of selling shares. The DTI consistently said that 'cold-calling' was serious enough to provide a reason for revocation of a licence. However, many dealers in the industry, under pressure to achieve sales targets, cold-called. Some did so on a regular basis. Their managers and directors usually turned a blind eye.

Before the implementation of the Financial Services Act (1986) many investors did not realise this practice was illicit, or if they did, never bothered to complain. If they raised the issue with their dealer, he would have an excuse, like: 'I sent out details of this investment to you, but they obviously got lost in the post.' If he had genuinely sent this out to clients who had expressed themselves willing to be telephoned, he was not cold-calling.

At one licensed dealer some whizz-kids wrote on the client cards that they had sent out information when they had been doing nothing of the kind; they even scribbled fictitious dates.

Technically if a client had dealt three times within a three year period, the dealer was not obliged to send him information before closing him. In practice, the dealer might just sell stock, regardless. The dealing room atmosphere tacitly egged him on.

A few dealers, in various firms, were in the habit of cold-calling stolen clients. They would come up with some plausible introduction line: 'You will remember speaking with me at my previous firm . . . ' (The client will usually pretend or imagine he does.) Or: 'You dealt with my close friend John Smith.' (Who may have been nothing of the kind.)

Dealing clients having an entrepreneurial streak in them, didn't care whether or not they had been lied to, until they lost money. They would then complain. They were probably best off talking to the Press, as licensed dealers would often do anything to compensate when the source of grievance was made public.

One Miss Beeby, who lost £38,470 trading through LHW Futures got most of her money back following a publicised outcry, and various inquiries into the hard sell methods of the firm's dealers. The *Investors' Chronicle* proposed: 'Is it too much, perhaps, to suggest that their concern is linked to their imminent re-application to join the Association of Futures Brokers and Dealers?'

Losers with other firms were, in certain cases, reimbursed, particularly whilst a firm was awaiting a decision from the regulatory authorities on its application for membership.

Many a naive British Telecom or British Gas or British Airways shareholder has acted on 'advice', which he assumed was impartial, to reinvest in some dubious unquoted stock. In many cases this was illicit, but went on at certain licensed dealers all the time. Some of the management knew about it.

What with cancelled bargains, new issues dealing, and options, etc, as well as joint ventures and client referrals, it was often a moot point whether a client had been dealt three times, twice, once, or indeed at all. Often the astute dealer could construct a convincing case which contradicted any complaint made by aggrieved buyers of dud OTC shares, too late.

Generally, licensed dealers have been required to disclose material interests in proposed transactions, and to observe good market practice. These rules have been laxly interpreted. If they sensed the client was off his guard, dealers would stray from the straight and narrow. It was simply a question of what they could get away with.

Many dealers, like their clients have never been interested in much beyond short-term gain. They have, furthermore, taken care of their own interests, at the expense of the clients'. Even when this had become obvious, a masochistic streak in certain clients would keep them buying.

Harvard clients would offer 'referrals': friends or relatives who would deal. Their purpose was probably more to sink or swim in companionship than to do their friends a favour. It was like forming a business partnership, or getting married. This points to the fact that the clients were as self-interested as their dealers.

According to Rule Seventeen of the Licensed Dealers (Conduct of Business) Rules 1983, dealers were not permitted to grant credit in relation to any transaction. Clients were obliged to settle on the normal settlement date. If a client was offered a longer time period to pay, the transaction could be thus rendered voidable. In practice though, clients at Harvard Securities were on occasions given longer to pay, and were pressed for payment by the rescheduled deadlines.

There was a frightening anomaly between the publicised risks attached to trading with some licensed dealers, particularly on OTC stocks, and the confident predictions made by dealers over the phone, their reassurances and self-projections of honesty. Top dealers at one firm were described almost admiringly in these respects by an irate client, known there as an 'old burn-out' due to the money he had lost in investing through them.

Harvard's standard 'wealth warning' read: OVER-THE-COUNTER SECURITIES DO NOT MEET THE LISTING REQUIREMENTS OF THE LONDON STOCK EXCHANGE. OTC SECURITIES ARE HIGHLY SPECULATIVE — SPREAD YOUR RISK.' This statement was carried in the Harvard newsletter *Market Maker*, as well as in the advertisements carrying latest prices of shares in which Harvard made a market — the *Daily Mail*, the *Sunday Telegraph*, and the London Evening *Standard*.

Harvard dealers usually encouraged clients to pick up as much of a particular OTC stock as they could pay for, conveniently or not.

Advice on 'spreading risk' was reserved for listed or USM stocks, where it was of course, not so crucial anyway.

Harvard advised that OTC investments should not form more than 15% of a client's investment portfolio, and also that clients should not be advised to sell all their listed investments to buy OTC investments.

However, many Harvard clients have had OTC stocks forming far more than 15% of their investment portfolio — not surprising when Harvard dealers have sometimes been forced to sell OTC stocks for days, even weeks at a time, on occasions through evenings and Saturdays, as well as during normal working hours. In 1988, with less Stock Exchange quoted stocks on their books, and fewer market-makers willing to deal with them, Harvard tended to concentrate on selling OTC stocks all the more vigorously.

The story must be told of a forceful sales campaign at Harvard in the few weeks preceding Christmas 1986. Dealers were then selling shares in Hilton Mining (unknowingly shortly before it almost collapsed) and in Bleasdale Computing and Weymouth Clinic (unknowingly shortly before the share prices noticeably suffered).

Dealers were told that Harvard wanted to have the stocks valued at their 'offer price' for that year's accounting figures, as opposed to the 'mid-price' which had been used for valuations in previous years.

It was further said that the new method of evaluation could only proceed if Harvard proved that the stocks in question could be retailed in certain quantities at the 'offer price'.

Dealers were offered the usual high 2% commission on their sales of stock. But extra incentives, icing on the commission cake, encouraged that extra effort. Harrods Christmas hampers and bottles of champagne were offered to individuals and to teams who generated the most business.

The dealing room turned into a madhouse. Rules against making guarantees were ignored more than ever. Dealers broke sales records, much to the admiration of the training officer working downstairs, who said: 'These guys are amazing. They know nothing, and yet are persuading investors to put hundreds of thousands of pounds a day into obscure little companies.'

At the end of the sales campaign, there were rows as to who should have the hampers which had turned out to be smaller than expected. It was, however, the prestige which the dealers craved. They were salesmen, not financial advisors, and *they would remind themselves of that fact with pride.* This shared knowledge helped to form a basis for their camaraderie.

A further incentive for the top salesman was introduced at this stage, in the form of two weeks' free lodging in Tom Wilmot's villa in Portugal, albeit with no travel expenses paid. You the reader must bear in mind that this, on top of other commissions and inventives, was offered as a reward for off-loading three specific stocks, at least two of which turned out to be unfortunate investments. Dealing director Neil Miller claimed that from the end of 1986 to May 1987, the dealers in his charge were bringing around £200,000 - £500,000 a day into Harvard.

Cash prizes were always the most popular with dealers. Awards of warrants or shares in OTC-traded companies were not attractive to dealers who had reservations about their value. More attractive were shares in recent new issues, such as TSB.

When under real pressure, dealers were likely to persuade clients to take profits (or losses) on listed stocks, even if they had only had them two or three weeks, so as to reinvest the proceeds into OTC stocks. Often, dealers would not even mention that the new investment had only OTC status. If they had done so, the client would probably not have consented to the switch. When they discovered it, via the obligatory risk warning on the paperwork, clients would be too late to reverse the deal (unless this was a first transaction).

Harvard dealers would often 'churn' clients out of main market stocks into OTC ones with impunity. However, Harvard dealers who churned clients specifically out of OTC into main market stocks may have been fined. Harvard's argument was that it was in the clients' interest to hang onto OTC stocks.

Clients of a number of licensed dealers, eventually guessed what a gamble the whole business was, but could rarely prove that the odds were loaded against them. They would just shout and threaten. Dealers were relieved they did not usually meet the dupes face to face.

Not all licensed dealers have used the hard sell technique, but the soft sell is an insidious tactic too, which may involve the dealer applying pressure, but only with persuasive sweet-talking.

Legislative loopholes have enabled the most amazing liberties to be taken. Dealers at Harvard Securities made enormous commissions for themselves, by dealing clients on the account, until the firm's directors put their foot down, fined offenders, and placed restrictions on such 'exploitation' of the commission structure.

At one licensed dealer many clients had made money buying and selling shares in Guinness or in condom manufacturers London International within the account. In the case of London International, the share price shot up in the throes of the AIDS scare.

The amount of the gain was confined for clients as they were not permitted to make more than £1,000 or so in London International, it came hard that their dealers insisted they come out. If they had stayed in, clients would have made significantly more profit. But the dealing director insisted on having the stock back on the licensed dealer's books, *even in one case when the client was not available on the phone.* He thus sanctioned an illicit discretionary deal that was apparently in the licensed dealer's immediate financial interest.

Dealers were taught not to accept cancellations if they could possibly help it. At Harvard a £25 fine was imposed for every cancellation, except for OTC purchases where the client was supposed to be allowed a five day cooling off period or longer, during which he was entitled to cancel.

To combat cancellation, a few Harvard dealers would try to deny the validity of the clause, saying: 'You can't cancel, it's not within five days', or, 'The cancellation clause doesn't apply to these sorts of bargains.' Dealers who suffered too many cancellations risked losing their jobs. The high risk warning attached to contract notes on OTC stock purchased proved a real nuisance to dealers.

In some firms, a popular way of dealing with clients who had cancelled was to smooth over doubts about risk, to pretend that no cancellation had taken place: 'I understand you're a little concerned about this share. You haven't received written information? I'll send you out something right away Sir, and perhaps you'd like to send us a cheque.' If a stock's value had risen, some licensed dealers would cancel the deal on the slightest pretext.

The likelihood of making a profit was sometimes constantly over-emphasised, until the client had been mesmerised into trying out the licensed dealer in question. After this initial experience, many a client would never deal again, and in some cases never see his money again either.

If a client insisted on cancelling, a desperate dealer might argue a fake moral obligation: 'We do have the technical clause, Sir, but that's for when the client's mentally ill, or for an old lady who didn't understand what she was doing. We expect you to keep your word, according to the Stock Exchange saying: "Dictum meum pactum", "My word is my bond" (ironic, since most licensed dealers were not Stock Exchange members). You'd expect us to stand by your sell order, and we expect you to stand by your purchase order.'

At one company, a dealer tried this approach on a client, who pleaded falsely: 'I have been ill you know. When I bought, I wasn't in a fit state to make up my mind . . . ' If a client, as in this case, still sticks to his guns, a dealer may really get aggressive. All he has to lose, he feels, is his own commission.

One dealer, regularly trotted out this line of patter: 'If you don't stand by this bargain, you will be blacklisted by the London Exchange. You will never be able to deal again . . . ' This was, of course, a blatant lie. The client though, almost invariably became alarmed.

By one or another of these means most clients who had initially cancelled would get cajoled into going through with the bargain after all. They would then become especially embittered if the share price went down — as at many licensed dealers it usually did. Settlement problems, late or non-delivery of share certificates, then the near impossibility of selling back, followed by the departure of dealers with whom they had built up the semblance of a rapport, only added to their resentment.

To keep a really big client, dealers would sometimes risk their own necks.

One female dealer whose biggest client was losing thousands of pounds, resorted to drastic measures when he begged her to save him from a debt he could not pay.

She added 'Ltd' to his name on the bargain slip, and told him to claim falsely that he had put the deal through in the name of his company which had now gone into liquidation. The client followed her instructions, and thus avoided paying monies due to the licensed dealer.

Dealers rarely help clients as much as that. During the bull market, several dealers used to fiddle the computers, so the bargains of other dealers went through with their own dealing codes attached. They applied the art of earning commission from other dealers' work. These most artful of dealers did not get caught.

There are times when salesmen in licensed dealing firms are expected to rally round and work extra hours:

On 10th June 1987, the day after the General Election, all Harvard's dealers were required to come in at 7.30 a.m. This was partly to compete with City brokers who were opening markets at 7 a.m., but also to provide reassurance to clients, should such a blight attack the City as a Labour victory.

On such fraught occasions, the rules sometimes go by the board.

From August to September 1987, Harvard dealers stayed working until late at night, punting out OTC and main market stocks at several pence below the market price, provided clients agreed to cash settlement, i.e. within forty-eight hours.

Dealers too were sometimes given extra incentives, for example 1p per share for every share sold in Rigby Electronics.

At an earlier stage, the Harvard dealing room was selling OTC when director John Harris said: 'Anyone who doesn't sell their OTC quota by 3 p.m. will get fined £100.'

Several dealers were given notice of this fine, including one ex-actor who promptly walked out of Harvard on the spot.

There has been a lot of discussion over the years concerning BIDS, and FIMBRA. What was at stake was how much control these two should exert as the major self regulatory bodies of the OTC market.

There was felt to be a need to strike a compromise between enforcement of rules through a self regulatory agency (SRO), which had its finger on the pulse of the action, and formal statutory legislation. A further issue under consideration was how much the private investor needed to be protected. The Financial Services Act (1986) gives him the sort of mollycoddling he has never had, but still he allows himself to get carried away.

The private investor needed most protection during the 1920s and 1930s, a time of share swindles indeed. The Board of Trade, in an effort to clean up the mess, appointed The Anderson Committee on Fixed Trusts (1936) and the Bodkin Committee on Share Pushing (1937). Their machinations culminated in the Prevention of Fraud (Investments) Act 1939.

This Act stipulated who could deal in securities. Only authorised licensed dealers, or exempt bodies such as Stock Exchange members, the Bank of England, a statutory Corporation, or a recognised association of dealers were so privileged. The Act was not before time.

However, once a licence was obtained, firms could go unpunished for what embittered clients would have described as appalling professional practice — despite the apparent Government approval that accompanied the granting of a licence. The ultimate sanction was the withdrawal of the licence to deal, and this was rarely invoked.

The Prevention of Frauds (Investments) Act 1958 was virtually unchanged from its predecessor. The Company Law Committee (1962) headed by Lord Jenkins, offered some suggestions for reform. These involved more stringent penalties for infringement of regulations on the part of licensed dealers, including not just revocation but also suspension of licences, as well as large financial penalties, and larger deposits to be paid by licence holders.

Furthermore, it was recommended that aspiring licensed dealers should provide fuller details than hitherto, and that the scope of dealers' work should be expanded. It was also advised that restrictions on the sending out of information to the public, and on advertising generally should be increased. It was said that agents of overseas companies should also be subject to the Act. Typically, given the bureaucratic inefficiency attached to such legislature, these suggestions were never acted upon.

In the early 1980s, the demise of the investment manager Norton Warburg, and other disasters, led to a watershed in investor protection, the Gower Report. It also led, less significantly, to an updating of the Licensed Dealers (Conduct of Business) Rules (1960).

Professor Jim Gower had the difficult task of being the Government's adviser on investment protection. He often spoke his mind, as in March 1986, when he said that the Department of Trade was 'always looking for grounds not to prosecute people'.

Once, in January of that year, the lion was bearded in his own den. A commodities salesman rang up Jim Gower at his Securities and Investment Board (SIB) Office, and Gower fired some pertinent questions at him.

The Gower Report on investor protection was initiated by the Government in mid 1981. It has given rise to all the new legislation. Professor Gower expressed his opinion that the Prevention of Fraud (Investments) Act made a dangerous distinction between the strictly regulated licensed dealers, and the exempted classes of dealers. He hinted that an Act entitled 'Prevention of Fraud' had contributed to the shady reputation of licensed dealers by its assumption of fraud in the offing.

Professor Gower included in his review securities, commodities, options, and futures, as well as life assurance, unit trusts, and other packaged investment schemes. His report evolved in 1985 into a white paper. Norman Tebbit was by this stage at the Department of Trade, and the emphasis of the report shifted from external legislative protection to self regulatory decision making. The originally planned Investor Protection Act was becoming the Financial Services Act.

Although the Insurance Industry has largely escaped the restrictions of new legislation, licensed dealers have not. They must now be sanctioned by a self regulatory organisation (SRO) such as FIMBRA, or directly by the overall watchdog, the SIB.

The SIB has been charged with implementing the provisions of the Financial Services Act (1986) and for making sure that a licence to deal in securities with the public is granted only to 'fit and proper' persons.

Either the SIB licenses and supervises these persons directly, or, more usually, an SRO acts on its behalf. The SROs must have rules at least as strict as those of the SIB, and are immune from prosecution.

Any person who acts without authorisation is committing a criminal offence, in which case fines or imprisonment can follow, with all the contracts being stopped by an injunction.

Surprisingly, authorisation is necessary for advice included in a tip sheet, but not in a bona fide newspaper. It must be pointed out that newspapers offer share tips often from the most untrustworthy sources, like PR managers of the companies concerned.

The Financial Services Act (1986) imposes other serious restrictions. It has extended the terms of the now obsolete Prevention of Fraud (Investments) Act 1958. No longer must there be a clear statement intended to deceive investors. It is now an offence to mislead by misconduct.

Furthermore, it need not be proved that a person involved knew he would deceive. It is enough if he deliberately performs an act which is likely to defraud. Nor is it even necessary for a victim to be shown.

Now, there is for the first time a duty to speak up and warn of any risks, something the licensed dealer has not always chosen to do. The old style licensed dealer has become redundant in the space of a few months.

Investor protection arrived later than anticipated. 27th February 1988 (P Day) was the deadline for application to one of the self regulatory organisations (SROs) for authorisation. The Act became enforceable from 29th April 1988 (A Day) and the compensation scheme came into being in August 1988.

As the SROs were unable to process all applications in the three months between P-Day and A-Day, the SIB granted interim authorisation to all whose applications were in by P-Day but were as yet unprocessed.

Investors have been faced with both fully authorised and partially authorised businesses for some months. Unless they asked, they had no means of telling what kind of authorisation a firm had. Sharks have been operating right up to the day when full authorisation was refused them, or later if they become representatives of fully authorised firms.

The Consumers' Association expressed concern that the compensation scheme was so late to come in. People who lost money with McDonald Wheeler Fund Management asked FIMBRA for compensation before it had even been recognised as an SRO.

After some initial battles, only the fittest bucket shops are surviving, in a financial community that will present the consumer with an annual bill of perhaps £20 million.

Already, the SIB has produced a most enlightening little booklet *Self-Defence For Investors*, which is available free. (Write to: Securities and Investments Board, 3, Royal Exchange Buildings, London EC3V 3NL.) Here the sales strategies of the professional share-pushers are explained in detail. For example, if the dealer says: 'This company has developed a miracle process which will completely revolutionise the industrial and/or medical world,' he is taken to mean: 'This company is trying one of the oldest cons in the world, popularly knowns as the "snake-oil" pitch from the days when travelling medicine shows in the Wild West used to convince frontier townsfolk that the bottles of snake oil would do everything from clearing baldness to pepping up their love life. Of course, it's all most sophisticated and full of technical jargon now, but the principle's the same. After all, if we were able to show a decent chance of achieving any of these miracles, why would we need to use hard sell telephone techniques to total strangers to fund the company?'

Respectable firms in the financial services industry are surviving the new legislation better than licensed dealers. It was an indication of future trends when in early 1986, the Takeover Panel decided not to penalise Kleinwort Grieveson for inadvertently buying more than 15% of S & W Berisford, for which the bank's client Hillsdown Holdings were bidding at the time.

If a less reputable firm had committed this slight mistake, a lot of City people felt that the Takeover Panel would have probably enforced the law.

Ambiguities in the new legislature will doubtless arise, over the next few years, and smooth operators may find a way. It is no easier now than it was to check the solidity of 'Chinese walls'. Rules on churning are vague, despite the SIB's claim that perpetrators 'usually' know when they're doing it. Likewise, it is hard to fathom whether a firm has charged 'exclusively' for its services, or whether research has been 'adequate'.

In practice, the SIB may in the long-term future show more partiality to some SROs like The Securities Association than to others like FIMBRA. Some decisions may remain hasty or prejudiced. As Ivan Boesky once pointed out: 'London cannot be taken seriously as a financial centre so long as the interpretation of crucial rules depends on what the authorities had for breakfast that morning.'

The main hope for unscrupulous bucket shops clearly still lies in bureaucratic inefficiency. Firms that commit fraud, or bring fraudulent companies to the market, have in the past evaded penalisation for too long.

The Fraud Squad's and the Department of Trade's investigative groups are understaffed, and in a court case, the jury sometimes fails to grasp the complexities of fraud. Difficult cases, and those involving small sums of money have sometimes not been followed up. Experienced fraudsters have woven elaborate webs — to be untangled too late, if at all.

Share swindlers started work from Amsterdam in 1979. The Dutch authorities were informed of the methods used by the Canadians operating there, and of their criminal backgrounds by the Toronto police in 1983. The Dutch police refrained from intervention at this stage because sales of shares were almost never made to Dutch citizens, so no Dutch laws were being violated.

The victims were known as 'pooches', and were selected because they had large disposable incomes. They were doctors, owners of expensive cars, etc. Lists were bought from data banks, and advertisements were placed in newspapers like the *International Herald Tribune.*

There was nothing illegal about such client selection or about the sales pitches, although everything was unscrupulous about both. The dealer would recommend the client to have his bank check a stock, would promise to advise when to sell, and would end the deal by saying: 'I'm a firm believer that you never go broke with a profit, do you?'

Continental salesmen operate under several names, to avoid sustaining a relationship with investors. They constantly refuse to allow people to sell back stock, pretending they have never received sell orders, or advising to send a telex, which subsequently appears not to have reached them. Bank account numbers, signatures, and other formalities can be checked and argued over, while a sell order is dragged out until it is no longer attractive.

The lavish lifestyles of the Amsterdam salesmen who only needed to work in sporadic bursts throughout the year, testified to the fraud which the Dutch authorities persisted in virtually ignoring. Peter Van Dijken, head of the Dutch fraud branch, once commented: 'We are becoming the financial slum of the world.'

Eventually, under worldwide pressure, the Dutch authorities consorted with police and regulatory authorities of Canada. The Dutch Government outlawed the boiler room operations, years too late.

Thousands of defrauded investors are still queueing for some return, but the receiver's fees and legal costs must come first. Most losses were small, but Jan Van Apeldoorn, receiver for First Commerce and other firms, knew of one investor who had lost 14 million dollars through a deal on worthless shares.

Changes are coming about in Gibraltar. The official consensus there is that there are not enough financial intermediaries to make the British self regulatory system viable. Alternative legislation is being drafted.

Gibraltar's Finance & Development secretary wants the law to prevent companies from registering in the colony, and calling themselves British, while they escape regulation by operating from another country.

Generally, UK investors still remain still unprotected if they part with money to continental bucket shops. The onus is on them to behave responsibly. Just as it takes two to make a baby, it takes two to arrange a share deal.

Just as legislation is sometimes lacking, it proves at other times burdensome. Harvard's launch of the astrology company Future Forecasts was delayed due to the need to comply with Section Four of the Vagrancy Act 1934, which said that those who profess to tell fortunes are rogues and vagabonds, and risk a three month prison sentence.

In March 1985, Stephen Isaacs appeared before the disciplinary committee of the General Optical Council, in connection with his OTC-floated, fashionable optician, For Eyes. The Council was not altogether content with the publicity he was getting, but For Eyes seemed to be making great strides.

Investors who eighteen months later lost money in this apparently promising company were not happy, some taking the view that their dealer had been over-enthusiastic as to its prospects. The question was: could they prove it? Their original dealers would probably have changed jobs, so they could not even confront *them*.

Prior Harwin's alleged shortcomings led to the Department of Trade effectively closing them down. Consequently, Cleveland Securities temporarily decided not to make a grey market in British Airways shares, i.e. buying and selling shares in this public issue before Stock Exchange dealings had started. This decision was in fact later reversed, but other licensed dealers besides Cleveland showed signs of panic, in some cases tightening up their standards.

When rumours floated around Harvard that a number of dealers may have been on the hit list, i.e. due to be sacked, the dealing floor atmosphere would become tense and quarrelsome. This happened at intervals and led to even less concern for the clients' interests on the dealers' part. Employees would become almost wholly preoccupied with saving their own necks.

Unlike the Securities & Exchange Commission (SEC) in America, the SIB is not supported by the State and its self regulatory function may serve only to protect itself — a view which has been expressed by the Labour Party. Private investors must not get complacent. The SIB itself has said: 'The existence of the SIB no more removes the need for investors to pay attention where they place their money than the existence of the *Highway Code* removes the need to look before crossing the road.'

The client must make his own decisions regarding investment, even if these are to delegate responsibility for decision making. He must never forget that the licensed dealer, in common with most businesses, exists to make a profit.

Chapter Seven

THE WEB

The spinning of the web began when the dealers' commission rates at Harvard Securities were drastically reduced in May 1987. The dealing director Neil Miller made clear his dissatisfaction to dealers: 'I'm not paid to motivate you into selling now. That's up to the team leaders,' he announced on the dealing floor. He was in the meantime almost openly looking out for a new position.

Miller parted company with Harvard Securities in May 1987. His hard sell tactics were by then finding little favour with the other Harvard directors. By this stage Harvard was seeking to improve its image and to impress the Stock Exchange.

He left, followed by a number of Harvard's top dealers. His conversations with them were, for obvious reasons, conducted after working hours. They would be coming to a new Stock Exchange firm, he said, where they could earn at the rate of £50,000+ a year, in other words, what some of the dealers were used to before Harvard's commission rates were cut. After a series of secret meetings, most accompanied him there like lambs.

Thus, some eleven new dealers walked out of Harvard Securities one by one in the course of a week. They were ushered into the new firm's swish offices in King Street, off prestigious Pall Mall. A smiling Neil Miller was there to greet them. He paid dealers an immediate £2,000 each, and then £2,000 a month by cheque — in all totalling £8,000 before they had even started dealing.

Not until some days after their arrival did Neil Miller tell them a name for the new firm. He called it Kingsley Paige, and told dealers not to tell clients yet. It gradually transpired that this company was a cover for London & Norwich Investment Services Ltd.

Curiously some dealers from the now crashed Sheridan Securities seemed to be operating from an office down the corridor. 'They'll be going soon. We want nothing to do with them,' said Neil Miller.

Sheridan Securities had been a high profile pusher of American Pink Sheet shares, some of which are now worth little or nothing. The dealers there had earned exorbitant commissions. The new recruits were not all aware of these facts, although some knew of Sheridan's rather unsavoury reputation.

Cleveland House, 19 King Street, London SW1, which housed the opulent offices of London & Norwich Investment Services Ltd, where the Silverton sales operation took place.

The lingering Sheridan dealers were suspicious of the influx of dealers. Were the new lot pushing Silverton shares? If so, at what price?

Sheridan dealers nosed about the offices, searching for contract notes, and asking of the London & Norwich dealers.

'What stock are you selling?'

'Trusthouse Forte', some retorted, or 'Nothing at the moment.' Certain of the ex Harvard whizz-kids here knew how to be economical with the truth, and not show it. Only, they had met their match in the Sheridan dealers.

Suddenly there was an Anton Pillar order (a legally authorised raid) on Sheridan, and the London & Norwich contingent retreated behind locked doors — where nobody could get THEM, but where some of them could get their CLIENTS.

Some Harvard dealers who had been invited to the strange new firm had declined to come. One dealer, still at Harvard, had shopped his colleagues before they left by informing on their plans to a director, on condition that he was made a team leader. He got his way, then later contemplated joining the London & Norwich gang.

Another top dealer refused to come until he was sent a letter headed with the name of the new company and indicating that it enjoyed membership of the Stock Exchange. This evidence proved not forthcoming, so he joined a firm of stockbrokers instead.

John Solleigh, Sheridan Securities' former managing director, addressed the new dealing floor every few days. He would say: 'We should be getting Stock Exchange membership next week.' Next: 'There are some technical hitches, but membership should be coming through in a few days.'

As yet, the name London & Norwich Investment Services was still relatively unknown to dealers. This mysterious outfit later became recognised as the FIMBRA company that Kingsley Paige was taking over.

Dealers were told to fill in forms for individual FIMBRA membership, 'so as to deal in Unit Trusts'. All complied, seeking three references each as required, and a secretary typed the forms out. Dealers did, however, query this. If they were supposed to be gaining Stock Exchange membership, why FIMBRA? Why Unit Trusts?

Dealers who had received P45 tax forms from Harvard were asked to hand them over. They did so warily, and were told this was essential for sorting out the tax which the company would be paying on their behalf.

Mysteriously the managers were overheard ordering computers, etc on the telephone in the name of the Sheridan Group.

The connection was beginning to be apparent to everybody. John Solleigh expressed his concern to divorce himself from any licensed dealers, but his association with Sheridan had been publicised in the national press.

Towards the end of August 1987, dealers started getting bored with just waiting for the brilliant new firm to start operating properly. If it wasn't for their £2,000 a month retainer, they might have just walked out.

Neil Miller's next move was to announce that he and his little team of dealers, despite limitations in their experience, would negotiate to take over Aberdeen Steak Houses, whose share price had been depressed for many months. Miller considered that this company was ripe for the picking.

For several days at a stretch dealers came in at 8.00 a.m. Pattinson Hayton, managing director of London & Norwich Investment Services Ltd, would pop in *every* morning, crack a few jokes with the dealers, and by 9.30 a.m. would be chauffeured away in his leased blue Mercedes 500 SEL. Some dealers would watch him go from the office windows above, marvelling at the sticker in the car's back window: "My lawyer can beat up your lawyer."

'Ha ha ha,' Neil Miller would chuckle, 'Now he's gone we can use the office space for our own purposes!'

The dealing room door would be bolted, and in whispers Neil Miller would explain the plan. Dealers would raise a combined total of £10 million from their clients. This would be loan stock, to finance the takeover of Aberdeen Steak House.

Once the takeover had been successfully completed, all dealers would be appointed directors of the company, each holding equity in it proportionate to the amount he had raised from his clients.

In whispers these meetings would proceed. Everybody was alert and interested. The use of office space, time and telephones secretly for their own purpose appealed to some of the more hardcore ex-Harvard dealers present. Here was their chance!

The burden of tasks was distributed. Two dealers went to Companies House to research details on the takeover target. One attempted to sort out a loan for £10 million from Coutts Bank. Another dealer obtained an Extel card. The restaurants were visited and criticised for the way they were run.

'We'll turn 'em right over,' boasted Neil Miller.

'Double the turnover in six months or so!'

David Watson was responsible for compiling the business proposal. Another dealer had the dubious honour of putting it into decent English.

A meeting was fixed with a leading chartered accountant in the City. It was reported that when Miller and a tiny cohort of dealers arrived at his offices, they were surprised but nonetheless delighted that the accountant had already guessed their bid target and had

Aberdeen Steak Houses . . . which London & Norwich dealers were plotting to take over under the leadership of Neil Miller.

the papers relating to Aberdeen Steak House ready on the table!

'This is the only possible one it could be,' said the accountant.

The contingent returned to the plush offices of London & Norwich Investment Services Ltd in a taxi. Swinging back in his chair, Miller showed his 'monkey grin':

'He reckons it's a goer,' he yapped.

'He reckons it's on.'

The bid was not so implausible as it might appear. Miller knew of a large stakeholder in Aberdeen Steak House who for a while earlier had wanted to sell, but had failed to find a buyer at the right price.

However, when the hard selling of Silverton Industries started, the takeover bid simply faded away. London & Norwich's unhappy clientele did not know what it had missed!

Pattinson Hayton was managing director of London & Norwich from the start, and became more powerful as Kingsley Paige's application for Stock Exchange membership proved unsuccessful. That was when London & Norwich Investment Services Ltd started selling shares in Silverton Industries, in which Hayton was the majority shareholder.

Neil Miller was away briefly on a trip to America, with Pattinson Hayton. He returned to the dealing room radiant; some dealers crowded around him.

'Pat Hayton's amazing,' he announced. 'He flew me over his oilwells and back by Concorde! We drove about in his £100,000 Porsche. This Silverton, whose shares we'll be selling, it's good! We spent a whole day going over one oil plant. I've thoroughly checked it out.

'Pat's offices on the Avenue of the Stars, California are incredible, with dolly-birds everywhere. Just my style.'

Some dealers listened in silence, gazing up at their leader as if he was a god. Most, like Miller, wanted to stick around where the money was. All some cared about was making a quick buck.

Originally, the 'special American situations' had been explained to the dealers as stocks they could place just four times a year. They didn't have to place them, explained Neil Miller, but they would earn huge commissions if they did. And they would make the clients money, he added.

Some dealers were already ringing up their clients. One was telling them: 'We've got this amazing chap here who handles special American situations. He only chooses four of them a year, but he gets four of them right.'

The clients, although puzzled as to the apparent gradual name change from Kingsley Paige to London & Norwich Investment Services Ltd, were getting excited alright.

They were being primed for the Silverton deal. In their hearts, some dealers may already have been realising what they were here for.

Meanwhile Pattinson Hayton was wandering into the dealing room, smiling at Miller, and muttering under his breath things like: 'I'm getting some shit sorted out.' And: 'we'll get the show on the road, and we'll piss on 'em all out there.' All the time his eyes would twinkle in his handsome tanned face, and Miller, as well as some dealers, would worship him.

'He's a multimillionaire,' one dealer put about. 'He's richer than Wilmot.' This was exactly the fallacy Hayton was designing to promote. In fact his spending was mostly on the back of a Company credit card.

He knew how to adjust his charm for the more refined dealers present. He was also a real ladies' man and would make sexual advances to female dealers, at which point his swearing would vanish into thin air. He was a master chameleon.

A team of Silverton directors headed by a Mr Christie, delivered several presentations on Silverton Industries to dealers in a special little room. Mr Christie, in his dry American accent, would drone on about oil prospecting, prodding a map. The dealers were bored to tears. To some, he seemed to be saying just a lot of technical mumbo jumbo. Some managed, however to ask him the odd question, so as to appear interested.

'Where are the biggest oil prospecting areas?' they would ask, or 'What will Silverton's agreement with ALCOA achieve?'

Mr Christie answered questions slowly and unintelligibly. Some dealers were giggling, yawning and winking at each other.

Events showed that the apparent optimism about Silverton Industries, of Mr Christie and his faithful band of oilmen was ill-founded.

There wasn't a great deal of information on Silverton industries available to dealers. Most would sell it as a quick in and out. The sort of client who wanted detailed information might not be the type who would buy anyway.

On the first day of selling, the ex-Harvard dealers were all at work early. One dealer, who had particularly wanted to sell fully listed stocks only, was white-faced. 'I'm not sure I can go through with this,' he said.

'You were happy enough to take eight grand from the company,' said one of the bosses. 'Now you're fucking selling the Silverton. Or piss off home.'

The dealer got on with selling, as did the others. The atmosphere started buzzing, as in a busy period in the old days at Harvard. That first day, dealers cleared a phenomenal £800,000 worth of Silverton shares.

The bosses walked about ecstatically.

'Come on, hurry up. We've not much Silverton left,' one manager shouted.

One dealer grinned: 'If we run out, we can just go into a back room and print out some more shares.'

Some of his colleagues roared with laughter. This was, however, an innocent joke. None knew at this stage just how much Silverton stock was available.

The next day, while dealers were still hard at it, the firm received a call from Michael Walters of the *Daily Mail*.

'Clients have been complaining', he said. 'How much Silverton was sold? What was this stock?'

'None has yet been sold,' claimed one of the managers. 'We're just taking orders.'

All sales were subsequently cancelled, to be deferred for six weeks.

Dealers now began sending out prospectuses on Silverton Industries, a precautionary measure, to fall into line with regulations which some had initially overlooked. By now public attention was being alerted by warnings in the press, 'Steer Clear of Silverton', said the *Daily Mail*. But would the punters heed the advice?

Some dealers were infuriated by such adverse press comment. Their £2,000 basic per month had stopped coming in now. They needed the promised 10% commissions. Who had alerted the papers? They looked within their ranks and found a scapegoat — a fellow dealer against whom threats were then made.

Some weeks later, the sales campaign was resumed. This time, most of the deals went through, for it was Harvard's old clients that London & Norwich Investment Services salesmen were ringing, and dealing.

At this early stage in London & Norwich's short but eventful life, director Neil Miller lunched with Harvard boss Tom Wilmot, in the restaurant of an expensive hotel.

Allegedly, Tom Wilmot had offered to do a deal with London & Norwich Investment Services Ltd. Neil Miller boasted he had turned this down, saying: 'I'm a lot younger than you Tom, and I'll be around for longer than you!' He set himself up as a rival to the Harvard boss, but was playing out of his league.

The bill for the lunch had come to £200. Neil Miller lounged around the offices of London & Norwich for what remained of that afternoon, boasting about how he had 'played' the lunch with Wilmot to all the dealers.

However, in the next forty-eight hours came the surprise blow that Harvard was threatening legal action against individual London & Norwich dealers, to retrieve its clients.

London & Norwich Investment Services Ltd successfully combatted this, using the services of solicitors Simmons & Simmons, and the private placing of shares in Silverton Industries went ahead.

Silverton Industries was the only stock actually sold. It was offered for the first time in the UK and presented as a quick in and out. Within a month, a minimum profit of 35 cents was assured — although clearly no guarantee could be made against fluctuations in the exchange rate. This information was passed on to the dealers, some of whom in turn passed it on to clients.

Clients were taken in. After all, certain dealers were promising them not the earth, but just enough profit to make the investment seem worth bothering about. Some dealers' warnings about a remote possibility of the exchange rate not being favourable, added plausibility to their sales pitches. They appeared to be concerned for their clients' interests.

London & Norwich Investment Services Ltd had FIMBRA membership from the days when the company had been selling Unit Trusts for some ten years, before it was bought out by Pattinson Hayton.

But the firm was breaking various FIMBRA regulations, some of which were arguably minor. The most horrific example was as follows:

After a tranche of Silverton shares had been sold to investors, the concept of Silverton Debentures was made known to the dealers. Silverton Debentures were presented as loan stock, convertible later into shares, paying 10% interest to clients in the form of a monthly cheque. Dealers were given a written sales pitch, recommending this as a safe investment for clients who could not face the rise and fall of equities in what was, after all, a bear market.

The next morning in London & Norwich's offices, an incredible scene took place. Some dealers quailed before what they were asked to do, which was to ring up the clients who had held unit trusts through London & Norwich Investment Services for a number of years. They were to tell them to switch over their steadily mounting funds, maybe £20,000, maybe £100,000, complete with the small but steady interest they had gained over the years, all into this safe and lucrative new investment fund called Silverton Debentures.

One of the bosses urged everyone on, without giving them time to think. 'Here are some leads,' he said, passing round details of clients from the original London & Norwich. 'Ring them up and tell them to convert. You yourselves get 10% commission on every deal.'

James Randall was a director of the original London & Norwich which had been taken over by Pattinson Hayton. Out of a sense of responsibility to his former clients, he remained on the premises, but it was only with the greatest reluctance and without any real knowledge as to what was planned, that he had released the names of his smaller long-standing clients to the firm's new owners. The more profitable names were coaxed out of him soon afterwards. Some dealers easily persuaded clients to convert, earning for themselves, in some cases, an apparent commission of thousands of pounds on single deals.

One of the bosses encouraged them as follows: 'Come on. Your calls are not being taped as they were at Harvard. Say what you like . . . All those flats you want, those holidays. This is easy money . . . If you want to be stinking rich' he added 'and to have two houses and two cars, get on the phone . . .' Most dealers did.

When the deed was done, the dealing director congratulated his dealers. Jokes were cracked about James Randall, London &

Norwich's former director: 'He's sitting in the far office, having a nervous breakdown.' said Pattinson Hayton with a smile.

'With a bit of luck, he'll have a coronary,' cackled a manager.

This particular chap, who had a stubborn honesty about him, was always rushing up to his senior manager and bleating: 'We're not sending out client application forms. We're not abiding by FIMBRA rules, we've got to be so careful . . . '

'Fuck off, will you,' the manager would reply.

Following the weekend, dealers discovered that James Randall, after learning what had been done, privately rung his former clients, advising that they should cancel their agreements. The clients clearly did so, almost to a man, and the Silverton Debentures ended up unsold. It was just as well, although feelings about the London & Norwich Investment Services' former director ran high. 'An interfering old man,' was one dealer's verdict. But none could deal his clients now. Some had only been able to gain audience from them by introducing the honest ex-director of the old London & Norwich as their close working colleague.

One client sent in a letter. 'I had conflicting advice,' he said. 'One person within London & Norwich told me to transfer funds into Silverton Debentures. Another, with whom I'd always dealt, decided against it. So I do not wish to go through with this transfer.'

This letter was produced for comment by the London & Norwich dealer concerned, when a year after (1988) he applied for membership of The Securities Association (TSA), so he could become a stockbroker. His application was successful.

It was quite late on that FIMBRA started visiting London & Norwich Investment Services Ltd. Officials would wander into the dealing room, chatting with salesmen. They saw that there was no work being done while waiting for the next deal. 'What do you do all day?' one asked. 'Sit around reading magazines like you are now, I suppose.' Dealers who didn't have individual FIMBRA membership stayed at home during FIMBRA's visit.

The officials would suddenly then incorporate sharp questions such as: 'What size is your average deal? What sort of clients do you have?' Their ploy was to catch them off guard, it seemed. But the dealers were wise to such tactics. Some gave replies that represented them in the most favourable light. 'Our clients have dealt with us for a long time. We brought them from Harvard. We always put them into amounts they can afford. Silverton Industries is a speculative stock, and obviously we make clients aware of that.'

London & Norwich played host to a succession of tea ladies. Young and trim, or old, fat and waddling, they came and they went, never understanding how the dealers were paid so much for doing so little.

Indeed, these young men to whom they brought tea and toast all day never seemed to have anything to do, except eat and drink. One tea lady described the dealing room as a chimpanzees' tea party.

Whenever a dealer fancied a cup of tea, he would not bother to go out to the kitchen to fetch it. Instead, he would lift the phone, and place his order with the tea ladies.

Sometimes for fun, the dealers would order one cup of tea after another, so the poor tea ladies got worked off their feet, one reason why they kept leaving.

One young cook would linger in the dealing room, chatting up the dealers. 'Ooh we're busy,' one young dealer would moan at her, with his feet propped on his desk as he thumbed through glossy car magazines. 'The strain of being a City dealer.'

'Go along with you,' the cook would say. She had a gamine figure, with a boyish freckled face and curly brown hair. She would roll up her *Daily Mirror* and prod him.

Pattinson Hayton, the managing director of London & Norwich Investment Services Ltd, remained the gregarious charmer. He was a tall, tanned Australian who boasted of playing polo with Prince Charles, leased a luxurious Knightsbridge apartment on his company credit card, and was chauffeur driven around London in a flashy Mercedes.

He used to tell dealers in his casual drawl: 'We're going to have a dog and pony evening in a hotel. So get your clients along. Get them to buy some Silverton too.'

The two evening presentations held at Claridges and The Berkeley Hotel were indeed splendid. Drinks and eats were served in private chambers. Presentations were given by Silverton's oil buffs. Mr Christie, with the aid of slides showing potential drilling areas around the Colorado basin, spelled out huge potential. He emphasised Silverton's recent deal with ALCOA (Aluminum Company of America). Nobody — dealer or client — understood much from these presentations. Some clients were, however, blinded with science. Most dealers didn't care so long as they were paid their 10% commissions. The 10% was, after all, more than twenty times what Harvard Securities was *now* paying for pushing OTC stocks. Was it what Tom Wilmot, in an internal memo to Harvard dealers, would later call 'dirty money?'

At evening presentations and elsewhere, Hayton was always popping up. He was courteous to dealers, always stopping them in the corridor and asking 'How are you?'. He had confidential discussions with the best, saying: 'Do bring clients up to our offices, for lunch or whatever. Get them into as much Silverton as you can.' He continued to make such approaches, even when dealers were no longer being paid.

Hayton was always darting off to the USA, and telephoning

London & Norwich's offices from there. He also used his car phone for this purpose. In the offices, he once noticed that computers had arrived, and were assembled on each dealer's desk. 'Do they work, or do they just look pretty?' He quipped.

The computer salesman had not been able to get the screens over there quickly enough. But after it was obvious that London & Norwich Investment Services Ltd was not going to pay for them, his firm whipped them away.

Those screens had proved great fun while they lasted. The dealers had at last been given something to play with. Harvard's former whizz-kids sat there building silly little two dimensional boxes, and solving crass puzzles on screens which as yet listed no share prices.

This was just another cover up for some dealers' increasing panic. This was all very jolly, but what lay in store for them? The question still haunts some dealers to this day.

Pattinson Hayton was adamant that dealers would sell their clients out of Silverton shares soon.

'We'll pump out this shit. We'll piss off to the mountains for Christmas. Then we'll get them out.' He once said.

In order to reassure dealers, money remitted by clients for shares in Silverton had been paid into a separate clients' account in the Dealing Director's charge, from which the dealers' 10% commission was due.

Even when this system was functioning, dealers were paid late, and cheques which dealers frantically express cleared tended to bounce, since London & Norwich didn't always have enough money in its account to meet them. Eventually, dealers were taking it for granted that they would not get their pay cheques on time, and were not surprised at the sudden suspension of their final commission payments. Little did dealers realise that some would *never* see the colour of their money.

During the London & Norwich's Silverton sales campaign, several dealers dropped out, not believing in what they were selling. One deserted to stockbrokers TC Coombs. Neil Miller tried to reclaim retainer money already paid to the dealer, ringing him saying, 'Pay us back or we'll take you to court.' The dealer, however, succeeded in not paying him back.

Another dealer who dropped out became unemployed for a long while, then ended up at the fated Anderson Kimble. Some dealers felt that he might as well have stayed, given the lucrative commission he had foregone, as they evaluated their work purely in terms of immediate financial reward.

Of the dealers who remained, several stayed away from the offices for most of the time; Neil Miller couldn't afford to sack them. After all, how would he replace dealers of this quality?

By this stage, Miller's authority was gradually diminishing; dealers who said they were going to lunch were usually off for the day.

Nor were clients held to bargains if they tried to wriggle out of them. Dealers were prevented from selling Silverton shares too hard on a regular basis. There was an emphasis on caution, on keeping a low profile.

Clients were beginning to query the state of the American market, the oil sector, and the OTC market generally. Some dealers, naturally gave favourable answers. 'The American market is bursting with opportunities. The oil sector is booming. The OTC is more sophisticated in the USA than in the UK.' Clients lapped all this up, greedy to get in on what they saw as a good thing.

The Observer revealed the link between Silverton Industries and Palmer Financial — which had previously been called Transworld Energy. Both were largely owned by Pattinson Hayton. Monies from sales of all these stocks were, in part transported to a trust in Liechtenstein. Also largely owned by Hayton were Galloway and Private Ledger, two further companies in the same mysterious network. London & Norwich dealers were on one occasion offered the opportunity of selling shares in Palmer Financial, likewise for 10% commission.

Silverton Industries had several market makers in the USA, where its share price, so *The Observer* pointed out, was quoted at around half that at which London & Norwich Investment Services Ltd was retailing the stock. After *The Observer* had revealed this discrepancy, clients started ringing up London & Norwich dealers querying why they had paid so much over the odds.

'*The Observer* has got it wrong. It's referring to a different Silverton,' some dealers said, quoting what one of the bosses had told them. In fact it was untrue. Silverton's share price in the United States was around $2.50 alright, although there was undeniably another 'Silverton' whose shares were traded on the American Pink Sheets, which was a company involved in the business of fire-fighting equipment.

A few clients rang *The Observer* and were assured that the facts were correct. Some London & Norwich dealers did not bother to research so deeply, and were misled like the majority of their clients. Pattinson Hayton sent *The Observer* a solicitor's letter, then breezily announced that he had got an apology out of them.

Not all clients took Silverton without question, and a few intelligent ones would not touch it with a bargepole. One potential client who, significantly, was an accountant, read the prospectus in detail, commenting: 'So many ambiguities and sheer meaningless statements — count me out!'

Another client asked for a bank reference from London & Norwich

Investment Services Ltd, and received one from the Co-op Bank, London & Norwich's original bankers. The reference proved good, but the client still shied away from such a risky investment.

When further warnings against investing in Silverton shares appeared in the national press, more clients than ever before claimed that deals they had done had never taken place, trying to wriggle out of their commitments. But Neil Miller urged his dealers: 'Don't press them. It'll only cause trouble.'

Complaints, in some cases valid, were made. The compliance officer was dismayed. However, a few dealers together with the bosses had a good laugh about them. Their attitude was exactly the same as it had been while previously employed elsewhere.

Several clients asked to be released from their investment if the price got below a certain level. This was very noble on their part, considering dealers had assured them of a minimum 35 cents profit after a month. Obviously, clients took such guarantees with a pinch of salt.

London & Norwich Investment Services Ltd was running out of clients and so started trying to recruit dealers with client bases. An advertisement was run in the *Financial Times* and in *The Daily Telegraph* for a chairman and dealers. The prospective chairman was offered £100,000 plus per annum, and a share of the equity. Dealers were offered around £75,000 per annum. These were perhaps the highest paid positions ever advertised by a licensed dealer.

Applications started trickling in, perhaps fifty in all, in many cases from highly qualified people, who had managed dealing teams in the City proper for years, or who had just come out of a major business school. Some graduates with minimal or no work experience applied, confiding their willingness to learn and their natural inclinations for hard work.

Some dealers read the letters and laughed at the applicants' earnestness. 'They haven't a clue,' said one dealer, wiping the tears from his eyes. 'I only want people who already have clients,' said the Dealing Director who was particularly interested in a bona fide stockbroker who applied.

The chairman's position proved hard to fill. Some applicants after closer enquiry, decided against it. The man who eventually took the post had good city credentials.

All London & Norwich dealers were invited to an evening at the American Club in Piccadilly, the heart of London's West End, in order to meet the new chairman.

Virtually all dealers turned up. They stood around awkwardly in a hired room, pinning name badges on their lapels.

The room was spacious and decorous. By the glitter of the chandelier, waiters in white coats and black bow ties glided about, offering dealers dainties on silver salvers, and refilling champagne glasses. This was proving an evening and a half.

The new chairman appeared bedazzled. He wandered about from group to group, smiling and chatting. He exuded, however, an indefinable air of puzzlement. How come he was *walking* into a job worth £100,000 per annum, plus equity? Something somewhere seemed wrong. Events were to force him to hasty action. Shortly afterwards, when London & Norwich Investment Services Ltd became involved in a court action with the DTI, the chairman understandably resigned, before he had even properly been appointed.

Gradually, London & Norwich Investment Services' connection with share-pushers Sheridan Securities became more apparent. News that an ex-Sheridan dealer had just died of a drugs overdose became known. Two dealers who had joined the London & Norwich dealers were ex-Sheridan. One had lived off just a few clients, persuading them to invest huge sums. Sheridan's principles of selling American Pink Sheet stocks of dubious value for high commissions had become those of London & Norwich Investment Services Ltd.

Clients who were strangers to London & Norwich dealers, occasionally rang up to complain about John Solleigh, ex-Sheridan managing director. One client who had lost tens of thousands from investing through Sheridan in Transworld Energy (related to Silverton) addressed a dealer as follows: 'Mr Solleigh seemed so nice. I checked with someone who knew him, who said he was as honest as the day is long.'

Another client proved more forthright, although his message was essentially the same: 'If you don't get this sorted out, I'm getting onto the DTI.'

'We're not Sheridan Securities, and have nothing to do with them,' the dealer said.

'But your advertisement in the *Financial Times* said that you would be making a market in Palmer Financial' (a Sheridan stock related to Transworld Energy and to Silverton).

'As a favour to you, yes.'

'The managing director of Sheridan is with you now, isn't he? I want a word with him.'

'He's not in. I suggest you put your query to him in writing.'

The team of ex-Harvard dealers had its own dealing room. As a reaction to the earlier Anton Pillar raid on Sheridan Securities in the office down the corridor, a combination lock was fixed on the door of the ex-Harvard dealers' office. The room was thoroughly self-contained, much to the relief of dealers, as they trusted only members of their own group. Later, locks were put on corridor doors too, and an amiable security guard was employed.

Dealers of London & Norwich Investment Services Ltd were initially opposed to recruiting dealers whom they didn't personally like, or who weren't the best. Then as client numbers were running low, London & Norwich were willing to recruit any dealers at all who would bring in the business.

A marvellous lunch party was held at the Meridian Hotel, Piccadilly, for established dealers at Harvard Securities who were potential recruits. New dealers would after all, have to be enticed into coming.

'Don't tell them much,' one of the bosses warned his dealers beforehand. 'Ha, ha, I think it's quite funny. The web's been spun once to get *you* in. Now it's being spun again.'

At the lunch, alcohol flowed abundantly and waiters served the most exquisite rice and chicken dish. Afterwards, Pattinson Hayton stood up and delivered an inspiring speech: 'London & Norwich Investment Services Ltd is a sharedealer in its own right,' he said. 'Nothing to do with John Solleigh and Kingsley Paige now.' He went on to say that Silverton Industries was a fabulous oil company. Investors would soon be coming out of their shares in it at a good profit. If Tom Wilmot caused trouble, they'd sort him out.

The potential recruits were suspicious of Hayton. Furthermore, everybody was smiling too easily. Former top dealers of Harvard Securities who had been at London & Norwich for a while seemed too relaxed. 'They're trying too hard to impress us,' one unsold recruit commented.

But many dealers didn't want to stay with Harvard Securities in any event.

After the lunch at the Meridian Hotel was over, some dealers lingered. One promptly ordered a round of champagne, to be put onto the bill. A crowd of somewhat merry young dealers was finally turfed out!

Just before leaving, one dealer dropped a flowerpot from the window of the gents' toilet, which landed on the roof of a passing cab.

Others sneaked out with a half-filled wine carafe under their coats. They were chased by frenzied waiters. 'Who's got it?' one demanded. 'Not I,' said each dealer in turn, slipping it to another.

Soon enough though, a new team of ex-Harvard dealers arrived at London & Norwich, led by an ex-Harvard stalwart who was shown documentation purporting to prove that the new firm was a member of the Stock Exchange. This was a reworking of the trick by which the 11 original top dealers from Harvard had been lured there. In blind faith, the stalwart whispered in the ears of his trainees at Harvard: 'I'm taking you all away to a Stock Exchange member firm.'

His last day at Harvard had not been uneventful . . . He returned to the office late in the afternoon after a heavy lunch, a little unsteady on his feet. Dealers noticed.

He then staggered outside to fetch something from his company car, curled up inside the back seat and fell asleep. A search for him was launched.

Upon his discovery he was threatened with the sack. However, Harvard's directors offered him one last chance. If he disclosed which dealers were about to leave Harvard, and the whereabouts of those who had already left, he would retain his own job. Ranting and raving he responded with a demand for payment, should he provide such information.

He was then asked to turn in the keys to his car, and to remove his personal belongings from the building. He refused. Eventually, Harvard retrieved the keys, dumped his personal belongings onto the street, and moved the car to a safer place.

After being thoroughly searched, he was then escorted off the premises. He turned up the following day at London & Norwich, and, one by one, curious Harvard dealers followed him there shortly afterwards.

However, once he was there he felt he had not made a wise move. His remuneration was delayed; he didn't at this stage suspect that it would never come.

Giving his new situation the benefit of the doubt, he encouraged the other new dealers to get on with selling Silverton shares, and how they did!

One dealer from the original group wandered into their room, warning that dealers' payments were long overdue *and that they would be lucky to get any money that they earned*. The ex-Harvard stalwart came after him with a vengeance. 'If you're going to demotivate our team, keep out of our dealing room,' he bellowed at him. He then complained to Neil Miller, who also rebuked the offender with: 'You'd better be saying the right things to them.'

Dealers in the new group idly speculated as to the outcome of their sales of Silverton shares. They essentially believed what Pattinson Hayton had said, namely that clients would come out of Silverton at a small profit shortly. In addition, Pattinson Hayton and his managers claimed that there would soon be the facility for dealing in main market stocks. One of the dealers was even stupid enough to believe that London & Norwich Investment Services Ltd actually had Stock Exchange membership.

One dealer, confronted with a Harvard director on the phone, who was berating him for his sudden, unexplained departure replied: 'Ask yourself why your dealers are coming here. What are *you* doing wrong?'

Another went back to Harvard and negotiated the possibility of returning there with better terms. She was offered incentives if she would sign affidavits enabling action to be taken against individuals at London & Norwich. Other dealers too were thinking of returning to Harvard, if Harvard would have them back.

Dealers left at Harvard were told that only the bleating sheep had gone and that London & Norwich Investment Services Ltd had nothing good to offer them. However, the dealers started daily looking further afield to other places of employment. To stay at Harvard was the last thing in their minds!

London & Norwich made half-hearted attempts to start sales campaigns in other stocks besides Silverton. The earliest proposition was Mintgate, a commercial property company. The Mintgate team addressed the dealers in the London & Norwich offices, finally standing them drinks at a nearby wine bar. Clients would be expected to hold their stakes in this unquoted commercial property investment vehicle for at least two years, and would regularly be paid interest; they could also inspect the properties held. One of Mintgate's directors, who said that he had been a Sheridan sales manager, took a London & Norwich dealer into his confidence: 'London & Norwich is Sheridan really,' he said 'If the King Street offices get raided, we can start up shop again at Mintgate's Baker Street offices.' Mintgate stock, however, was not to be sold by London & Norwich, since the dealers knew it would be difficult to offload, and found themselves uninspired by the 5% commission offered.

Ex-Harvard manager David Watson, now at London & Norwich found himself squeezed out by the management there. This, coupled with distaste for the way the operation was going, led to him walking out without ever obtaining certain monies due to him. Watson then almost immediately became managing director of Magnaquote Ltd, a new company that would be selling shares in Mintgate from Mintgate's own premises in the back offices of an estate agent in Baker Street, central London.

David Watson tried unsuccessfully to woo key London & Norwich staff to his new operation. He claimed: 'We'll be dealing in listed stocks through Russell Wood Stockbrokers. We'll eventually be working for them.' In fact, the deal with Russell Wood was one that he had originally been fixing up on behalf of London & Norwich. However, when London & Norwich directors had ousted him, feeling sore, he had taken the deal away from under their noses. Not that Neil Miller admitted this for a while. Miller was worried that his dealers might desert him, and sneered at David Watson's new set-up.

One of the London and Norwich bosses heard rumours that some dealers were planning to 'do a runner' over to David Watson's set-up. He telephoned one of the ring-leaders one Sunday morning and warned him in no uncertain terms against taking his team over to Magnaquote.

By arrangement with David Watson, Russell Wood directors interviewed two London & Norwich dealers in a City winebar. The idea was that they would be planted in Russell Wood, to process deals on main market stocks for the Magnaquote team.

The Saudi managing director of Russell Wood said to them: 'We're offering you £20,000 a year.' 'We want twice that,' said one of the dealers cockily. 'We won't accept less.'

Next, the two dealers visited Magnaquote's offices. They were a shambles compared to London & Norwich Investments Services'. At that stage, there weren't even any desks!

David Watson, backed up by an ex-Sheridan dealer he had recruited tried, not for the first time, to persuade them to come. 'Start here if you want, rather than at Russell Wood,' he said. 'Sell Mintgate, and eventually some main market stocks. We'll soon be FIMBRA members and we're amalgamating with Russell Wood anyway. We'll also have access to Merrill Lynch's dealing room.' It was becoming obvious that he was being over-optimistic.

Over the next few weeks, Magnaquote's team of ex-Sheridan dealers was only selling Mintgate. The company was desperate to recruit new dealers, and tried various ploys.

Potential recruits recognised Magnaquote's over-optimism and put on a show of accepting jobs, but didn't turn up; continuously and slyly deferring the starting dates. Watson and his small band of ex-Sheridan dealers were kept on tenterhooks as Magnaquote Ltd fought a losing battle for survival. Nonetheless, David Watson put a commendably brave face on the tide of events.

Meanwhile, the original dealers at London & Norwich had been told that the newly arrived team would be selling on Silverton to new punters, thereby enabling themselves to take their existing clients out of it. But the original dealers could not quite see this happening! In the back of their minds they were wondering if their clients would ever see their Silverton money again. It was by this time becoming increasingly more difficult to placate clients, who were daily ringing up and wanting out, even on occasions resorting to threats.

How would it all end?

The October 1987 stock market crash came very conveniently for London & Norwich. Some of the original dealers, who on instructions had told their clients that they would keep Silverton shares for just a month, had now the perfect excuse for their inability to take back the shares. 'The market's gone for a Burton, sir, in the States even more than in the UK. The dollar's collapsed,' they said.

'When can I sell out of my shares?' clients asked.

'Give it a few days sir' or 'In a few weeks', some dealers said, smoothly continuing to put clients off. Neil Miller told the dealers that London & Norwich was under no legal obligation to take its clients out of Silverton because it had, thankfully, sent out prospectuses which emphasised the speculative nature of the shares, and which most importantly, indicated that they would only be dealt on a matched bargain basis, meaning that sales could go through only when buyers could be found.

It was only as a precautionary measure, after the Press had been alerted, that some of these prospectuses had been sent out, but, in retrospect, it was just as well they had been.

Certain dealers were by now openly evading clients. The switch-board girls co-operated, telling callers that certain dealers were in meetings. Pattinson Hayton had told office staff to do what they were told, without question, and never to talk about their work to anybody.

Dealers had to take some calls to avoid complaints. When asked point blank at what price Silverton shares traded, only the most honest said no two way market was being made. Many quoted $5, which was the price at which they were being pushed in the other dealing room. These original buyers, who had paid $4.75 a share, felt satisfied. Had not their shares risen 25 cents, despite the general market collapse? 'Your shares are safer in Silverton right now than in any other investment,' some dealers were saying, and this seemed plausible.

Some dealers went so far as to exaggerate the price-level to which Silverton shares had supposedly climbed. 'They're trading at $5.50,' one dealer would say.

Clients had in some cases put large sums of money, even £100,000 plus into Silverton. A number had raided building societies, taken out bank overdrafts, etc, all on the basis that it was only for a month.

Meanwhile, Neil Miller was resorting to techniques that were used in certain continental firms to promote sales of Silverton shares. At one stage, he pinned two £50 notes on the wall, offering these to the day's best salesman. Nobody, however, got them.

To the newer dealers he proffered a fan of dud leads: 'I'll bet you £200 I can sell Silverton to any client you choose from this pile,' he said.

Nobody quite dared take him up on it. His tactic nonetheless inspired them to further sales. This was astute leadership on his part, and deferred the stage at which dealers would start whispering about him in corners, making their future plans behind his back.

Dealers moaned that their clients needed another stock besides Silverton, and they gleefully went on strike until they got it. Some were bothering to come into work even less frequently than usual.

Consequently, a new Canadian stock was produced for London & Norwich dealers to sell. This was a cosmetics company, whose glamorous female representative made a short speech on its prospects on the London & Norwich dealing floor.

The company manufactured middle to up-market beauty products, distributed through client friendly salons. Shares were tradeable on the Vancouver Exchange which is currently in the process of becoming more regulated.

The dealers proved more enthusiastic about eyeing the representative's body than about listening to what she said, and they consequently did not learn enough about the stock to sell it. Not that they would want to sell it, as Neil Miller was offering them only a 4% commission to do so, and besides some were owed thousands of pounds in long-overdue commission on their sales of Silverton shares. More than a few dealers were openly querying why Pattinson Hayton had not paid them. There was no doubt that being paid their commission was more important to most of them than raking in the clients' money.

So the next morning, the dealers just lounged about when one of the bosses yelled: 'Get on the phones and sell.'

Miller sat at his desk with his head in his hands. He was not usually to be seen in such a depressed state. London & Norwich Investment Services Ltd was already starting to appear ineffectual, and dealers were turning against him. Meanwhile Harvard Securities was applying the thumbscrews. FIMBRA and the DTI were, so to speak, not far away.

Alarmed at witnessing their leader's depression, one of the dealers asked him: 'What do you want us to do?'

Sell more Silverton!' he ordered. 'I don't really care about this Vancouver stock. But we must get rid of this Silverton!'

'But we've no more clients,' protested the dealer.

'Clients be damned! You were Harvard's top dealers. You're just not trying.'

Nor, however, was he. He made no sustained effort to motivate the dealers or even to get them to come into work every day. He just talked and lounged about, and his team did the same.

'We want to deal in main market stocks!' his dealers would moan.

After its original plans to deal in stock market listed shares through Russell Wood had been transferred to Magnaquote, London & Norwich made one vain attempt after another to set up deals through other stockbroking firms. There was a tentative arrangement with another broker, soon cancelled due to a succession of unpaid debts. The firm threatened to sue.

A dealing facility in listed stocks was finally arranged through Henry Cooke Lumsden, a stockbroker highly rated for private client service. London & Norwich clients would be obliged to deposit 25% of the value of any stock purchase they made, as an insurance for the broking firm, and the minimum dealing size was fixed at a quite substantial £5000.

This time it was the London & Norwich clients who refused to co-operate. They were already panicking that they were not yet out of Silverton Industries, as their dealers had promised them. Were they locked in? Some dealers at Harvard Securities warned them they might have lost all their money.

At this stage London & Norwich Investment Services Ltd was in serious debt, to the tune of hundreds of thousands of pounds. Debts, including hotel bills, had simply been run up on a company credit card.

The Department of Trade and Industry started investigating in its usual quiet way. Neil Miller admitted to dealers that clients had complained to this body about being sold shares on a month's hold. 'No crime,' he said. 'You were just being overzealous.' Although it was he who had represented the shares to dealers as a month's hold, he now urged that they should blame, if anybody, his fellow director Pattinson Hayton, who had cleared off to the States.

Hayton had left a mass of unpaid bills. It was reported in *The Observer* that solicitors acting for First American National Bank at Nashville, Tennessee, had filed bankruptcy proceedings against Hayton in London, arising from a judgment for more than $1 million obtained against him in Tennessee in April 1983.

London & Norwich Investment Services Ltd's lately arrived dealers, unpaid for the Silverton shares they had sold onto their ex-Harvard clients, were getting restless and sore. They didn't feel able to look wholeheartedly for jobs, as they were still hoping against hope that London & Norwich might pay them.

Meanwhile, some were desperate for money. A few were living off overdrafts, and were even being threatened with eviction from their rented homes. So skilfully had they been manipulated that they saw their unfortunate circumstances as a blow of fate, and felt that London & Norwich was operating in good faith.

Many had given up good jobs with Harvard and, in one case, a company car. They had worked at London & Norwich for nothing and had ruined a major part of their client base. Now they effectively had dwindling financial resources, no job, and reduced prospects of getting one.

London & Norwich had taken a while to sort out its tax affairs. Dealers had been told firstly that they were employees, then that they were self-employed. The London & Norwich compliance officer had, without any intention of deceit, informed FIMBRA in August 1987 that the firm was operating a PAYE scheme.

In November 1987, when dealers had been unpaid for weeks, and London & Norwich was already under scrutiny by the DTI, dealers were ordered to set up limited companies, and to backdate all previous commission cheques into their companies by issuing belated invoices for services rendered.

London & Norwich went to great lengths to persuade dealers to get cracking with this, setting up interviews for them with an accountant who argued: 'Whatever your particular circumstances, it will be in your interest to set up a limited company.'

This manoeuvre, if successful, would obviously have let London & Norwich Investment Services Ltd off its own tax liability. One dealer protested: 'The firm's due to pay this tax. I'm not paying it!'

London & Norwich tried to dissuade him from this, firstly by pleading: 'You're not treating us very nicely. You know the money wasn't taxed.'

'We were told London & Norwich was paying the tax,' the dealer repeated.

'If you don't pay it, London & Norwich will pay the Inland Revenue, but we'll take you to court,' said the firm.

Most dealers did set up companies, but delayed giving London & Norwich back-dated invoices as there were doubts voiced by professional advisors about the validity of this. More alarmingly, London & Norwich looked as if it was on its last legs, although Neil Miller denied it almost to the last: 'We've got over all our problems now,' he said calmly. 'We'll be around a good ten years yet.'

Right to the end, Pattinson Hayton sought to be liked. He was displaying one of the con man's chief characteristics, which was to ingratiate himself with the authorities, and with more decent people, to keep his own name clear of the mud. Thus when his London & Norwich Investment Services Ltd was wound up by the Official Receiver, after its court appeals against the DTI's winding up had petered out due to lack of funds to pay lawyers, Pattinson Hayton, by now safely ensconced in the United States, rang up one of the London & Norwich dealers. She was a sexy lady who had not been paid for around £100,000 of business she had done.

'I'm so sorry everything's collapsed,' he gushed. 'I just didn't have the money to keep paying the lawyers . . . But I'll clear London & Norwich's debts, and I'll pay you your commission. I swear it.'

'Yes . . . ' she said, blinded by an apparent sincerity in the Australian's tone. She could not help pitying him. He had striven to build an empire, and now it had collapsed in a heap round his ears. After all, was it Hayton's fault that she hadn't been paid?

When she had put down the phone, her fellow dealers persuaded her that this was a ploy. Hayton didn't want the dealers bad mouthing him.

She reacted by cancelling all her sales of Silverton shares and she joined the queue of dealers, clients, and creditors on Hayton's trail.

Shortly before London & Norwich was wound up, there was a further move by Harvard Securities' solicitors.

There had been constant battle between the two companies, each of which had been harnessing the national press to its own ends. Harvard Securities had helped supply news about London & Norwich to certain newspapers. London & Norwich had retaliated by supplying information about Harvard for the *Daily Mail*, *The Daily Telegraph*, the London Evening *Standard*, and *Private Eye*.

On the Harvard Securities dealing floor, Tom Wilmot had distributed an internal memo virulently attacking London & Norwich to the following effect:

'Virtually all of the people working at London & Norwich used to work at Harvard. We trained them, we gave them a career, and an opportunity of a lifetime. They are encouraged to steal from Harvard, to take records, to cause as much disruption as possible. This is not an honourable way to behave. The products being sold to clients by London & Norwich are appalling. No company can afford to pay commission rates as high as 10%. The industrial norm is around 30-40% of 1% (i.e. 0.3-0.4%). To pay higher levels shows desperation and a need to 'buy' the dealers, to an extent that he does not look closely at the type of security that he is pushing to the clients that London & Norwich have stolen from Harvard . . . '

Ironically, Harvard had been paying 2% or more on all OTC stocks sold, up to May 1987. This too was well above the 'industrial norm'. Was this not a case of the pot calling the kettle black?

In the same internal memo, Tom Wilmot claimed: 'You will probably recall that the now defunct Sheridan Securities was pushing one hundred and forty-four restricted securities in valueless American companies. London & Norwich are controlled by ex-directors of Sheridan. They are playing the same games again.'

He omitted to mention that his second in command, Harvard director John Casey, had been a director of Sheridan Securities for almost five years, in fact until the previous year — again, a case of the pot calling the kettle black!

Furthermore, Harvard Securities, after this outburst proceeded to try to make a market in one of the very categories of shares it had been criticising. By September 1988 it was quoting 80p mid price for the ex-Sheridan stock Denning Robotics.

For days, a photographer lurked outside London & Norwich Investment Services Ltd's offices, taking snapshots of dealers whenever they appeared. Always obvious, he was at first given a wide berth, then ignored. The dealers were more entertained than scared. This was like a live spy drama.

One Friday, a contingent from Harvard Securities appeared at the premises of London & Norwich Investment Services Ltd. Directors

John Harris and William Holden, complete with solicitor, had been chauffeured there in Tom Wilmot's car, and were bearing an Anton Pillar order, which is a legal authorisation for a raid.

In the corridor, John Harris bumped into a London & Norwich dealer he had trained personally.

'You should never have come here,' he whispered; there was more compassion than anything else in his look.

'Neil Miller said it was a Stock Exchange member firm,' the dealer replied.

'You shouldn't have believed him.'

The office premises were then thrown into a turmoil, as the intruders instigated a search for Harvard's leads — little pink cards that were Harvard's exclusive property. A dealer who had come briefly to London & Norwich had returned to his old firm, Harvard Securities, and had given testimony against London & Norwich dealers, saying they had Harvard's leads.

Whilst Harvard occupied the offices, one London & Norwich dealer managed to slip Harvard leads out, leaving them in Silks Restaurant next door.

Another dealer refused to let Harvard's men search his bag. He closed the lift doors almost on the fingers of Harvard's solicitor!

Harvard was proposing to instigate legal action against Neil Miller, David Watson (now at Magnaquote) and three other key London & Norwich people who had previously worked at Harvard, but this manoeuvre came to nothing.

However, one highly placed Harvard man had sworn he would get even with the ring-leaders who had enticed his staff away. What would be his next ploy?

In London & Norwich's last weeks, some dealers were playing cricket in the offices with paper bat and paper ball. One quieter dealer, negotiating property purchases on the telephone, had to dodge about constantly, so as to avoid being hit. When they were tired, some settled down to playing cards for money. Most read no financial magazines or did much to indicate they had been stockbrokers in the making, except for a few account trades through their own brokers.

One trick certain dealers enjoyed playing on the public at this stage was to ring up numbers taken at random out of the phone book and to say: 'This is British Telecom testing your phones. Please whistle into the phone. Now say something . . . ' They would giggle at hearing people making fools of themselves, then would hang up!

A yuppyish dealer there, in his early twenties, would dial through to the open chat lines announcing to anybody who happened to be there: 'You working class peasant! What's your name, Tracey or Sharon? Darren? Are you a dustman or a shop assistant? Or are you just on the dole?'

If any calls came through on the direct line to London & Norwich some dealers would lift the phone and say: 'Save the Whale. Have you rung up to make a donation?'

The caller would mumble apologies and hastily put the phone down.

If he rang the same number again, a dealer would repeat, 'Save the Whale', only this time aggressively. That would usually be an end to the matter.

One London & Norwich dealer borrowed £10,000 from a client to invest in a Docklands warehouse. He did not repay the money as quickly as he had suggested he might, and the client later complained about this to the London & Norwich Unsecured Creditors' Committee.

Another London & Norwich dealer openly declared his intention to find a position in a *real* Stock Exchange member firm.

A manager, who had introduced many dealers to stocks and shares, said: 'Don't even bother to look. You will never fit into the City proper. You haven't the uprightness, the breeding. The only way you'll stay in the business is by peddling Mickey Mouse shares, like you are now!'

The dealer stared at him. The manager shrugged: 'We're a special breed of workers. We're worlds removed from a proper stockbroking environment. We're a school of fish, and we must swim together if we're to survive!'

The manager spoke a profound truth and from the heart, although it was not applicable to the dealer he was addressing. His father had achieved eminence in his career, and this young, wild upper-class rebel appreciated how hard and how honourably the 'old man' had worked. Parents were a source of embarrassment to some young sharedealers.

In the last days of London & Norwich, the impression was conveyed that the firm might just be getting off the ground. A golden company emblem was now hanging in the hallway, and a hired photographer was snaphappy all over the offices, preparing for a high gloss prospectus.

Neil Miller was photographed sitting back grandly in his chair, his hand gripping the telephone receiver. The dealers gaped, and a last thrill of excitement ran through the bones of the company. Was there hope yet?

In London & Norwich Investment Services Ltd's last days, some clients rang their dealers in panic. Some threatened legal action. One even said to his dealer: 'Get my money, or I'm personally coming up to your offices to finish you off!' Others pleaded 'Help me!' A few clients threw a combination of tactics. A fair number of clients declined to ring their dealers at all. Were they too afraid of discovering the Silverton investment had not worked out?

One afternoon at 3.30 p.m., the liquidator came into London & Norwich Investment Services Ltd's dealing room. The dealers gathered to hear him. Although nerve-racking, this was also quite exciting. Neil Miller, however, looked overwhelmed.

'I'm closing this company down,' announced the liquidator slowly. 'I'm sorry this comes just before Christmas, but that's the way things are.'

A manager stood up: 'I'd like to thank Neil Miller on behalf of all of us present, for the effort he's put into the company,' he said.

The dealers cheered and clapped. There was a certain sadness in the air. Never would they all have such a wonderful time again. All that remained was an inquiry into what had actually happened. While this was underway, some of the dealers had spent their earnings, and were back in the City working in such firms as Tudorbury Securities, Empire Futures, DPR Futures, InstantRate, AJ Bekhor, and Bailey McMahon.

Even after London & Norwich had been closed down, in the public interest, the offices remained open. Dealers, some of whom had hardly appeared in preceding months, came in to carry on their card games. Plenty of personal calls, in some cases international, were made on the telephones. The photocopier was used extensively.

Six electronic typewriters, some sophisticated telephones, and some business cassette recorders vanished. They were all newish, and of the highest quality as well as being unpaid for. Some dealers and office staff alike were stocking up.

Certain dealers raided the stationery cupboard like paratroopers. One dealer was spotted loading a box of expensive stationery items into his car boot in the private car park below the offices.

One thing was sure. Most London & Norwich dealers would not be buying envelopes, pens and staplers for a while to come. If this was their last fling, it was a good one.

Many did not bother to look for new jobs, but rather clung to their good times, as if they would go on for ever.

Meanwhile, investigations were underfoot. Neil Miller asked one of the dealers to sign an affidavit saying business had been conducted according to the rules, but he and other dealers were reluctant to become involved. A creditors' committee was formed to realise London & Norwich Investment Services Ltd's assets, to discover the whereabouts of funds raised through the Silverton offering, and to seek an explanation for the firm's impecuniousness from Pattinson Hayton. Tom Wilmot gave this committee his full support. The web was not yet broken.

There are gullible clients, just as there are gullible dealers. Many such clients, and dealers alike, have been attracted to firms like London & Norwich Investment Services Ltd.

Some clients, despite reading warnings in the *Daily Mail* and *The Observer*, had been stupid enough still to pay for their purchases of shares in Silverton Industries.

Will the mugs never learn their lesson?

Chapter Eight

THE AFTERMATH

Following London & Norwich's dreadful lingering descent into liquidation, and with the ensuing disgrace that fell about the directors' and dealers' heads, a cloud was cast over the entire licensed dealing community.

The professional lives of dealers invariably ran into their personal lives. Unemployed ex-London & Norwich dealers, trying to relax and spend their earnings, found themselves plagued. Investors pestered Neil Miller, in person and on the telephone. Miller claimed that one also got through to his parents, despite their number being ex-directory.

Several ex-London & Norwich dealers changed their telephone numbers, which were being given out to clients by an anonymous source.

An embittered holder of worthless Silverton shares rang up his ex-London & Norwich dealer, saying: 'You'd better pay back your commission earned on the deal. We either settle this out of court, or in court . . . ' The dealer cleverly called his bluff and legal action never ensued.

On one occasion, clients of an ex-London & Norwich dealer visited her home and sat on her doorstep for two hours waiting for her to come home. When she didn't, they left a note for her demanding the return of her commissions earned on Silverton shares sold, and saying they would be back.

Another ex-London & Norwich dealer received a surprise and unwelcome visit from one of his former clients at his parents' house, where he lived. The client demanded the dealer's commission on his sale of Silverton shares. 'We'll come to some arrangement,' promised the dealer. He never did.

A rumour came about that bank accounts of ex-London & Norwich dealers might be frozen. One dealer started making arrangements to convert £20,000 of his earnings into bonds. Another claimed he had transferred £25,000 earnings in cash from his bank account into a safe deposit.

Ex-London & Norwich dealers became paranoid about associating with their former colleagues. They wanted just to fade away. One ex-London & Norwich dealer occasionally popped into a stock—

broking firm to pick up her new boyfriend. She turned her back on the ex-London & Norwich dealers who were broking there, although they had once been her good friends.

Where could the London & Norwich dealers move on to? What was left for them? One dealer who had a relation ensconced in a City stockbroking firm, embarked on negotiations to join a Stock Exchange member firm that principally served private clients.

The dealer boasted of his own considerable number of private clients each of whom would perhaps spend £5,000 a time. He claimed he had shown them good profits even in the adverse conditions of Harvard.

He then made the mistake of slipping into the discussions a mention of London & Norwich Investment Services Ltd. Immediately the recruiting broker's attitude cooled: 'Oh, you were involved with that company,' he said. We'll have to reconsider your application now in a new light.'

The dealer concerned found the broker seemed from then on to be 'unavailable'. Deciding to cut his losses, he embarked on a tour of Europe with his girlfriend. He had plenty of funds, having earned himself a small fortune selling dud shares in Silverton Industries.

London & Norwich dealers were bad news, so the feeling went in the City particularly, but also in licensed dealing circles.

Fox Milton & Co were wary when interviewing an ex-London & Norwich dealer around March 1988. Director Grant Raisey said: 'We're shortly expecting to attain authorisation from The Securities Association. Will you attract bad press if you come here?' In the end Fox Milton & Co refused to touch *any* London & Norwich dealers.

Some ex-Harvard dealers, including a couple who had been briefly at London & Norwich Investment Services Ltd, wound up at AJ Bekhor, the stockbrokers who employed half-commission men.

Most of the London & Norwich dealers were named in an edition of *Market Maker,* the Harvard Securities newsletter. Harvard warned clients against dealing with these individuals, and offered a telephone number via which further inquiries could be made.

A significant number of the ex-London & Norwich dealers ended up at futures and options dealing firms. One such firm was advertising in the London Evening *Standard* for dealers used to servicing private clients. This was 'InstantRate,' an options dealer based in somewhat shabby basement offices in City Road, EC1, where outgoings were relatively cheap.

One morning in the early days of InstantRate's existence, some ten ex-London & Norwich dealers flocked to its City Road offices.

They were greeted by an ex-Harvard, ex-Buckingham Corporate, ex-Eyas Securities veteran, now director of InstantRate, who asked them how many clients they could bring.

The offices of InstantRate Ltd, City Road, London EC1 where dealers were offered a staggering 10% commission to sell traded options.

'We can't deal clients who have lost all their money on Silverton,' one dealer said.

'Nonsense,' said the InstantRate director. 'Nobody can stop you.'

The jobs were there for the taking. The dealers had to make up their own minds.

'You get 10% commission on all monies brought in from your sale of options on the FT 100 Index,' another director explained. 'So if you do £3,000 worth of business a day, you make £300. It's the client who loses out financially by paying large commissions. This is your last chance to make a killing, before the Financial Services Act really bites.'

InstantRate would provide clients' names from a list that had been provided by Chartsearch. The new dealers were told to bring whatever clients they could too. InstantRate appeared to be operating on the principle of short-term profit, maybe over a span of months rather than years. In fact, InstantRate was never to be granted membership of the AFBD (Association of Futures Brokers and Dealers), but survived by becoming representatives of David Coakley, a fully fledged member.

For the benefit of potential recruits, a red-faced dealer produced a brochure which explained the concept of options in simplified terms for private clients: 'Merrill Lynch offered me ten grand for the copyright to this,' he claimed. 'I've not said yes yet.' Some of the potential recruits, unsurprisingly, did not believe him.

'At least by dealing through us, the small investor stands a chance,' argued one of InstantRate's directors. 'We may charge him exorbitant commissions, but that's the only way we can pay you dealers so highly.'

He then explained in more detail the dealers' commission structure: 'Every time you roll on money which clients have invested from one traded option into the next, you get a further 10%. You only need a handful of clients, and you're earning a bomb out of them.'

How did one sell traded options? Advisable first of all was a simple explanation of what they actually were. Next came InstantRate's coup de grace. The dealer was told to ask what direction the client thought the market would move in. Whatever the answer, he would pretend this was his opinion too, as a means of securing business. The following line is cited from the sales script distributed to all dealers:

'Where do you see the market going, Mr X? (I see you put down . . . on the card.)

'In fact we absolutely agree with you and we are currently recommending the call/put or the FT 100 Index.'

Dealers met with the directors individually or in pairs after the general introductory talk. At this point, one of the directors outlined the employment terms: 'Sort out your own tax. You're self-employed. We'll pay cash weekly on clients' cheques cleared. It's up to you if you want to use false names, you're salesmen, here today, gone tomorrow. All we insist on is that you put through a certain minimum level of business.'

At the local pub that lunchtime, InstantRate's directors were bunched on one side of the bar, the potential recruits on the opposite.

'Very hard hitting,' said one dealer sarcastically and a little too loudly.

'Shut up. The money's right. Where else can we go?' said his colleague.

A couple of dealers had already wafted away from the group. This seemed too risqué for their liking after their involvement in the London & Norwich fiasco.

The next morning at 10.00 a.m. some eight dealers were due to start. One turned up. He did a couple of quick deals, then vanished at lunchtime, embittered that his colleagues had deserted. This character had been a dealer at Harvard Securities, and since leaving that firm had appeared like a lamb without its shepherd.

InstantRate's secretary was taking phone messages all that morning.

'My washing machine's broken down, so I can't come in today,' claimed one dealer.

'I've got food poisoning,' said another.

'I'm seeing my accountant to sort out tax,' said another.

By this stage, the secretary was giggling as she answered the phone. None of these dealers ever turned up at InstantRate again.

A director rang the ex-Harvard dealer who had come in for the morning: 'Bring everyone back, and I'm sure we'll work something out,' he pleaded.

'I'll think about it and get back to you,' he replied. InstantRate, however, never heard from him again.

One dealer rang up the Association of Futures Brokers and Dealers (AFBD) to inquire after InstantRate's status: 'So far they've not applied for AFBD membership,' said an official. In fact, InstantRate was to put in a last minute application.

The AFBD official encouraged the dealer to talk but didn't comment. The dealer mentioned that there were no computer screens in the offices, because, as a director had put it, 'they would distract the salesmen'. The official laughed: 'Well you must draw your own conclusions. You've obviously got your head screwed on; why don't you visit our offices, and we'll discuss the situation further?'

The next port of call for ex-London & Norwich dealers was Empire Futures, later to be de-authorised by AFBD. An advertisement for dealers appeared quite frequently in the national press, to this effect: 'Earn up to £22K a year in a City Commodities Firm!' A telephone number was given, for Alexander Mann Recruitment Agency.

The World Trade Centre, near Tower Bridge, home of Empire Futures, and, perhaps more notably, of Sheridan Securities whose clients were parted from substantial sums of money.

One ex-London & Norwich dealer, following up this advertisement, undertook various tests provided by Alexander Mann, and was told that the sales manager of the firm in question had a magnetic personality.

The firm proved to be Empire Futures, whose sales manager was indeed a 'magnetic personality.' He had previously worked at LHW, the well-known futures dealers, and had learned his hard sell methodology there.

Although the dealer who had investigated Empire Futures through Alexander Mann declined to take a job there, several other Harvard/ London & Norwich employees did in fact start at this firm, where they were told: 'After a while here you could be very rich.'

The best salesmen at Empire Futures were ex-LHW. The sales manager once remarked: 'I've rarely seen anyone good come out a licensed dealer.' Stories abounded in the firm about the fabulous LHW methods, as the star salesmen remembered them.

It was said that the client buying futures from LHW in the 'good old days' was exposed to three levels of dealer, one after the other, until every last penny had been squeezed out of him. The Senior Account Executives (SAEs) at Empire Futures worshipped such an approach.

Sadly, three out of four funds which Empire Futures had offered clients had dropped substantially in value during the 1987 stock market crash.

However, the fund they were retailing in early 1988 had risen in value during the crash, as salesmen were quick to point out. They presented it with the aid of newspaper clippings that showed the Futures Industry in a glamorous light.

The fact that Empire Futures had not attained AFBD membership did not in itself seem to affect business turnover. The main reason for the dealing room's poor sales figures was the failure of potential clients to understand what financial futures actually were, coupled with the devastating effect of the obligatory risk warnings.

The average account executive in futures or (as at Empire) in futures managed funds had a longer negotiating task, to be rewarded with fewer and smaller sales, than his counterpart selling shares at a licensed dealer and often made correspondingly less commission for himself.

All this is evidence that business turnover cannot be generated by willpower alone. Willpower works wonders only on interested clients, via a product that seems desirable.

Nonetheless willpower was harnessed at Empire Futures to maximum effect. Recruits were swiftly made aware that it was mostly their sales figures that counted. This in itself was a major cause of the high staff turnover.

The theoretical training in figurework and in background knowledge, culminating in a stiff written examination after only two weeks of employment weeded out the men from the boys. The course was just to satisfy the AFBD, new recruits were assured. The working hours — 9.00 a.m. until 8.00 p.m. every night except Friday (5.00 p.m.) seemed a ridiculous constraint. Few were able to concentrate that long, even if they had had enough interested clients to keep them busy.

The Empire Futures sales manager made some applicants feel small during interviews by firing at them extremely hard questions about the precise state of the dollar, the latest US trade figures, or by asking them to calculate difficult percentages on the spot. However, he was looking out for the way they handled the pressure more than for the quality of their answers.

Account executives (AEs) employed the tricks of the trade in worming business out of clients. They were trained to get work telephone numbers (when unavailable) from clients' wives by a plausible lie. AEs would ring the home telephone number, and say to the wife: 'Is that Mr . . . 's secretary? Oh, it's his wife. Sorry I thought this was his work number. What is it then?'

Generally they would play on clients' weakness: 'You lost money on stocks and shares during the crash? This fund increased in value during the period . . . '

Potential clients were enticed into filling in and sending Empire Futures its forms, giving their permission for an account executive to contact them. Anybody who filled in a form was at one stage offered a free calculator. This turned out to be a cheap model that sometimes reached clients late and occasionally broken, into the bargain.

Business at Empire Futures was a rare event, so any AE who achieved a sale was well clapped and cheered. The eleven hour day was broken up by commentaries on the price of metals, etc, and also by stints of mailshotting clients on the part of AEs.

Desperate measures were needed to pep up the daily sales figures. One morning, AEs were instructed to write on white cards details of the expensive houses, the Porsches, etc they aspired to own. They pinned those cards to the front of their telephones, to remind them as they were dealing . . .

The account executive (AE) at Empire Futures (and other futures firms) would instruct his client to attach to the cheque he sent in a note to this effect:

'These funds must not be cashed, banked or traded without my express verbal permission.'

The smooth AE found a brilliant use for this prima facie millstone round his own neck.

As he was nearing the end of his sales pitch on the telephone, he would read these instructions aloud, telling the client to write them down first, and then to read them back to him.

If the client went so far as to read them back he was usually closed. What a clever sales technique this was. And all so respectable, so apparently in the client's interest.

If clients weren't worried about AFBD membership, AEs certainly were. All the time AEs were told 'Membership of the AFBD is just a week or so away.' This was the kind of pipe dream with which ex-London & Norwich dealers were all too familiar. Sure enough, the advent of membership was delayed. Senior managers had been seen showing AFBD officials round their offices: 'If we're doing anything wrong, tell us,' they would say.

After a sale was made, a courier would promptly turn up on the client's doorstep and collect the cheque, before the client had too much time to think about the wisdom of his investment. At this stage clients of futures dealers have been generally known to back out, and have occasionally become involved in fights with the firm's couriers who were 'fed up with waiting' for clients who were having second thoughts about handing over their cheque.

After Empire's courier had brought the client's cheque onto the firm's premises, the client was telephoned for his confirmation that he still wanted to proceed.

AEs of Empire Futures were often expected to stand up while selling on the telephone. The sales manager would patrol until he came across some AEs still seated: 'What's this? Bear Corner?' he would announce. 'Chairs are for bears. Stand up.'

The apparent hive of activity, with dealers screaming into the 'dog and bone' (i.e. telephone) was at times a miserable pretence. There was nothing more soul-destroying than putting on a show of working hard, in order to generate an atmosphere. Was the business expected to come by magic?

Maybe Empire Futures should have learned from techniques used at the Porchester Group (now the MI Group) where salesmen were constantly inviting clients into their West End offices. If someone bothers to pay a visit, he is more likely to pull out his cheque book and get something done.

One by one, the ex-London & Norwich dealers who had started at Empire Futures vanished, each to do his own thing.

One of this group received a phone call from Bailey McMahon, a Dublin based dealer in little known American stocks.

The offer sounded enticing, given that he had been earning insufficient to even cover his mortgage commitments at Empire Futures. The firm claimed it would pay his fare to Dublin and back, as well as his accommodation costs for the first month. He would receive

10% commission for all business cleared, plus he could draw £100 a week in advance of business.

The prospect of this big money blinded him. He assented to go, and before leaving England, opened an account with the Union Bank of Switzerland.

A scheme was initially proposed whereby dealers would pay tax on around £10K a year, via a PAYE system, and would pocket remaining earnings in hard cash, without paying the tax.

Many dealers at Bailey McMahon appeared ignorant of their exact tax obligations, whether to Ireland's or England's Inland Revenue.

Bailey McMahon was the foreign affiliate of JB Power Securities of Denver, Colorado, a company registered with the Securities and Exchange Commission (SEC) which had been denied permission to trade in Iowa. Its founder, Gene Olson had been censured and fined by the National Association of Securities Dealers (NASD) for activities violating its rules of practice, i.e. failing to supervise an employee who practised fraud; selling shares to people prohibited from receiving them; improper distribution of shares.

Not knowing or caring about such things, the ex-London & Norwich dealer flew out to this share-pusher. He went out drinking with the Bailey McMahon team, and admired what he saw as their cosmopolitan sophistication. Much of the talk was about the Gibraltar based European Equity Research which some had just left.

The new owners of European Equity Research were allegedly investigating a former employee who had ended up at Tudorbury Securities. He had walked out of European Equity Research with a sizeable client list, which he was now attempting to trade piecemeal with other dealers at Tudorbury.

Bailey McMahon was pushing shares in a company called Daytona Spyder Motor Corp, which manufactured a custom built imitation Ferrari, as used by Don Johnson of 'Miami Vice' fame.

Bailey McMahon dealers on the phone to their clients glamorised this stock. Some would claim that the car in question would soon be on display at Saudi Arabia's biggest airport, and they would further indicate there had already been a major television documentary about this rarest of collectors' models.

All who bought shares in the company at the inflated offer price, were mailed a colour photograph of the car, while information on the stock was faxed to them. The shares were sold as a likely sixty day hold, a short-term capital gain situation.

The possibility of General Motors taking over the company, since they made some of the car's parts, was mooted. This was unrealistic, but there were no tape recorded phone conversations, so there was no incriminating evidence of anything said.

The clients were genuinely international. Mailings had gone to

Saudi Arabia, England, and Switzerland. Bailey McMahon's salesmen would come into the offices early in the morning, perhaps at 7.00 a.m., to sell to the Saudi Arabian market. So familiar with their own sales pitches did they get, that as one dealer commented, they almost came to believe them.

Most salesmen there were Irish, American or British boys, in their early twenties, and green about shares. Most had never worked in the securities business before, and virtually none had Stock Exchange professional examinations under their belts.

They survived by mimicking the sales pitches of the afore-mentioned ex-London & Norwich dealer, and of one of his ex-London & Norwich colleagues who joined him shortly afterwards.

These young wide boys warned clients in their breezy cockney accents against Harvard Securities, though they had personally never been near the place. Repeating what the ex-London & Norwich dealers were saying, they advised: 'If you get approached by a Harvard dealer, sir, my advice to you is to slam down the phone.'

These green dealers gave assurances as to share performance which could not be substantiated. Some of the Arabs proved easy game. They conveniently understood little English, and could play with tens of thousands of pounds as if it was Monopoly money.

One Bailey McMahon dealer claimed, 'We're FIMBRA members', which was totally untrue. Another claimed, worse still, 'We're stock-brokers.' Indeed, one of the switchboard girls answered the phone with, 'Bailey McMahon Stockbrokers.'

Daytona Spyder Motor Corp's biggest claim for respectability was its quotation on the internationally available Reuters screen. This calmed the suspicions of the unsophisticated punter.

Only the most gullible clients could have been impressed with the Bailey McMahon newsletter. This was called *Market Watch* and was sent out free to investors, although printed at the top of the front page was an impressive: 'Yearly subscription $72.00.'

The text appeared hastily scripted, and was not without grammatical and spelling errors. The reasoning in the articles was simplistic to the point of fallacy. The ploy of financial overview served indirectly to promote shares in Daytona Spyder Motor Corp, which was mentioned, as if en passant, amidst an overenthusiastic eulogy of smaller companies and their prospects. Here is an extract:

'Investors have rediscovered small stocks after virtually ignoring them since 1985, but now, the City and Wall Street are developing a love affair with small issues which has all the earmarks of a hot and heavy romance . . . The biggies . . . are constantly on the search for small companies willing to sell or be taken over at inflated prices.'

This newsletter then says of Daytona Spyder Motor Corp: 'With only 10 million shares outstanding, earnings for the company reflect in a very obvious way. Were the same earning applied to a 500 million share company, it's doubtful if they would even cause a ripple.'

Similar vagueness characterised the sales pitches dealers delivered to their clients on the telephone. There was no mention of profits, or achievements in accounting terms. It was all a question of prospects, of potential.

The good sales records, notwithstanding frequent cancellations of these inexperienced dealers was a tribute to their talent for sounding plausible. Their clients were the inexperienced, the out and out gamblers, or perhaps most frequently businessmen laundering money — this last category of investor being the least likely to complain if he lost it all.

At Bailey McMahon were hatched some extraordinary sales lines. One dealer constantly claimed to his clients that he was a stockbroker with ten years' experience. This was an exaggeration.

One experienced dealer approached his Arab clients like this: 'Listen Mahommed. We both wipe with the same hand . . . Take the camel by the reins.' Or: 'Listen Mahommed. We're both businessmen. What's your line? You're in oil — fine. If your pipes are flooding, you get in a plumber. If you're feeling ill, you consult a doctor. If I need advice on oil drilling, I come to you. Well likewise, if you want to make money, you come to a stockbroker. That's me . . .'

The camaraderie beamed down the telephone lines, half way across the world. It spurned any hint of alienation, fostering a relationship built on instant trust in the common pursuit of capital gain.

Dealers were paid 10% on monies received from first time clients. Once opened up in this way, these clients were passed onto the loaders.

The loaders were skilled hard sell merchants who had worked in bucket shops operating in places like Amsterdam. They knew the ropes. They told how Bailey McMahon had business connections with Tudorbury Securities in London, which had offered them both stock (e.g. House of Holland) and redundant dealers.

The new ex-London & Norwich recruits learnt of the Bailey McMahon connection with two companies: Prime Times Ltd, and T & I Commodities, both based in Richmond, Surrey.

Another ex-London & Norwich dealer replied to an advertisement in the *Guardian*, in which Mr Layman offered telephone salesmen a six figure income.

Mr Layman spoke on the phone with a slow American drawl. 'Would you like to raise finance for promising young companies?' (i.e. sell shares for Bailey McMahon.) Or, 'Would you like to sell Art? Imitation John Lennon paintings?' (from Prime Times Ltd in Richmond.)

Bailey McMahon's loaders were paid 5% commission on sales they made to any client who had already been opened up, the remaining 5% commission accruing to the dealers who had first opened up the client, and who were thus implicated in the whole process.

With the expensive international mailings — far more than many stockbrokers could afford — and the expensive international phone calls, the 10% commissions accruing to dealers, the dealing manager's override, and directors' profits, one shudders to evaluate the mark-up on the share prices.

The loaders had a more hard hitting sales technique than anybody the ex-London & Norwich dealers had ever seen. Perhaps the fact that they were in their thirties, and had some experience of the world, helped them succeed in their approach. Here is a re-run of their patter:

Loader: 'Good morning sir. This is probably the most important telephone conversation you will have this year. Unless you have at least £50,000 liquid, you might as well put down the phone here and now.' (Occasionally the client will admit he can't match this prerequisite. The loader does actually slam down the phone.)

Client: 'Go on.'

Loader: 'We've got *the* stock for you. It's $4 now. We have a tranche of these on our books. You will need to hold for sixty to ninety days, and then we're looking for a premium of $3.'

Client: 'Let me think about it. I'll have a word with my wife.'

Loader: 'Right. You go home tonight and ask your wife if you can buy these shares, and I'll go home and ask my wife if I can sell them to you.'

After the client has bought, there is a sixty to ninety day lull, following which the stock is quoted at a higher price on the Reuters screen. This seems to bear out the salesman's earlier assurances. The client is then encouraged to double up.

In practice, clients can buy, but often find it hard to sell such stocks. However, the client who really insists on selling may be allowed to do so, to stave off a formal complaint, or even legal action.

The loader in such firms, when confronted with a hopeless case, resorts to the 'Columbus technique'. He imagines the prospect confined in an octagonally doored room. The aim is to close all doors on him, one after another. He says: 'Right, I've tried everything. I admit it, you've got me beat. Why don't you want these shares?' He then raises *every* possible reason: 'Have I not explained enough about the company? Is it because they're unlisted? Is it the price?'

If, for example, the client says 'Yes' at this point, the loader replies: 'If I can get you a better price, will you be happy?' The client may at this stage succumb.

To the client who claimed he already had a good stockbroker, the loader would respond with this classic line: 'I appreciate you already have a stockbroker. But if you make a small profit here on a good tip from me, maybe you'll put a bit of business our way in the future. Just as when you've been to a good restaurant, you recommend it to your friends . . . '

At Bailey McMahon, clients who cancelled were known as 'croakers'. They were not small in number, since any respectable financial advisor they checked with advised them to have nothing to do with this Dublin based outfit.

Salesmen were encouraged to do any size of deal. Once opened up, the clients would be finished off by the loaders. Salesmen had been known to earn £2,500 in a good week, and the loaders twice that amount.

The Arab clients were so obsessed with cars that they could be coaxed into risking big money on Daytona Spyder Motor Corp via what was presented as an IPP — 'Initial Public Placing' in the shares.

One of the ex-London & Norwich dealers at Bailey McMahon received a telephone call in his new dealing room from RAI Hamilton, the chief executive of Tudorbury Securities, and business associate of Les Williams (ex-Harvard, ex-Tudorbury), who initially ran Bailey McMahon's dealing floor. He introduced himself as 'Mr Hamilton', and invited the dealer to visit Tudorbury's Westminster offices when he was next in London.

The offices of Tudorbury Securities at 5 Old Queen Street, London SW1.

The two ex-London & Norwich dealers decided to leave Bailey McMahon. First, they embarked upon a lead removing operation. Sneaking back into the offices after work, they crammed their pockets with names and addresses of rich Arabs. The photocopier became heated with overuse. These client details might be useful at any future employer, so they felt.

The two dealers then vanished overnight, emerging from Gatwick Airport with a suitcase containing some of Bailey McMahon's leads. They hadn't waited to be paid, and had only a few pounds in their pockets.

Perhaps they were financially no worse off than typical wealthy loaders who, as one dealer put it, 'pissed away' their money, buying and wasting whisky bottles at £100 a throw in expensive nightclubs, and indulging drug habits.

Bailey McMahon was desperate to recruit good dealers. Another dealer now became the manager there, and forbade personal calls on the dealing floor. One of his staff, ex-Harvard, was once speaking on the phone to his father in England who was ill, when the receiver got wrenched from his hand and slammed down by his manager: 'I said, no personal calls,' he snapped. A fight broke out and dealers in split factions urged on the combatants.

When that employee left, the new manager made vain attempts to recruit people who would 'do the biz', who would 'do the numbers'. He rang up another ex-London & Norwich dealer who said: 'How did you get my number? How on earth did you get it?'

The new manager put down the phone on him. 'He's off the game,' he muttered. In fact the manager himself was soon to leave Bailey McMahon, and ended up working as a dealer at Tudorbury Securities in London.

The most successful salesmen in bucket shops are sometimes rootless people, often orphans and bachelors, with a lack of social conscience. They match their wits against the police, the Government, and the Inland Revenue as much as against clients. In cocking a snook at the establishment, they may go one step too far. What starts as a gesture may become instinctive in them. A few start negotiating oil deals, dealing in drugs, and searching out other opportunities to make money, under the cover of sharedealing.

In order to maintain their lavish lifestyle, dealers hop from one outfit to another. One Bailey McMahon dealer dreamed of working at Kettler Investments AG in Switzerland. He thought he would 'learn a thing or two' there.

Indeed a salesman from Kettler Investments AG cold-called the author, trying to sell him shares in Messidor. He had picked on a time-waster, but it took him a while to realise it.

He intimated that investment in Messidor was likely to make him a fortune. He alleged that the stock had three 'top' market makers and constantly reinforced his arguments with reference to world business trends: 'As you will have read in the *Sunday Times* . . . ' he kept saying.

He finally came out with this classic line: 'In Switzerland we only know about three things. Watches, chocolate, money. I don't sell time. I don't eat chocolate. But I do know how to make you money.'

The salesman tried to press for an order there and then, saying he would send round a courier for the cheque, and oozing flattery: 'You're a shrewd man, Mr Davidson.' He repeated the author's name and address — 'to get it right on the computers'. He was a wily so-and-so, omitting to mention various facts.

The prospectus stated: 'This offering is termed a "blank cheque" offering because (1) the Company has no specific business plans or business in which to invest. (2) the investors will bear an inordinate degree of risk, beyond that of normal business uncertainties.'

The prospectus further pointed out that Messidor with its net tangible book value of just $375, was then taken over by Triton, a company which had in the previous year made a loss of $3,000 on a turnover of $41,000, and which had no significant assets.

Messidor had declared they had an option on a group of 'outstanding' mining claims in Nevada. However, the option was not acquired for some considerable time, and Messidor put down only $25,000. In a filing with the Securities and Exchange Commission, Messidor stated: 'There can be no assurance that the company will commence or complete any sampling or exploration.'

The author was offered shares in Messidor at $3.25, then regularly later at an ever rising price. Only months previously two million of these shares had changed hands for $3,000, a price of $0.0015 per share. The price had been marked up 216,000% and more.

The bucket shops, then, stand to make massive profits. For this they must find suckers. It is no wonder they will spend so much time and money on mailshotting operations. They will stop at nothing to get clients.

One ex-London & Norwich dealer was offered through the grapevine a chance to sell the London & Norwich client list, of which he had an illicit copy, to a Mafia representative for £100 per name. This is some one hundred times the going rate on the legitimate London market. He would exchange the list for cash in the presence of an intermediary, who would take his cut, in a London hotel room.

Immediately he got excited at this apparent money for old rope and started copying out the list. He plotted to sell the names, but to keep a copy for his personal use as well. Colleagues first dissuaded him from this treachery, next from the entire enterprise. 'You don't cross the Mafia, they'll cut your legs off,' one warned him. A former manager of his advised: 'Have no transaction with the Mafia. They'll mark you as one who is prepared to do anything for money.' It transpired that the Mafia wanted the list for nothing, suggesting that if the names were so good, why did the dealer not come out to the continental bucket shops and deal them himself?

In the end he opted to just keep the list for his own use. The hours he and his girlfriend had spent copying it out for the Mafia were wasted.

Client leads are unsafe in most licensed dealers. A dealer at Tudorbury Securities was once advised to put leads in the safe overnight, although this is generally a risky practice. In the event of the company going into liquidation immediately afterwards, employees might be denied access, as happened at Anderson Kimble.

One friend of a Tudorbury dealer raided the dealing room of Eyas Securities in April 1988, shortly after Eyas had been suspended from trading. He sneaked into the building with a partner late at night. They photocopied all the best leads, working through the early hours of the morning and left around 7.00 a.m.

A Tudorbury executive had previously told the dealer: 'Tell your friend, just get hold of those leads, no matter what he has to do. But to be careful of any night watchmen outside the building.' He had hinted he would pay for them but later retracted saying: 'I'm not doing any private deals with salesmen here.'

A Tudorbury manager, who had heard about the raid and was at that stage responsible for getting in new leads, said to the dealer: 'Hand them over, or I'll sack you.' Buckling under the threat the dealer gave him some leads which were then filtered through into Tudorbury's dealing room.

Salesmen who join certain licensed dealers are expected to bring clients with them. When the chairman of one firm interviewed an ex-Bailey McMahon dealer, he said: 'It would be worth you popping back there for a week or two, just to get some more leads to bring here.'

Raids on dealing houses were commonplace. RAI Hamilton of Tudorbury officially bought up the Sheridan Securities client lists, and his dealers started trading the clients, some hoping they would prove a soft touch. However, other firms were also dealing the same clients.

Tudorbury's main rivals were Magnaquote, a sad phoenix from the ashes of London & Norwich Investment Services Ltd, who were attempting to retail shares in Mintgate (property investment vehicle) to the same ex-Sheridan clients. RAI Hamilton raised an objection to this unofficial competition. He had, after all paid for the clients.

Mysteriously, one weekend, Magnaquote's Baker Street offices were raided. Files were ransacked, leads were stolen, computers were tampered with, and even the office furniture was whisked away. Magnaquote became no more.

The identity of the culprit was never discovered. If however, this raid had been perpetrated by another bucket shop, it would doubtless have been a ploy to stop Magnaquote from trading. As such it would have been quicker and more effective than an Anton Pillar order, as well as being considerably less expensive.

Raids on dealing houses, by now quite common occurrences, serve as plausible cover for other nefarious deeds.

News came in of a weekend raid at another London based licensed dealer. It was said that all documentation, leads, etc had been sifted and photocopied by professionals. A broken window, coupled with a dislocation of furniture and of files, seemed to substantiate the story as a whole, as well as did the disappearance of certain vital documentation.

As regards this break-in, there were suggestions of the raid being instigated from within, so that certain documents could be removed, prior to an investigation of the firm.

Clients who have lost umpteen thousands of pounds by rashly agreeing to invest in companies that have subsequently fallen by the wayside, are easy targets for further high pressure sales tactics.

However, even the worm will eventually turn. There comes a point where clients have lost all their savings, or can't bring themselves to invest further in the same sort of dodgy shares, only with a different name. Special tactics are called for.

Harvard Securities evolved a scheme which would harness the resources of investors who had lost substantial sums on the firm's recommendations.

Clients who had invested in Berkeley Leisure, VTC, Future Forecasts, and Towerbell Records would be offered free 'A' shares in Medivest plc, a new company set up by Harvard, that would serve as an investment vehicle.

These 'A' shares would be convertible for cash into ordinary shares. It would seem in the clients' interest to thus pay out more money.

Harvard made this move at a time when they had not yet obtained the full authorisation that would soon be prerequisite for their survival under the regulations of the Financial Services Act (1986).

Members of the Harvard Complaints Committee, a group formed after the £6 million collapse of VTC, were wary of this offer. If they accepted it, they might appear to be withdrawing their complaints about Harvard's past recommendations.

Another way a licensed dealer might obtain clients is to make a market in the shares that have been monopolised by another share-dealer, maybe one that has just gone into liquidation.

To take just one recent example, after Afcor Investments collapsed, Harvard Securities indicated that it would like to deal in the following shares Afcor had been trading, mostly on a matched bargain basis: Systems Control, Telesnaps, Rumours, Cosmerique, and Camden Palace.

Negotiations reached a stage whereat Afcor was referring to Harvard Securities investors who were asking about certain shares they had bought from Afcor.

Prior to this, London & Norwich Investment Services Ltd, shortly before its demise, failed despite frantic efforts, to find an alternative market-maker in the UK for shares in Silverton Industries.

Some investors who had lost their money on Silverton Industries were all the more indignant that this had been the only share London & Norwich Investment Services Ltd had dealt in, despite the firm's constant promises and endeavours to offer either a full stockbroking facility in its own name, or to put business in any shares through a bona fide stockbroker.

Thus ex-London & Norwich clients, even more than the ex-Sheridan clients who had been losing money for three years, were loathe to buy from licensed dealers again.

Some ex-London & Norwich dealers ended up at Tudorbury Securities, where RAI Hamilton seemed particularly keen to recruit them, doubtless because they could be rated amongst the top share sales people in the business.

Tudorbury came up with a potentially brilliant scheme for re-harnessing ex-London & Norwich and ex-Sheridan clients. A letter was sent out to them, proposing in very general terms an investment vehicle pooling all that was left in Silverton, Transworld Energy, and other stocks in which no real market was currently being made. But the proposal never took off.

It has to be said that dealers of Tudorbury Securities had great difficulties in getting some ex-Sheridan clients to trade. They were still waiting for certificates and money.

Sadly, through Sheridan, many of these clients had put much of their money available for investment into Transworld Energy/Palmer Financial, which was connected with Silverton Industries.

Although they had recently heard from Sheridan's liquidators, Touche Ross, these clients were for the most part remarkably vague as to how much money they would recover from their investments, or even as to whether stocks like Transworld Energy were still tradeable.

The Tudorbury dealers were offered £10 cash on top of normal commissions for every new ex-Sheridan client that they opened up over a limited period.

The better dealers — a tiny minority — started to deal these clients.

To deal them, it was helpful to subtly misrepresent the situation vis-à-vis Sheridan. Concealment of certain truths made for easier sales.

The positive news was bona fide, although these dealers hyped it up. Yes, clients might be able to trade in the USA Sheridan's NASDAQ or pink sheets quoted shares — Paperback Software, Denning Mobile Robotics, Tyron Inc, Systems Technology, in fact everything except Transworld Energy/Palmer Financial. Shareholders' certificates would be delivered in a few weeks time.

Dealers didn't go out of their way to mention that some holdings would be diluted in proportion to the extent Sheridan Holdings had been short of them.

With regard to Transworld Energy/Palmer Financial, dealers were vague. 'Nothing's been sorted out yet, we're waiting on news,' they said. They knew that the clients had lost most or all of their money on these, but many didn't suggest this.

If they annihilated the client's hopes of recovering his money, or of seeing his shares reach the heights that the Sheridan salesmen had originally suggested, there would be no further business.

The client would grunt and say something to this effect: 'Hmm. I've lost quite enough money. You can't be asking me to throw good money after bad.' Indeed since Roman times, bearers of bad tidings have always incurred disaster.

The client who is made to feel good about investments which he has already made will respond the more willingly to a salesman's own proposal for future investment.

Many a tearful ex-Sheridan client would say something like: 'I still believe in Transworld Energy,' although his voice might falter, and contain a note of query.

Such clients are not necessarily idealistic by nature. They have just been brilliantly pitched by the canny Sheridan dealers, and are reluctant to admit that they have been duped.

Some Tudorbury dealers have proceeded to say something like: 'We may be able to sell your Denning Mobile Robotics etc for you through our broker in New York, once you have the certificates.' The client is left with the impression that here is someone who cares, who knows, who will hold his hand during the perplexing period of the liquidator's assessments.

To which stock was the ex-Sheridan client likely to be directed by Tudorbury? Swanyard Studios was a likely proposition, as the company's shares are a perpetual buy recommendation from Tudorbury.

The astute dealer would glamorise Swanyard's Islington-based recording studios, occasionally introducing this selling point towards the end of his pitch: 'We believe in the stock so much that we, Tudorbury Securities, have taken a more than 5% stake in it.'

The North London premises of Swanyard Studios whose shares Tudorbury tirelessly promoted.

The argument put this way impressed the naive investor. In fact RAI Hamilton's family at one stage has owned a significant stake in Swanyard, and RAI Hamilton's wife, Margarita is Swanyard's managing director. These links were pointed out in the *Daily Mail*, but did not appear a problem due to the fact that Swanyard Studios was quoted on the Stock Exchange Third Market, so had been subject to a degree of regulation. Tudorbury salesmen are correct in stating that Swanyard is not an over-the-counter share, even if its price is only three or four pence.

At the end of May 1988, after Department of Trade & Industry (DTI) officials had been inside Tudorbury Securities for some days, RAI Hamilton formally announced that he was resigning as non-executive director of Swanyard Studios, to pursue other interests.

Dealers at work . . . dealers at play.

One dealer, in selling Swanyard to a client, blinded him with science: 'When you were dealing with Sheridan, did you have shares in Sunflower Inc? Good Wines Ltd . . ? ' These and other invented stock titles rolled all too glibly off his tongue. The client never suspected. He was fair game to that dealer, and his money appeared up for grabs.

A few dealers felt bound to Tudorbury Securities due to substantial debts they owed the firm which arose through their dealing on their own account. This is perhaps why they stayed there for a comparatively long while.

Most dealers at Tudorbury were young — on average in their early twenties. Many looked and felt ropey, drinking too heavily and sniffing too much cocaine. One dealer there would delight in occasionally offering cocaine to new recruits in his firm.

Sex for young sharedealers in various firms still a roll in the hay. Some go out to local pubs in groups, seize on any female flesh they can, then lure it to bed.

Their chat-up techniques are backhanded. They have been known to describe themselves as stockbrokers and to discuss the market as if they are out there on the floor of the London Stock Exchange.

Their sexual appetites are pepped up by their relatively easy day. Most live off a few big clients, and are too lazy to open up new ones.

A few will spend vast sums of money taking naive, easily

impressed girls to discos, clubs, restaurants, and finally to nearby hotels, or else in taxis back to their flats.

The next morning, the boys roll into work, sometimes looking as if they've slept in a haystack. The girls, it has to be said, may look no better — they too may have spent the night out in happy company.

Almost all dealers have in common an extraordinary level of sexual athleticism. But the boys run into trouble sometimes. Up against young men in more decent, less glamorous and less lucrative fields of life they pale and cower.

One dealer brought back a girl to her own flat shortly after midnight. She unlocked the door, and there stood her regular boyfriend, smiling at them from the hallway. He stepped forward and belted the intruder in the mouth. He was a construction worker, a real man. The dealer saw stars and came into work mid-morning the next day, a sadder, wiser human being.

Chapter Nine

FROM DISSOLUTION TO RENAISSANCE

Dealers are frankly best keeping mum about what they do for a living, how they do it, and most importantly, what they are paid. Revelation is bound to rouse resentment. Even silence is not without its dangers.

One Yuppie dealer who had just joined a stockbroker from Harvard Securities was driving his posh car through the City when two cars sandwiched his own, causing him to stop.

Two skinheads hurried out of their respective cars towards him, dragging him out of the driver's seat. Passers-by stared as if watching a violent film on TV, while the hooligans smashed a front tooth, broke his nose, bruised his jaw, and left him with concussion, a heap of bones fit only to be transported to hospital.

It has to be said that the majority of dealers bear little resemblance to Yuppies and so run little risk from spontaneous assault at least. They look more like used car salesmen.

Sex and violence outside working hours are not enough for some sharedealers who require significant doses of each on the job. Not infrequently, a fight breaks out at Tudorbury Securities for instance, usually because one dealer, rightly or wrongly, thinks a colleague has been ringing his clients. Clients are, of course, a dealer's lifeblood and many dealers will fight tooth and nail to retain control of them.

Thinking that he had dealt one of his clients, one teenage share salesman nearly throttled a dealer ten years his senior, leaving him as red as a beetroot, puffed out and sweating. Even the most hardened dealers were somewhat alarmed at the severity of the attack.

RAI Hamilton, chief executive of Tudorbury Securities, has sacked and then reinstated one female marketing executive on several occasions. In her last farewell speech, she said pointedly: 'I'm going on to better things.'

'Don't forget to come back every week for your Friday afternoon fuck,' said RAI Hamilton, in front of the whole dealing room.

After she had gone, dealers criticised the way she had run the firm's leadbank. 'She kept all the leads stuffed down her knickers,' growled a senior dealer.

'They must have been hot leads,' mused RAI Hamilton.

Neil Miller, by now ex-director of London & Norwich and ex-associate director of Harvard, had been taken on at Tudorbury Securities. This brilliant manager, who had trained so many in the industry was now engaged by RAI Hamilton, theoretically on a consultancy basis to advise on problem over-the-counter shares. In practice, he was making his voice heard on the dealing floor, from his second day onwards.

At first he kept a low profile, wandering about chatting to the dealers, many of whom he had trained when dealing director of Harvard Securities. The dealers treated Miller with a mixture of suspicion and begrudging respect. He had banked up many enemies in his time. His attitude while at Harvard towards sales people, as chronicled earlier in this book, had been ruthless: 'Keep up the figures, or get the hell out.'

After Harvard, he had led a team of dealers to London & Norwich Investment Services Ltd, where he had swiftly damaged his own reputation, but now, after a short lapse of time and partly due to the intervention of a top Tudorbury dealer, he was back in business.

After a few days of nosing around, Neil Miller confided in a dealer that within a month or two he intended to be running the Tudorbury dealing floor.

At the end of one day, he announced his presence formally to the dealing room: 'Most of you here know me. I've been watching what goes on here. Selling shares is a numbers game. Most of you are just not making the calls. Not doing the work. Well, I've got news for you. No one knows better than me how hard it is to get jobs in the City at the moment. Those of you who are at least making an effort will keep yours. The rest of you will be facing the sack. Dealers are two-a-penny nowadays, and you're all just taking us for granted.'

His audience at this point stirred. Here were some of the toughest sharedealers in the business. A match for Neil Miller even. Real veteran share salesmen who had their own client books, who had worked for bucket shops such as Buckingham Securities and Eyas Securities.

Amongst them were several dealers whom Neil Miller had, in September 1986, spent days trying to persuade to stay at Harvard Securities, and not to go to start up the Tudorbury Securities dealing floor. This pack had left, notwithstanding, and the existence of that very dealing room was evidence of their start-up operation's success. Neil Miller had helped Harvard Securities wage war on this new Westminster-based sharedealer. Now, irony of ironies, Miller was here trying to establish roots.

One of the founder dealers of Tudorbury Securities said loudly: 'Neil, perhaps you could define your role here, so we know if you've got any authority over us.' Neil Miller retired from argument, and soon Hamilton appeared on the dealing floor to say: 'I've got Neil here *not* to run the dealing floor — he'll never get a FIMBRA licence anyway — but to advise and help me. This room is only doing £40,000 worth of business a day right now. It's not enough, so I have to take measures. I'm giving Neil my full support. He's a quality person, even if he has worked for the wrong firms. So when he says "Jump", you jump!'

After this minor uproar, Neil Miller became accepted on the dealing floor, albeit not liked. He wandered about, observing dealers in action, and his very presence provoked a buzz, pepping up dwindling enthusiasms. These boys knew from hearsay or experience how good a motivator Neil Miller had been, at Harvard for instance where, unlike now, his wings had been unclipped.

He noticed two young novice dealers sweating away at their work, but failing to notch up sales. One of these had been sacked from his dealing room at Harvard.

Crouching between these two, he murmured: 'You should suggest to those clients that there could be good news on the horizon. Tell them you can't say more at this stage, but that you're putting a big recommendation on the shares.' This was quintessential Miller. He was the best trainer in the business.

He was meanwhile looking for ways to consolidate his precarious position at Tudorbury. His was a controversial presence, and correspondingly insecure.

He started to implement a plan to create a tip-sheet under the auspices of Tudorbury after getting some ideas for its contents from an ex-London & Norwich dealer. This would be something a bit special.

A provisional title was 'Gutter Mutter'. It would contain several startling features: an agony aunt column, offering guidance on investors' queries about shares; a financial horoscope; a comic strip featuring a dumb investor; profiles of important personalities — the first might perhaps be Michael Lucas, director of BOM Holdings, a prominent Tudorbury stock (now suspended); a market report. However, this particular blueprint never got beyond the dummy stage.

Neil Miller had bigger things on his mind. Michael Walters, the *Daily Mail* journalist whose bête noir seemed to be the licensed dealing community, had recommended investigating what he was up to.

Walters had interrogated Neil Miller extensively about the London & Norwich affair. After the first sales of Silverton Industries were made, back in August 1987, he had rung Miller at his London & Norwich office. Miller had said that they were only taking provisional orders for the Silverton shares as opposed to actually dealing in them.

The clients who had been sold the shares might have disagreed with him!

Later, Michael Walters told the author that he had found Neil Miller's ready justification of Silverton Industries — as a good risk stock for speculators — both 'amusing' and 'ridiculous'.

In April 1988, Walters followed Miller into the Tudorbury offices. On the following Monday he wrote in the *Daily Mail:* '*A cool reception at Tudorbury for the invisible man* . . . At Mr Miller's new place of employment, however, he is hardly known — the invisible man who comes and goes without a trace . . . the receptionist did not know a Mr Miller when I asked her to call him back down. She turned the pages of her directory, felt sure I had made a mistake; there was no Mr Miller. It took several minutes before she could be persuaded to ask another young lady, "What extension is Neil on?" And down he came.'

Neil Miller was very nervous when he came into work that morning. 'How do you think RAI will react to the article?' he asked one dealer To the others he said: 'The article's saying nothing.'

Most dealers at Tudorbury knew better than to comment, to take sides. Suddenly Neil Miller departed for a week holiday trip to Spain. He returned very briefly, only to leave the company soon afterwards.

The publicity surrounding this incident put the fear of God into the remaining licensed and futures dealers. Some hastily cancelled plans to take on ex-London & Norwich salesmen.

Some days later, RAI Hamilton appeared on the dealing floor. 'Somebody in this room's been leaking information to the press,' he said. 'That person's greatest punishment will come when the rest of you find out who it is.'

He drifted from the room as abruptly as he had entered it. One dealer groaned: 'I wish I could be working for a company that doesn't have to be worried about press coverage,' he said.

The next thing everybody knew at Tudorbury Securities was that an ex-Sheridan salesman with a formidable dealing reputation was sacked. RAI Hamilton hurried onto the dealing floor with a fellow director, and stood over the dealer while he was removing personal belongings from his desk.

'Hurry up,' said Hamilton.

'Wanker,' said the dealer.

'Get off the premises while I'm still able to restrain myself,' said RAI Hamilton.

Tearing up the ex-Sheridan leads which had been issued to him, the dealer laughed: 'I'm the one who's restraining myself.'

As he left, a friendly dealer slipped him a bundle of Tudorbury leads.

A few days later, RAI Hamilton announced to the dealing floor:

'He's talking to newspapers and to brokers, making out we're carrying on Sheridan's dirty work. He's trying to get Tudorbury closed down.'

The sacked dealer ended up at a respectable firm from where he telephoned his contacts, still at Tudorbury, asking them to put such clients' business as they could not handle through himself.

One dealer at Tudorbury was attempting to run his own book in shares, selling what he chose, at his own price. Many dealers there were trading for themselves on the account in large quantities of shares.

Tudorbury's share recommendations since October 1987 had frequently lost clients' money. Amongst these were: Colorgen, Chemex, AJ Cohen, The Norton Group, Indo Pacific, BOM Holdings, Downibrae and Hampton Trust. Not surprisingly in the circumstances, dealers had burnt out many of their clients, and were in need of new ones, but had little impetus to create them. They wanted big clients to be handed to them on a plate.

They sat around waiting for the big deal that would pay the week's wages. Sometimes it came. More often than not they were forced to open up new clients which they achieved with a veteran grace, and with an air of being above it all. Their opening lines were sometimes unctuous, e.g.: 'Good morning, Sir. My name is Paul Smith. S-M-I-T-H. I'm a senior equities trader with Tudorbury Securities. Have you heard of us, Sir?'

Tudorbury dealers would occasionally ring up a client who had been on the brink of buying and would say they had reserved for him a certain number of shares.

This is one step removed from the tactic of AEs at DPR Futures who would ring as yet uncommitted clients, saying: 'The courier's on his way, sir, to collect your cheque.' The courier would genuinely be travelling there, and this assumptive approach often led to a sale. The method was known as the 'bike treatment' and one DPR AE specialised in it.

At this point, Tudorbury Securities on the one hand badly needed business done, while on the other hand had to behave, as the DTI was presently in the process of investigating the company.

Neil Miller delivered another motivational speech to the dealing floor. 'OK, I know you haven't got new leads yet, but a lot will soon be coming your way. I'd rather see you on the phone all day, talking to clients but achieving no sales, than just lazing about. I've organised selling of all this Harvard OTC stock which went down the plughole, like VTC and Towerbell Records. Here, you've got the opportunity to sell fully listed shares, so I don't know what you're all grumbling about. Get on the phones . . . '

The room got excited. Neil Miller broke the dealers up into teams, in the old Harvard style. By thus instilling competitiveness, he put an end to the habit dealers had picked up of not bothering to work until a new cash incentive offer was made, on top of the ordinary 2% commission — and only then putting in a hard stint. Dealers who were about to leave the company would fake bargains purely to obtain the cash bonuses.

Selling now took place as an intensive team effort for shorter hours than usual, i.e. between 9.00 a.m. and 4.30 p.m. Every member of the winning team would pick a prize out of the lucky dip at the end of the day. The lucky dip was a box filled with sealed envelopes in a bed of straw; each envelope contained notice of a cash prize between £10 and £2,000. The £2,000 prize never seemed to materialise, but there was an abundance of prizes at the lower end.

Tudorbury's chief executive, RAI Hamilton, seated, offering extra cash incentives in the form of a "Lucky Dip" to one of his dealers, standing.

The room's business trebled almost overnight as dealers regained their old competitive instincts, which in some cases had lain dormant since their Harvard days.

Leads were becoming available, obtained from Eyas Securities, Anderson Kimble etc.

It was around this time that a dealer rang up InstantRate, mid-afternoon when his own dealing room was buzzing. Gordon Beshaw, a director of InstantRate, answered the phone.

The dealer didn't give his name, recognisable as that of a one-time applicant to InstantRate, but just announced: 'This is what a real dealing room sounds like.'

He held the mouthpiece wide. From the other end, Beshaw listened for several minutes, perhaps trying to detect which firm's dealing room it was, before quietly putting down the receiver.

In efforts to obtain clients, female sharedealers in various firms have traditionally gone to bed with the male dealers. Several good client leads, plus a meal out and nightclub = one 'fuck' — was about the going rate.

Thus the girls who went in for this came expensive. For every male dealer who didn't want to pay the price, there was a score who did. The more attractive girls angled for higher game: managing directors and chairmen of sharedealing firms.

A notorious female dealer slept with one dealer after another, taking their clients from them, and leaving them sore. She advised the clients to cease dealing with the company forthwith, and took their business with her to another firm.

Tudorbury's male dealers generally derided marriage. Like adolescents, they scorned its conventionality, dismissing it as society's instrument of confinement. Nonetheless some fell for the bait. One dealer was so ashamed to be married that he went about pretending he was single. Even while his wife was pregnant, he was out at nights chatting up women.

Some dealers worry increasingly about catching AIDS. If several have all been with the same female employee, they may push one of their party into a VD clinic. If he emerges squeaky clean, the rest may reckon they are clean too. A fallacious reasoning no doubt, but a short life and a randy one, that's a sharedealer's.

Sharedealers delight in corrupting the novices in their profession. They like to call it initiation. At one country wedding, in front of some fellow dealers, one old hand drank, on his own admission, sixteen pints of beer. He claimed afterwards that he had also had five marijuana joints, and three lines of cocaine. He still, however, found energy to satisfy the 'tart' he had been chatting up.

Later, back on the dealing floor, he made his view clear that he was achieving something virile and splendid by this sort of behaviour. The younger dealers obediently admired his stamina and his recklessness, hovering around their mentor like bees round the proverbial honeypot.

A party was held for all Tudorbury dealers at Swanyard Studios. Experienced dealers escorted round the novices, occasionally offering them twists of cocaine as they filled their glasses with bubbly. All were allowed to wander through the studios at leisure. A young musician with a spikey, blond, punk hairstyle strolled around in macho leather clothes. *Time Out* lay open on a swish smoked glass table.

A black back-up singer was curled up on a chair in one of the recording rooms. Her black bikini was so brief that she set some dealers' mouths watering. Her frizzy hair was stunningly waved.

After a buffet dinner, RAI Hamilton addressed his dealers: 'My thanks to everybody. Let's stick together as a company and we'll make it big.' His wife Margarita Hamilton said: 'Thank you all for raising money for these studios. You're not as boring as I thought you would be, for financial men. And you are doing such good by your sales work. You're creating music.'

The dealers were touched. Most didn't see their work in such a useful light.

Afterwards, dealers played billiards, snorted coke, and drank the night away. One dealer groped for any female flesh he could find. Several dealers moped, following a quick prize-giving ceremony, because their achievements seemed not to have been recognised.

But the prize-giving rewarded only winners of specific competitions in a grand general contest which had started when a poster headed: RAI's 40th Birthday Bonanza' had been pinned to the dealing room wall.

The colourful poster had outlined competitions, deadlines, and prizes. For instance, a holiday for two in Vienna was the reward for the dealer who sold most shares in Renaissance, an unquoted American stock. Prizes for other sales achievements included: a grand piano, a mystery weekend for two, solid gold cutlery, a telescope and a holiday for two in New York — travelling there by QE2 liner and back by Concorde.

This provision of incentives to sell, for instance, Renaissance over and above other stocks was contrary to the spirit of the Financial Services Act (1986). When FIMBRA visited Tudorbury Securities, the poster was taken down. Likewise when the DTI visited, a few dealers urged that sales scores should be wiped off the white glossy board.

But RAI Hamilton was obviously prepared to take risks to get the Renaissance sold. The dealing manager of Bailey McMahon claimed that RAI Hamilton, with whom he enjoyed a business relationship, had offered Renaissance to the Dublin share-pushers to punt out to its own clients, but that he had declined the offer.

RAI Hamilton had for months been offering his own dealers at Tudorbury every incentive to sell Renaissance. He had been forging private cash deals with individual dealers, i.e. an extra 3% cash, on top of 2% commission for any Renaissance deal, as soon as the client's cheque had been cleared. This was necessary as when he put the whole dealing room on selling Renaissance, literally nothing got done.

Consulting Neil Miller, he put together a new sales pitch for the stock, which he gave to specified dealers only by word of mouth.

'The share price should move in three months,' he said. 'Its major market-maker is Drexel Burnham Lambert, who are big in the States. Another market-maker is trying to get hold of stock but can't manage it. This is a ground floor opportunity for investors . . . '

The basic facts about Renaissance were as follows: The company would be offering charity donors increased tax savings, at a time when the charity industry was worth a substantial $87 billion a year in the US. Amongst the directors was Dan Dane, who, it was alleged, was connected with the merger between Abbey Life and Hambro — now Allied Dunbar. This gentleman was to be seen at Tudorbury from time to time.

Renaissance was expected to capture at least 1% of the charitable market for the forthcoming year. There were only 3½ million shares in issue.

RAI Hamilton suggested that dealers should incorporate into their sales pitch the suggestion that Renaissance might be obtaining a price quote in the *Financial Times* and further said that he would run a book in Renaissance. Clients could buy at £1.20 or sell at £1.00 — making for a respectable enough spread, although sell orders would not be encouraged.

A glossy fact sheet on Renaissance, for sending out to clients was eventually prepared. It proved full of optimistic projections, with little in the way of figures to represent solid achievement.

Some dealers made no mention of risks and pitfalls over the telephone for investors in Renaissance. According to Hamilton, FIMBRA had not disapproved sales of the stock, but this meant little. FIMBRA had not disapproved the Silverton Industries prospectus for London & Norwich.

It may have been a measure of RAI Hamilton's reservations about the stock that he asked certain dealers to sell a little Renaissance here, a little there, and not to offload too conspicuously onto the bigger punters — although this was to some extent going on.

Renaissance's recommended three-month hold was to stretch into a six month, year long, or still lengthier hold.

In the meantime Drexel Burnham Lambert, Renaissance's market-maker, was in trouble. The bank had been publicly associated some years back with Ivan Boesky, the insider dealer. They were now facing civil action from the Securities and Exchange Commission. The possibility of later criminal action was highly likely.

A manager of Harvard Securities, telephoned *The Observer* with a story linking RAI Hamilton, Renaissance, and one or two ex-London & Norwich dealers. *The Observer*, however, rejected his suggestion.

Michael Walters said of Renaissance in the *Daily Mail*:

'Mr Hamilton claims great hopes for Renaissance, and says some of his investors have already made a profit by selling it back to Tudorbury.

'Selling is a good idea. Small investors are ill advised these days to buy any shares which are not readily tradeable on the London Stock Exchange.'

Such adverse publicity was most damaging for sales figures. In his desperation, RAI Hamilton hired an ex-London & Norwich dealer: 'I want you to sell Renaissance for me,' he said.

'Can I sell other stocks too?'

'Occasionally. But it's the Renaissance you're here to shift.'

As it turned out, the dealer refused to cooperate with the spirit of Hamilton's demands and left. Tudorbury's sales of Renaissance continued for a while, but by early 1989 had reduced to a trickle.

Chapter Ten

A-DAY BLUES

After the great International Stock Market Crash of 1987, share salesmen and stockbrokers alike were faced with a trial of a very different nature. 1988 ushered in the impending Financial Services Act, redundancies in stockbroking firms, and insurmountable debts for many licensed dealers. Numerous small firms' futures now hung in the balance.

Business was painfully slow within licensed dealers, as most clients declined to gamble on the faltering stock market. Flashy sports cars were being sold at bargain prices. Yuppified flats in sought after areas of London were flooding the market at a rate which made headlines in the national press.

'The Yuppie is dead,' claimed a leading left-wing politician. Filofax mania was grinding to a halt. Weekends in New York were becoming a thing of the past. Would the bulls ever stampede the stock market again?

Few sharedealers at this stage cared whether bulls or bears had the upper hand. 27th February 1988 (P day) was the deadline foremost in their minds. By that date, every firm and every individual had to have filed an application for authorisation under the newly implemented legislation. Share salesmen operating under false names or with dubious pasts now dreaded that their careers were over.

29th April 1988 was A-Day. Dealers in every walk of the City were not sleeping at night. Would they qualify as fit and proper under the new legislation? They would not have to wait long to find out.

The less respectable share salesman started looking for ways to cover up their past records. Even the few reputable ones felt snowed under by a mountain of bureaucratic paper work. To be declared fit and proper was in no sense an easy matter.

Salesmen at various licensed dealers in competition with each other closed ranks. The panic spread also into the less reputable futures firms.

Dealers started working in increasingly erratic patterns. Dealing floors became hothouses of paranoia and of drug abuse, all of which reflected an experimental new market place that scarcely seemed to know its own regulations. How quickly could licensed dealers make the necessary temperamental adjustment?

Anxiety got its grip on the dealing rooms. The dealing manager at Tudorbury Securities found inspiration from the writings of Tom Hopkins on self-motivation and on selling. He kept pinned to his phone a card that read: 'I do the most productive thing possible at any given moment.' He urged all dealers to sell in Tom Hopkins' hard-hitting American way. He would say: 'Go in expecting "Yes" and your willpower alone will generate a sale.'

His approach might have once gone down a treat at Harvard Securities. Tudorbury salesmen found it reeked too much of hard work, as well as being risky under the looming legislation.

One dealer, who had earned a small fortune previously with Sheridan Securities, was suddenly facing possible legal action over the biggest deal on Transworld Energy/Silverton that any of the Sheridan or London & Norwich salesmen had done.

At this stage he preferred to sit about in the dealing room, chatting and smoking, revelling in his past glories. He didn't presently need an income, and so cast himself in the role of a great securities dealer in retirement. When problems arose with FIMBRA, he resigned without batting an eyelid.

Dealers at one firm were still ringing their clients, pitching them on ill-fated OTC stocks. The clients would ask: 'What SRO do you belong to?' Dealers replied: 'We're members of BIDS — The British Institute of Dealers in Securities' — conveying the false impression that this was a recognised SRO.

Following criticism of Harvard in the national newspapers, clients were flocking to sell back stock. The dealers were getting restless. One was complaining that his income had dropped by 50%. But where could they go?

Ironically at this very time, Harvard was advertising specifically for registered representatives, a qualification that it had not previously demanded in its new dealers. Was Harvard trying to change its image at this late stage?

The reins of power on Harvard's dealing floor were constantly shifting. Meetings were held at which the dealers were told: 'Don't worry about the bad press. We've had it all before, and survived. Just keep selling stock.'

When clients said: 'I don't want to buy OTC stocks. The OTC is finished . . . ' some dealers would reply; 'No. Don't you know? The OTC stocks are about to go onto the Third Market.'

This was true of a few, but if the clients had stopped to think, they might have wondered how even the grand old Harvard Securities could sponsor some fifty or more OTC companies onto the Stock Exchange.

Not long previously, one share salesman of Eyas Securities who had formerly been a Los Angeles antique dealer and who knew almost nothing about the stock market, had blurted out to a

The Victoria Casino, London W2, where dealers played in the same manner as they worked, winning and losing vast sums in a single night.

colleague: 'What must I do to be fit and proper? How should I change my sales pitch? I've just bought a brand new Ferrari — it looks as if I'll be kissing goodbye to that.'

Certainly A-Day was a day of judgment. On its approach, dealers at Tudorbury Securities and elsewhere were terrified their source of income would die out. They clutched at their jobs like drowning men at straws, mindful of how many dealers came and went like special guests. Some still needed to finance their cocaine habits.

Dealers also had gambling debts. One dealer at a well-known firm had made £40,000 from a personal account trade. In their rush to emulate him, dealers throughout the fringe City did not think to inquire as to his losses on account trading over the previous few months.

Dealers would occasionally blow huge sums of money in casinos. The managing director of one licensed dealer would take his favourite dealers to casinos, giving them money. When they had squandered this, they would run up overdrafts on their American Express cards, caught up as they were in the excitement of the gaming table. The late night would result in their making a haggard appearance on the dealing floor the next morning, like so many Banquo's ghosts.

With all their expenses, dealers wanted to rake in all the money they could, before regulations became too hot. In selling stock they harnessed the help of their companies' analysts. The analyst at one firm was a young cocaine freak, who gleaned much of his financial information from the Hambros Guide — just like some of the clients.

This analyst was sometimes quoted by dealers who wanted to impress naive clients. 'Our analyst says . . . ' they would point out. Clients were impressed, conjuring up a fantasy of a bespectacled wizard with figures, who, when he wasn't putting company directors through the third degree, was sweating over minutiae in company reports. They assumed he was dedicated to the clients' interests.

Dealers would sometimes put clients onto this gentleman, who would stop throwing paper darts, stub out his umpteenth cigarette, and talk to them in low civil tones that conveyed an impression of worldly wisdom, even if he was a little light on hard facts.

Various other little tricks of the trade were used to sell shares:

After BOM Holdings had its rights issue in late 1987, the shares were split into two classes — the 2½p and the 25p shares.

Some dealers selling BOM Holdings would announce cheerfully to clients: 'You can follow the price in the *Financial Times*, Sir.'

The price quoted in the *Financial Times* referred to the 25p shares, as opposed to the 2½p shares. At this time, certain licensed dealers were only retailing the 2½p shares.

Thus clients often followed the wrong price, which gave them an over-optimistic view of their shares' prowess *at that point*. Some dealers knew this and didn't enlighten them.

A dealer who was briefly the tops at Tudorbury stopped working for some weeks, immediately after his father died. He lazed about, living on his past reputation.

Then one day, in a sudden spurt of new life, this dealer rang his clients. There was a brilliant new stock, he said. Had they funds? Not just their usual couple of grand. How much could their building societies answer for?

They hung on his words, half starved with greedy impulse, as he milked the dupes dry this last time. He tempered his aggressive closes with a dash of sentimentalism: 'Life is too short to be missing the best opportunities, Sir . . . My father has just died. He went to his death-bed in the garden, with a spade in his hands, and a prayer on his lips . . . ' The clients whom he persuaded into trading with him in huge quantities of stock may have been embarrassed into it.

Other dealers tried more blatant tactics. Off one salesman's tongue would roll the following line: 'I'm a senior dealer here. I get eight out of ten of my recommendations right, *provided* that you sell when I recommend it.' This conveyed the implication that the dealer cared enough to advise when to sell.

Following the stock market crash of October 1987, Tudorbury Securities needed fresh money in, not money taken out. In the wake of Tudorbury's various short-term disasters, such as the overnight 30p price drop in Hampton Trust, or the price drops in Colorgen and Western Industries, the Tudorbury dealer would have his story ready: 'A temporary lapse. A bit of profit-taking. As you know the market's dodgy at the moment, sir. Hang on, and the share price should be up in a jiffy.'

One Tudorbury dealer had introduced the phrase 'On Your Way Smiler' as his last word to clients, after he had dealt them and had put down the phone. Some of his colleagues had gradually incorporated this phrase into their own repertoires as a means of boosting personal morale by putting down the client after the deal had been done.

Hardly any dealers at Tudorbury were prepared to sacrifice even a little of their leisure time to take more interest in economic affairs. Their job was mainly quickfire salesmanship, worlds removed from serious investment advice. Even under the new Financial Services Act, some could get away with knowing little and still selling plenty of stock. It was a kind of magic.

Most Tudorbury dealers were interested in the Chancellor's Budget speech as it would personally affect their tax situation. A dealer brought in his portable TV on the day of the 1988 speech. All dealers assembled that afternoon to watch, breaking attention occasionally to do the odd share deal. A few took notes of the Chancellor's words, so they could reproduce them for clients' benefit. It might pay to sound well informed.

Unusually, the Chancellor's speech was interrupted a number of times. To restore quiet, the Speaker shouted, 'Order Order'. The dealers found his need to do this amusing. The next morning, on the dealing floor, one dealer shouted out 'Order. Order . . . ' The others roared with laughter.

For the next couple of weeks, when dealers came to work, instead of saying 'Good morning', they said 'Order, order.' During the day, whenever the dealers got slack or merry, someone shouted out 'Order, order . . . '

'Order, order' became remembered when the rest of the budget speech was forgotten. This childish obsession may even have helped to cause the significant drop in sales figures at the time.

For a while, even after the implementation of the new Financial Services Act, telephone calls to and from Tudorbury's dealing room were unrecorded. Dealers could be wide, and Tudorbury retained no evidence of it. Of course, clients too could later deny what *they* had said. Around the A-Day period, Tudorbury suffered plenty of cancellations.

When licensed dealers get desperate to bring in money, the credit control manager is the first to feel it. Salesmen are largely protected, as their morale must remain high if they are to continue shifting stock.

The credit control manager at Tudorbury was a lady who had a knack of wheedling money out of clients. She would ring up the many who had not settled, and would say: 'Listen, I'm only Credit Control. All I know about, love, is pounds, shillings, and pence. I know nothing about shares.'

She had a high success rate. Dealers, faced with clients who would not settle, requested her intervention. She would comply, grumbling: 'You think you have problems trying to get your clients to settle. I get this twenty times a day, love. Twenty times a day.'

Sometimes she needed a specific client to be rung by his dealer. Not always knowing which dealer handled which client, she played this trick to find out — she would announce on the dealing room something like: 'Mr Harrison wants to pick up some Blacks Leisure. Whose client is he?'

The dealer concerned would immediately make himself known and she would laugh: 'I might've known it was you. Mr Harrison owes us money. Ring him up, will you, love, and remind him to send us a cheque.'

One Tudorbury salesman teamed up with a female dealer on the floor. She would make and take calls, pretending to be his secretary. This invariably impressed clients.

One upright Tudorbury dealer who was waiting to register with FIMBRA before he felt able to deal, used to answer some of his calls for him with: 'I'm just a clerk. I'll hand you over to a dealer.' After a week however, he left in disgust.

Insult is an effective motivator. One Tudorbury dealer asked RAI Hamilton for the profit figures of A & M Leisure. He stabbed the written sales pitch on her desk with his finger. 'It's there in black and white. You must be dyslexic. Any chance you might actually do some business now?'

Stung by his sarcasm, the dealer swiftly sold £19,000 worth of A & M stock in the next couple of hours. Hamilton likewise incensed another dealer into working hard by calling him a 'mediocre salesman'.

One dealer at Tudorbury used to prowl around the dealing floor, muttering he must have a 'charlie' (a line of cocaine) before he started work.

Once his nostrils were thus relieved, he would grunt: 'Let's see what client I can rape now.' as he reached out and grabbed other dealers' client cards. He always used to deal big.

He once took the cards of a younger dealer whose girlfriend he had chatted up in the pub the previous night. The boy seized his collar: 'You've got my bird. Now you've got my clients. What more do you want?'

Clients were by now pulling as much money out of licensed dealers as they could, realising that it was at risk. Bad press comment about Harvard Securities, for instance, or a dealer's sudden departure made them suspicious. If the share price dropped dramatically, clients often would not settle. Many took advantage of the sensitive timing. Firms out to survive in the new moral climate did not press too hard for unpaid debts.

Inevitably clients were becoming more aware. The London & Norwich Unsecured Creditors Committee may have floundered helplessly, but the Harvard Clients' Complaints Committee was gaining public support.

Much to Wilmot's rage, Labour MPs Mr Dale Campbell-Savours (Workington), Mr John Evans (St Helens North) and Mr Maxwell Madden (Bradford West) put down a formal motion in Parliament advising investors to withdraw their business from Harvard.

Sharedealers viewed this development, first announced in *The Times* of 29th June 1988, with consternation more than with pleasure, even if they hated Harvard. Once the father of licensed dealers collapsed, so might the whole industry. All their positions were on the line.

At this stage, Harvard's shares were trading at 27p, as opposed to 40p a year earlier.

The legendary licensed dealer was facing other problems. The DTI had been investigating. Clients were trying to sell out of stock. The firm was still not fully authorised.

By way of adding fuel to the flames, Channel 4's *Business Daily* featured a special investigation into Harvard Securities and the OTC market.

Many of the arguments raised were old hat. Should Harvard have suspected beforehand that VTC, one of the OTC stocks in which it had been making a market, might collapse? Could the investors' losses of £6 million have been thwarted?

Harvard's statement of defence, read out on the programme, was brilliant. Amongst other things it claimed that clients who had invested in all its OTC stocks from the time of issue would have made money.

Yes, but Harvard's clients buy largely on dealers' *specific* recommendations at *specific* times. These are not always in their best interests. Moreover, do all clients receive the same quality of treatment?

One dealer was going to appear in shadow on television to talk about Harvard Securities, and some Tudorbury dealers were contemplating a group television appearance for the same purpose.

There was no love lost between the two companies as Harvard had tried to close Tudorbury in its early days. But the dealers would only speak out for the right fee. As this fee was not forthcoming, the idea came to nothing.

This goes to show the mercenary nature of dealers. They will sway with the wind, if the price is right. They will also turn on their own kind in their weak moments. Some, for reasons of professional rivalry, did not wish Harvard to gain authorisation under the Financial Services Act (1986).

The vultures were scenting blood before it was spilled.

At this stage, a Munich lawyer acting on behalf of forty-six German investors who alleged that they had lost DM 378,511 by trading in obscure shares through the German based Harvard Securities AG, was threatening legal action against the firm's directors, management and even its founding shareholders.

Harvard AG had been founded in March 1984 as a partnership. John Casey, one of the partners, was a director of Harvard Securities in London. The bone of contention was that Harvard Securities AG was not supplied with DM 1 million (£300,000) share capital, as stated in its partnership articles.

No longer were certain dealers asking, 'Why are clients such suckers?' and thanking their lucky stars that 90% of the UK's population was financially illiterate. Clients were getting wise.

An association to 'promote, protect, and represent' the interests of private clients in London was launched in June 1988 by the magazine *Private Investor*. This club was striving to cater for investors as the AA or RAC does for motorists.

Its strength doubtless lay in the names on the advisory panel: Sir William Rees Mogg, Norman St John Stevas (Lord Fawsley), John Biffen (previous leader of the Conservatives in the Commons), Baroness Elles, and solicitor Sir David Napley.

More clients were learning to put their complaints in writing. The following is an extract from a letter from a dissatisfied client to his dealer at Tudorbury Securities on 25th June 1988:

'I see that Chemex International fell by 6% on Thursday, and is expected to fall further after the plant explosion in the USA.

'You seem to have a knack of selling me stock before it falls. Point is, how long will it be before I get my full investment back? Total invested so far, £6,231.'

Clients' letters of complaint can be considerably more cutting than that. One dealer at Harvard Securities sold a client shares in Herbert Woods PLC, whose price plummetted immediately afterwards.

The client wrote to Harvard something to this effect: 'The dealer is now ringing me (from London & Norwich Investment Services Ltd) saying he has been headhunted by a member firm. On the basis of this recommendation. I will be hunting *his* head.'

Harvard sent a copy of this letter along with a note from their own solicitor, to London & Norwich. Clearly Harvard felt a strong obligation to intervene on the client's behalf.

Another client of Tudorbury Securities wrote in (October 1988) as follows:

'As recommended by your company, I bought 30,000 shares of Meridien Oil at 10.75p on 10.06.87. During the last 17 months, I have neither received dividends nor financial statements of the company. It is being quoted at the level of 4p. Another sad story is Airship Industries, 2,000 shares sold to me at a price of £0.30p on 15.10.87 again no dividends, no financial statements sent to me, none updates me (sic) on this also. It is now quoted around a fabulous price of 8p!

'York Trust Group PLC: I don't know how many, like me, fell a victim to the hard selling tactics for this share. Your company sold me 6,100 shares . . . at a price of 0.78p on 27.06.88, assuring that in the short-term this share should touch £1.00, but to my horror, I find this slipping on a continuous basis, falling as low as 0.48p!'

On 2nd November 1988, another Tudorbury client wrote in, listing his portfolio as follows:

'10,000 Norton worth 10p, purchased at 18p, 20,000 BOM Holdings, 55,500 Swanyard Studios, 9,000 Colorgen, 15,000 Honorbilt, and commented:

'All these are *down* on my purchase price, and there seems to be few signs of imminent profit. What has gone wrong?'

These letters reveal typical complaints of Tudorbury clients. The problem is that clients so often take their dealer's word on blind trust. On 8th October, 1988 one client wrote to his Tudorbury dealer, admitting:

' . . . since I did not really want to dabble in shares before I knew a little about them, perhaps you could explain to me, what happens to my shares, when do I get them, what expense is involved in selling them, and also do you advise me when to sell them?'

More clients than you would think are in this predicament.

Client complaints about Harvard Securities have been too numerous to present a sufficient sample. Here however are some extracts from a letter by one frustrated client:

'My only hint of deception up to now had been the incredible reasons the dealer had been giving me for the lack of movement in the stock price. It seemed everything was depressing the OTC market: British Telecom, BP Oil, market fluctuations etc . . . etc . . .

'My first real cause for concern came in October and November '85, when the share price of 'Associated Furniture' began to make a nosedive. I naturally phoned to make enquiries, and was told there was no problem, the shares were selling fine and the movement was due to just a bit of profit taking. However, I had become very worried about the whole situation and asked the dealer to send me all information, past and present, about "Associated Furniture". This information was not forthcoming. I then wrote a letter to Harvard; asking the same.

'The next development was the suspension of the shares. I phoned the dealer and asked what was going on. He, to my surprise, announced it was good news; there had been a takeover bid by a listed company and the shares would be coming back on the market at least double, if not more, than before they were suspended . . .

'The next development was the reintroduction of the stock back on the market at some 2p per share. I found it impossible to get hold of the dealer. As soon as I mentioned my name, the answer would be he was busy, and when I asked for any dealer they were all busy . . . I finally got to talk to the dealer on Wednesday 15 January. He told me the share price was 2-4, but still maintained he had no details of the takeover and I would get these through the post. By Friday 17 January, I had made repeated attempts to contact the dealer. The usual evasive methods were employed, leaving me on the phone unattended, until I had to hang up because of the sheer expense . . . '

Occasionally, clients will write letters in support of Harvard Securities. Here follows some extracts from one such letter. The client's motivation becomes obvious:

'I am writing to advise you that I wish fervently to continue to use the dealing and advisory service currently provided by Harvard Securities PLC . . .

'Like a gambler ever plunging deeper to recoup his losses, I have tempted to invest in speculative shares in the hope of increasing my capital. This policy has proved disastrous, particularly since last October, and I am now down to four figures. The fault is mine and I am not attempting to apportion blame.

'73% of my money is invested in shares handled by Harvard. If they were suspended from dealing, the effect would be hardly less than catastrophic . . . '

Clients in general were by this stage guessing that certain licensed dealers ramped stock, selling a proportion of a bulk load of shares to a client at a high, then dumping the rest on the market, so the price would sink. This bulk load might have been picked up very cheap, some months earlier, by the licensed dealer. But the clients could prove nothing.

Why do clients sometimes continue investing through licensed dealers even when it seems not in their best interests? Some may be laundering money or evading tax A few may belong to highly organised political or criminal organisations that are looking to hide illicit funds. One bought many of his shares from a licensed dealer, rather than from a stockbroking member firm, because he didn't want to bring his dealings to the attention of the Stock Exchange, who might suspect he had specialist knowledge. He once boasted about this to a favourite dealer who admired his cleverness. Dealers have a soft spot for anyone who so works the system. This derives from their temperament.

However, to find out further what drives the more typical client, the author interviewed one of his *own*, Mr Morris, a successful forty year old chartered surveyor, who was in the habit of ringing his dealers daily from the car phone. This is what he said:

'I dealt before the crash with the whole gamut of licensed dealers at once. Harvard, of course. Tudorbury. Eyas. Anderson Kimble. Chartwell. Fox Milton. Equity Share. Sheridan. You name it.

'My interest in the market has grown over the last four years. I read all the Sunday newspapers, and pick up a lot of tips that way. The bad press about licensed dealers does worry me. It never seems to stop. I did pick up shares in Transworld Energy from Sheridan, but I saw the warnings in *The Observer* and never paid for them, thank God. I would have lost every penny.

'The most frustrating side-effect of trading with licensed dealers is their high staff turnover. No sooner do I establish a rapport with some dealer than he vanishes. He won't always get in touch with me later, but I'm stuck with the fruit of his recommendations.

'I have all sorts of shares in my portfolio. Lots of dead wood. Pavion, Central & Sherwood. Denning Robotics. Crane Holdings. I have to keep detailed files. The one thing that really annoys me is waiting six or nine months for certificates. Even then they don't always come . . .

'Why can't dealers have some basic facts at their fingertips? They sometimes get the stocks right, but their buy recommendations are not always timely. I've often been better off following my own instincts.

'I am led to believe some dealers are more interested in offloading stock for their own commission purposes than in showing me a profit. For instance, I'm glad I went into Blacks Leisure when it was recommended to me (mid 1987) at 21p, but I should've gone in earlier when it was only 16p.

'I admit I can't resist a good share, a quickie. It's my weakness, I just can't say no. I'm sure you must have a lot of clients like that.

'I've dealt with several stockbrokers in my time. Why is it they don't tip shares? They sit back and wait for me to ring them. What use is that to me?

'I've always been after the hot tips. A bit of specialist knowledge, because let's face it, without it how am I going to make money? All right, I'm a compulsive gambler, but I only use money I can afford.

My wife gets mad with me because she thinks I throw away good money. I get mad with her when she is fined for not returning her library books. 'At least I'm trying to make money' I tell her.

'Mind you, I'm a bad payer. You see I don't always settle until I've got in finance from my property deals. I don't like to delay settling for too long; the firm might close my account, selling me out at current prices, and I could lose a fortune.

'I'm a short-term punter really. Don't get me wrong. I'll wait a few weeks. I don't expect returns within the account, although naturally I'm pleased enough if they come. I don't mind holding for two or three months or longer if something is really going on. I prefer to take a quick profit when I can though, even if I only make a few pence. I came in and out of Hard Rock Cafe when it had first come onto the over-the-counter market, and made about 20p a share. OK the shares soared afterwards, but I have no regrets. I'm not greedy. What I resent is a 60% loss.

'My profits have not been so good on shares, particularly during the crash. I've lost £15,000-£20,000 or so in the last year.

'I think the property market is more predictable than the stock market, but perhaps that's because I know more about it. I've been buying fewer equities since the crash and I'm slowly trying to close my position with Harvard at the moment. How long do you think they have to last?

'Property and shares. These are my two great loves. In that order, thank God, or I'd never be making a living . . . '

Here is the authentic voice of the client type who is a licensed dealer's bread and butter. Mature. Idealistic. A natural gambler — keen to make a quick buck, but in a position to foot losses.

The dealer is trained to squeeze every last penny from this type. The good dealer will never warm to him, but will turn on the charm, so he can catch the client offguard, and so squeeze him the harder.

What he gets out of him on the day is what counts. Tudorbury's dealing director, for instance, praised dealers who notched up high sales figures on the day, regardless of how they had performed on preceding days.

Since A-Day, clients have been gaining an increasing rarity value. Salesmen need clients on personal recommendation. Many have started trying to buy client lists from dealers who have left the profession.

This proves almost impossible. Ex-sharedealers have somehow developed a new moral distaste for the 'churn 'em and burn 'em' lifestyles they have just left. On the other hand, if they ever decide to return to it, they will need what clients they previously had.

Dealers now found they had to make do with their existing clients. Many neither understood nor cared about regulations, selling shares like clumsy amateurs.

Their continued carelessness and ignorance was revealed in their sales pitches. One dealer said, 'Renaissance is quoted on NASDAQ, Sir.' Another said: 'We've formally taken over the Anderson Kimble lists.' Both these statements were untrue.

In summer 1988, stolen client lists were being peddled from firm to firm by sacked dealers. These were worth more than share registers as the names were exclusively from one dealing firm.

Some Anderson Kimble clients, disillusioned with financial losses therefrom, were reluctant to trade with Tudorbury Securities, whose dealers were selling to them from May 1988 onwards, from a purloined client list. Many were awaiting an outcome of the Fraud Squad's investigations into Anderson Kimble.

FIMBRA was criticised after Anderson Kimble went into liquidation approximately a month before A-Day. They had been informed that they should act fast since Anderson Kimble was going bust, and that the firm was late in paying a substantial sum of money due to a stockbroking firm whose name and telephone number were given.

FIMBRA had replied that it was common for members to be late in payment, and asked the informant, who was close to Anderson Kimble, to put the complaint in writing.

An investigation team was not sent to Anderson Kimble until nine days after FIMBRA had been alerted. The creditors blamed FIMBRA for this.

Many people were absent from Anderson Kimble's first creditors' meeting, since the details of it had been insufficiently publicised. At the second creditors' meeting, one of the directors, David Bennett, was absent, although the liquidators had asked him in writing to attend.

It transpired that clients of Anderson Kimble could have lost £750,000, and it was unclear how many who had paid for shares would be issued with certificates.

At the meetings, all sorts of tangled issues were raised, such as from where had Anderson Kimble got the money to reduce their overdraft with the Midland Bank, in excess of £250,000 at one stage, to £7,000.

Anderson Kimble had in fact been advertising its services nationwide shortly before it went into liquidation. One client present at the first creditors' meeting had not heard of the firm four weeks previously.

Furthermore, Anderson Kimble had been advertising for dealers in its London office, days before the company went into liquidation. The recruitment advertisement, placed in the London Evening *Standard* had not mentioned the firm's name.

An ex-London & Norwich dealer went for an interview there. Inside the small offices, the interviewer looked him up and down: 'Are you a University graduate? Most of us here are,' he said.

The dealer smirked: 'I'm twenty-two years old. I earn £40,000 a year. I think I've made better use of my time than I would have done at University.'

He was offered the job but didn't turn up on the Monday. The firm looked as if it was on the rocks to him, and as it turned out, he was right.

To many others in the industry, Anderson Kimble's preference for graduates had seemed pretentious. This had been a tinpot little firm, with offices spread over the country, but with few dealers to fill them.

Given that dealers had been paid commission of 30% on stock spreads, i.e. differences between buying and selling prices, they had recommended mostly penny shares, as this breed has a larger spread. Of course, an excess of penny shares is not in *any* client's interest, but this is what some of the Anderson Kimble clients had been lumbered with.

Indeed in some firms, dealers were paid commission on stock spreads and have been known to widen these spreads, purely to increase their own commissions.

The official rights to the Anderson Kimble client list were auctioned by the liquidator. Two individuals outbid the rest, and bought the official client dealing cards and records for £2,250. It was a moot point how many of these clients would deal, as Anderson Kimble's crash had lost them much money.

The two new owners of the list were ex-London & Norwich dealers. One was working with Tudorbury Securities, the other with Empire Futures.

These two dealers then offered RAI Hamilton a proposal. If he would give them a basic salary and a separate room, complete with their own screen, they would sell stock to the Anderson Kimble clients. Wherever possible, they would sell the clients out of the stocks they had purchased through Anderson Kimble — stock market listed penny shares such as Kalon, Downibrae, Bristol Channel Ship Repair, Pavion, BOM Holdings etc, in order to put them into Tudorbury recommendations.

RAI Hamilton, upon being presented with the idea, tried to persuade them to sign over the list to Tudorbury Securities. 'I'll pay for the list. Not now. In a couple of weeks time,' he said.

He was perhaps more interested than he let on. Official ownership of the list was worth something. A little while back, some ex-Anderson Kimble dealers had arrived at Tudorbury to work there. A manager had proposed they should stay until they had transferred their dealing clients onto Tudorbury's computer. Dissatisfied, however, they left after only a few days of employment.

The two dealers refused to sign over their list. Instead they started hawking it around Stock Exchange member firms, and obtained provisional job offers from Russell Wood.

Licensed dealers were by now starting to make their exits as demonstrated by the sad demise of another London based sharedealer, the short-lived Eyas Securities, who were the first to feel the axe of the Securities and Investments Board (SIB).

Many dealers at this firm had not known that their firm's directors were also directors of the over-the-counter traded stocks Osprey Financial Trust PLC and Crane Holdings PLC, in both of which Eyas was the sole market-maker. What they did not know, they could not pass on to clients.

This directorship tie-in had attracted official attention. It was also noticed that Eyas Securities was proposing, so it seemed, to deal after A-Day in OTC stocks in which it was the sole market maker.

The authorities found that Eyas Securities' computer system was not up to date, and that its filing system was substandard. But this information was not made available to investors until it was almost too late for them to sell out of stock.

FIMBRA ordered Eyas Securities to cease trading altogether on 15th April 1988, until The Securities Association (TSA) should grant them authorisation. It was the TSA's responsibility and no longer FIMBRA's to authorise market-makers in OTC shares.

Eyas Securities, notwithstanding, continued to trade. On A-Day, FIMBRA turned over the case to the SIB which was responsible for handling problems relating to firms that had not been accepted by any self-regulatory organisation (SRO).

On A-Day, the SIB ordered Eyas Securities to cease trading. The licensed dealer obeyed. The SIB said that Eyas Securities had 30 days in which to lodge an appeal. This swiftly became public knowledge.

Salesmen at one licensed dealer rushed to cold-call Eyas clients.

In the meantime, Harvard Securities started making a grey market in the shares of Crane Holdings. Was there yet hope that the price would rise to its former heights?

Two ex-Eyas Securities dealers who had filed claims with the firm for commissions due to them, were now plotting to wind up Eyas. One of these dealers was in addition owed a backlog of overrides on the dealing room's business, which he claimed had been promised him in a meeting. Few dealers take kindly to being forgotten by their ex-bosses, as if they were merely clients.

Grade One Investments went into liquidation in March 1988. Its clients had been hoping for huge returns on capital that was, with their full knowledge, placed in bets on horse races — but managing director Marcus Rae made heavy losses at the Cheltenham Races. Do punters have no limits to their greed?

The Bristol firm, Reyd Services had been closed down by FIMBRA after a number of alleged rule breaches over the selling of shares in an Australian garage company, unquoted on any Stock Exchange.

Prior to the closure, Reyd had tried to resign from FIMBRA on grounds that they were being taken over by an overseas company. FIMBRA, who had already started investigating, did not allow this.

The SIB was conducting investigations into firms such as Acorn Financial Services which was allegedly dealing without authorisation in investment bonds, and into unauthorised sharedealer LEV Investment and Management, which was to become voluntarily wound up.

Even the continental share-pushers were not necessarily untouched by the new legislation. For instance, the writing on the envelopes of Madrid based share-pusher Timezone indicated that they be returned to a Dover postbox in the event of non-delivery. Did this put Timezone under UK jurisdiction?

Firms who were not yet authorised sometimes exaggerated their status in order to recruit dealers.

A new sharedealer, GOW Securities (sister company to GOW Commodities) started advertising in the London Evening *Standard* for experienced securities dealers. An ex-London & Norwich dealer rang up. 'Are you FIMBRA members?' he asked.

'Yes,' he was told.

He explained he had a top dealing record, and a substantial client base. 'Are you definitely FIMBRA members?' he asked again.

'I've told you once, we are. Are you deaf?' snapped the manager.

When the dealer attended an interview, the manager qualified what he had said earlier as follows: 'We've put in an application for FIMBRA membership, like all the other firms. We'll have to wait and see how it all shakes out.'

His exaggeration on the telephone demonstrated how keen the firm had been to recruit experienced dealers.

FIMBRA membership was in demand. Britannia Mercantile Company Ltd, another sharedealer, was sending out contract notes with a FIMBRA logo. FIMBRA, however, had no record of the firm. James Hay, who was running the show, claimed he had FIMBRA membership via his previous place of employment, the crashed Anderson Kimble.

FIMBRA passed the buck onto the SIB who in turn passed it onto the DTI, since the potential breaches of regulation had occurred prior to the implementation of the Financial Services Act.

Some weeks later, Hay was being hunted by the police. It appeared that he had financed Britannia Mercantile, and other companies, using funds from a company called Database Design & Development, whose bank account quickly became overdrawn — at which point the Fraud Squad was called in. Hay, it appeared, was not a signatory on the bank account.

Fox Milton & Co Ltd was clearly determined to get TSA membership. They prompted the departure of three new recruits, all previously stalwarts of the recently crashed Afcor Investments, so as to maintain a clean image.

Fox Milton had been criticised for cold-calling — something they deny, and also for selling shares in Mandarin Resources which was subsequently suspended — something they pointed out they could not foresee. In fact, Fox Milton had an excellent reputation in the trade. It was sad but, of course, not conclusive when The Securities Association (TSA) gave Fox Milton notice of its intention to refuse them membership. The company was run in a highly professional way by Methodists, and had always offered clients a realistic chance of making money. Sadly again, but inevitably, dealers started deserting Fox Milton for Tudorbury whose full FIMBRA membership had been confirmed. As it turned out, Fox Milton & Co Ltd were fully authorised by TSA on 19th December 1988.

Meanwhile InstantRate Ltd, referred to earlier, was soldiering on. The company offered potential clients £25,000 cash, and other spectacular prizes for correct forecasts of the gold price, the sterling dollar rate, and the FTSE 100 Index.

Entrants had to sign this declaration: 'I would like to receive full details of the InstantRate financial services and market information, together with any advice I may need in financial investment. I would also like to be kept up to date with information regarding the options market.'

Entrants had further to telephone InstantRate to confirm receipt of the entry form. There is some doubt whether this was not conflicting with the rules of the Securities and Investments Board (SIB).

The SIB referred the competition to the AFBD. The whole caboodle was looked at in *The Daily Telegraph's* Family Money-Go-Round section, on 28th May 1988. Suddenly, pfff . . . InstantRate was in the public eye.

In an effort to make his dealers feel secure in this somewhat trigger-happy climate, Tudorbury's chief executive RAI Hamilton, grandly announced to the floor: 'Don't be frightened to advise your clients. Remember, you are the experts. Tudorbury is one of the few licensed dealers that have survived. We will be around in ten years time.'

Meanwhile he appeared very keen to recruit new dealers. An advertisement for experienced dealers in *The Daily Telegraph*, had yielded a disappointing response.

One morning a motor-cycle courier popped into Tudorbury Securities, so it appeared, to find his bearings. He was later to tell dealers that he had been sent for.

The next day, RAI Hamilton ushered him into the dealing room and proudly showed him round it. New desks were in place. A screen had just been hung on the wall with brackets. It all looked highly professional. 'Would you like a job as a dealer?' asked Hamilton.

The courier paused: 'I need a few days to think about it.'

Hamilton nodded, and waved to indicate the entire dealing room: 'Wander about. Ask a few questions . . . ' he said.

The courier casually questioned dealers, and they all told him the same story. They were a FIMBRA company, and provided a good dealing service for private clients.

The courier asked if they churned clients. No, no churning. Was Tudorbury solvent? Of course. He admitted then how he knew what questions to ask. Before his present job as a courier, he had been a futures salesman at LHW. He had quit, despite 'earning the dosh', because he was sick of hard selling people.

If he came to Tudorbury, would he be walking into the same trap? No, the dealers reassured him. Hard selling was vetoed. It was all above board here. Clients had a real chance to make money. Tudorbury would still be around in ten years time.

Just before the courier left, one dealer slipped him a piece of paper bearing her phone number. 'Ring me tonight,' she hissed. 'I'll tell you the score.'

After the visitor had gone the dealers whispered uneasily amongst themselves. 'Was he planted?' they demanded, and 'by whom?'

He started at Tudorbury and turned out to be an innocent after all. But the deep suspicion of the dealers on the one hand and of himself on the other demonstrates the terror and uncertainty that prevailed. It was an atmosphere that lent itself to absurd practical jokes.

For some days, DTI officials had been visiting Tudorbury's offices. The lucky dip referred to previously was always staged *after* they had gone.

Late on one of these afternoons, RAI Hamilton was on the dealing floor, setting up the lucky dip, when the telephone rang. A dealer answered it as follows:

'Tudorbury. You want RAI Hamilton? He's quite busy at the moment. May I ask who's calling? Oh yes. Um . . . I'll interrupt him.'

The dealer turned to his boss: 'RAI, it's Mr Pink of the DTI' he gasped. 'He wants to know if you're doing a lucky dip.'

RAI Hamilton started. He quivered, parting his lips noiselessly. Was this the end?

Dealers watched him pick up the telephone. The silence was sudden and heavy. All the thrills of the lucky dip were forgotten.

As he spoke into the receiver, Hamilton started panting with relief. The caller had turned out to be his wife. The dealer had tricked him. Everybody clapped and cheered.

But alarm bells were constantly ringing in Tudorbury dealers' heads, and by the end of June 1988, a new bi-weekly compliance meeting had superseded the familiar sales training.

The dealing manager at one of these new sessions explained that churning a client out of Alpha stocks such as ICI, so he could buy penny stocks such as BOM Holdings, was against the rules these days. Such churns also impeded Tudorbury's cash flow, he said.

This was because the client would receive his contract note for the BOM Holdings purchase in forty-eight hours, but Tudorbury would not receive money from his ICI share certificates until the settlement date of the following account, i.e. after several weeks' wait.

The dealing manager explained further that Tudorbury could not afford too many letters of complaint about churning, since they all had to be filed, in keeping with FIMBRA regulations.

One aggressive senior dealer next told how he had pulled off a massive deal without needing to churn.

He had said to the client: 'I have a stock you ought to be in on. the company is BOM Holdings. That's all I'm telling you about it. I've two million shares on my books. One million are already allocated. The other million are for you . . . ' The client bought without question.

In late June 1988, one Tudorbury dealer, nicknamed 'Horse', partly as a skit on his surname, partly for the way he had used to 'bull into' clients, told a new client, ex-Anderson Kimble: 'Send in a client application form please, Sir. We can't deal until you've done that.'

The client groaned: 'Oh, for the days before the Financial Services Act, when all these dealers would ring me up and tell me fabulous stories about the companies whose shares they were selling. Ooh, I loved it. I invested so much money then. With all this bureaucracy now, I'm not so sure I can be bothered . . . '

Clearly a few clients, like all the dealers, were regretting that the clamps were being applied.

However, given that other clients were seizing the opportunity to register complaints, a little caution was necessary. Tudorbury dealers, for instance, no longer dared to sell stocks that they knew too little about. Many took to checking out Tudorbury's special recommendations with their favourite brokers.

For instance, one dealer checked with her 'mate' at Collins Coombs on an 'Aussie' mining stock called Paragon. She hung on the broker's words, then relayed to her clients Paragon's good points, intensified into a sales presentation.

Not long previously, the dealer and the broker had been working together at Harvard Securities. The rapport was still there.

Chapter Eleven

THE WEB REVISITED

Once upon a time there were two firms with full FIMBRA membership, London & Norwich Investment Services Ltd, and Tudorbury Securities. London & Norwich bit the dust! But Tudorbury remains . . .

After the closure of firms such as Anderson Kimble and DPR, and the takeover of Empire Futures, Tudorbury Securities attracted dealers like the ray of hope from a lighthouse.

Some Tudorbury dealers were discarding the old hard sell tactics, and were worming their way into the confidence of clients they hardly knew, in order to ease them into share transactions.

Tudorbury dealers were spotted frequently in the company of RAI Hamilton in various smart nightspots. They would dance until 4.00 am in the morning, sleep for one or two hours, then stagger onto the dealing floor, anaesthetised into readiness to place stocks that may not have suited their fancy.

Swanyard Studios, BOM Holdings, and Chemex International were a typical menu of the day. It was a varied enough dish, only, in the dealers' words, "not horny enough."

More clients lists were now trickling into Tudorbury and thousands of names were being mailshotted to bring fresh business into the company.

Glossy brochures and a smart newsletter were being proposed. Clients were to see a new and improved Tudorbury. The fresh image had already been portrayed in an advertisement for Tudorbury Securities contained in the programme for the prestigious Berkeley Square Ball. In this, Tudorbury's status had been enhanced by an accompanying picture of the busy New York Stock Exchange.

In its mailshots, Tudorbury sent out the new newsletter with a chairman's letter, and a prepaid card, but not the glossy brochure. Was Tudorbury going so upmarket as dealers had been led to believe? Whatever the case, the trickle of new clients was welcome. One dealer said gleefully: "It's like Manna from Heaven!"

To dealers' astonishment, the punter was ringing into Tudorbury on his own initiative to buy shares. In their experience, this was almost unprecedented.

Many male dealers who were single and unattached frantically sought to chat up the blonde temporary receptionist. Each was hoping she would fancy him enough to transfer the bulk of phone-in clients to his line. One dealer succeeded in this manoeuvre, and found great pleasure in thus enlarging his client base.

Tudorbury's prime recommendation to new clients was the Norton Group. Within a few weeks, the shares had not performed the way dealers had suggested. The new client base was diminishing fast.

'For fuck's sake,' cried out one dealer as he watched the Norton shares plummet:

RAI Hamilton scrutinises an envelope in his ''Lucky Dip''.

'I'll never be able to call that client again.'

Tudorbury's lucky dip, introduced earlier in the book, became a lifeline to the dealers. At the end of the day, they would demand like panting wolves whether RAI Hamilton was on his way with the envelopes containing cash prizes.

At one lucky dip session, the dealer who had secured the top sales figures for the day had to pick four envelopes. The room came to a hush, and all eyes were upon him. He seized one envelope, opened it, and pulled out a piece of paper stating £10. The dealers to a man said: 'A a a a h!'

As he rummaged for the fourth envelope, some dealers began to jeer and heckle as if he was on the television programme Wheel of Fortune. As he pulled out his choice, one very tall dealer growled: 'Choose another one.'

Lucky for him, the recipient ignored this advice. The piece of paper in the envelope stated £1000. As he read it aloud, the dealer started jumping for joy. The dealing room was immediately reverberating with dealers' roars. This might have been the FA Cup Final.

The dealer for the rest of the afternoon walked around the dealing room like a king who had just inherited his throne.

News of Tudorbury's lucky dip travelled beyond the company on a private underground grapevine, helping dealers to entice former professional colleagues to Tudorbury. Cash prizes were the norm here, they said. And: 'Never will you go hungry.' Referring to Tudorbury's high (2%) commissions, and the lucky dip, one new dealer remarked: 'I can have my cake and eat it too.'

At this stage, the dealing room at Tudorbury Securities was to starting to resemble an overcrowded parking lot. Too little space, not enough telephones, and not enough desks. Two dealers were often sharing one internal extension and usually the dealer who did the least business suffered because he was shifted from one extension to another. One dealer commenting on this state of affairs said:

'There's no room at the inn.'

New applicants galore were now being interviewed, and the thumbscrews on present dealers were being applied. Some Tudorbury dealers did not by and large approve of this pressure, turning their backs on the motivational speeches, and threats of the sack.

Dealers would walk onto the dealing floor holding cardboard boxes loaded with coffees, crisps, mineral water, sandwiches and sweets. They would have stocked up from the cafe opposite the Tudorbury Building, whose most prominent server was a not always lucky Tudorbury client.

Like the vendor at an American baseball game, a dealer would parade on the dealing floor and distribute these items, maybe while a speech was being made.

Tudorbury dealers were often bored. Some dealers would roll up written sales pitches and memos of the day into balls, to chuck them at their colleagues. Dealers everywhere were aiming and ducking, finding it amusing that colleagues were distracted while talking to clients on the telephone. The dealing manager would hardly bat an eyelid. He was preoccupied with handling the ever mounting complaints which were pouring into Tudorbury's offices.

Another favourite pastime was pasting adverts and share tips on the pillar in the middle of the dealing floor. In one edition of *Private Eye*, dealers found a picture of a band of marksmen on a roof, in the context of the controversial IRA killings in Gibraltar. Dealers gathered round one afternoon and with a few deft strokes of the pen transformed the marksmen into imaginary clients, writing in those gentlemen's suggested comments regarding the failed performance of a Tudorbury recommended share. The picture was then enlarged onto A3 size paper, and pasted onto the pillar.

Another pin-up was a four or five line share tip whose print size was extremely small. A dealer enlarged it about 300 times, which seemed to make a mockery of what was actually written.

Basically they were deriding the shares they were selling, as well as giving their creative minds something to get to grips with.

After the August Bank holiday, dealers were back enjoying a round of selling on the Norton Group. Their enthusiasm, along with the lucky dip that helped to promote it, was curtailed by the arrival, not for the first time of the DTI's official, Mr Pink.

Mr Pink stayed two and a half weeks this time. One dealer expressed the opinion this was two and a half weeks too long. Most were worried. Was this Tudorbury Securities' last tango?

One black dealer was told he had been selected to talk to Mr Pink. In a panic he started analysing why, of all people, him. A colleague whispered in his ear: 'Don't do it.'

Fortunately for the dealer, this order turned out to be a practical joke and he was not required to proceed.

Tudorbury Securities had provided for Mr Pink an office on the second floor wherein he could plough through his paperwork in peace. Meanwhile some hoped the company could get on with *its* work in peace.

Mr Pink was spending much time going through Tudorbury's books, and some randomly chosen share transactions. Dealers' morale, never stable, plummeted to new depths.

Mr Pink expressed a desire to listen to the recently installed dealing room tapes, and dealers dreaded this might come about.

All sales pitches were confiscated after RAI Hamilton appeared on the dealing floor and announced: 'Hand over any sales pitches you have lying about. I must let Mr Pink see a sample.'

Two dealers were very wary of this, and agreed: 'We will never see our pitches again.' To date they have indeed been proven right.

Dealers were now left without vital written ammunition as old Tudorbury recommendations such as BOM Holdings and Swanyard Studios were reappearing on the daily selling menu.

New dealers who knew nothing of these stocks desperately needed proper written sales pitches, and the dealing director assured them that new ones were being prepared.

The Tudorbury compliance officer, who was suffering from a bad bout of flu, escorted one dealer into Mr Pink's office one afternoon. Straining to speak, he introduced both parties, and carefully announced to the dealer:

'We are here to help the DTI in their investigations. We have nothing to hide. So don't be afraid. Answer all Mr Pink's questions to the best of your ability.'

Mr Pink interrogated the dealer on matters such as sales tactics and training methods. He threw in here and there a few tricky questions related to the management of the company. At one stage, RAI Hamilton put his head round the door to check all was going well, and made a few wisecracks. After a full two hours, the DTI inspector said:

'I know you're busy, and so I'm grateful you've given me so much of your time. You can now get back on the dealing floor and sell stocks.'

Another dealer who saw Mr Pink proved less composed. From outside the office, a raising of voices could be heard. No doubt Mr Pink was doing his job. The dealer was also doing his.

Dealers upstairs were agog to hear feedback on what some termed 'The Inquisition'. All were curious to find out what Mr Pink might be searching for and what tactics he might use.

A few dealers who had not already done so started to query their professional future, and the goodies that came with it. Could they hang onto their nice cars? For how much longer could they maintain their luxury flats? Could they keep enjoying £25 a head gourmet lunches? Would they carry on fattening their waist lines and wallets, and thinning their work-loads? One dealer remarked nervously to another:

'The Indians are catching up with the Cowboys.'

Worries vanished with startling rapidity after Mr Pink's departure. Dealers were reassured as to the company's future prospects. Mr Pink's stay had taken him through the annals of Tudorbury Securities, top to bottom, round and round, inside out, dealers were told. And Tudorbury Securities was still around.

The DTI inspector had been told that the tape machine was broken, making it difficult for him to listen to any of the dealers' sales pitches. Nonetheless, for future reference, individuals would bear responsibility for what they told clients, RAI Hamilton made clear:

'It's you they'll be going after, not me,' he said.

Dealers were supposed now to be back into the high gear of selling stocks and shares. However, the postal strike had delayed the arrival of many potential leads. Some dealers had worn down their frail client bases, and had no one new to ring.

It was not long before dealers started hovering around the dealing director, moaning: ' I need new leads.' Their lack of business kept dealers interested in 'Acid House'.

Some dealers found this new craze more exciting than their familiar drink and drugs exploits. They seized on every exposé article on the subject in the tabloid press, reading it aloud. Dealers identified with the subjects of these press reports, yet made sure to deride them too.

At around this time the controversial pop-song: ' We call it Acieed ' was top of the UK Charts. One female dealer enjoyed ringing a pop music telephone line, and would bop at her desk, with the receiver jammed to her ear.

'Acieed! Acieed! ' she would chant dreamily, and the dealers would join in.

Certain dealers would appear to be plotting their own escapades into Acid Houses in stage whispers that could sometimes be heard all over the dealing floor.

Competition at this stage was introduced to encourage subscription sales of the Tudorbury Investments newsletter. The five dealers who in a single given day gained the most new subscriptions from regular clients were to be awarded a 'night out on the town' with RAI Hamilton.

The prize turned out to be a mundane visit to the theatre for ANY Tudorbury dealer who wanted to go. The production to be seen was ' Dreams in an Empty City' by Stephen Sewell, at the Lyric Theatre, Hammersmith. RAI Hamilton had already seen it, and so would not show up. He urged all dealers not to miss the play as its theme was the stock market crash of 1987.

Most of Tudorbury's staff showed up, and were on their best behaviour. Some put on a show of being real theatre buffs, although night-clubs were more their thing.

' Dreams in an Empty City' was an intelligent play that required concentration in its viewers. As the play started, the merry band from Tudorbury, naturally the noisiest in the auditorium, gave the audience of about 50 an unwelcome lift.

One young dealer, restless after five minutes, began to squirm in his seat like a goldfish that has been removed from its bowl. A colleague furiously whispered in his ear that he should call on the few manners he knew for the rest of the evening.

The intermission at last arrived, and dealers made a beeline for the bar, ordering double gin and tonics, rounds of white wine, and pints of their beloved beer.

The young dealer referred to above announced:

'I'm popping out to McDonalds. I'm starving.'

His colleague who had previously reprimanded him snapped:

'For fuck's sake, didn't you eat earlier? Nobody leaves a theatre for a Big Mac and fries. Isn't it about time you learnt some manners?'

Notwithstanding, the dealer nipped out to McDonalds. Meanwhile the second half of the play started. By this stage, dealers had a new freshness about them. A few drinks, a few snacks, and a few minutes to unwind had brought back their worldweary tolerance, perhaps even with some hope of their understanding the next half.

Five minutes into the second half, the dealer who had gone to McDonalds rushed back into the darkened auditorium, clutching a gin and tonic. He was a little taken aback to discover Tudorbury Securities staff had changed its seating arrangements just for the hell of it.

Some of the Tudorbury administration staff present were particularly inept at grasping the details of the production due to its technical nature. Some of the dealers, however, were starting to identify with certain characters portrayed.

At the finale, the Tudorbury Securities contingent gave the cast a round of wholehearted applause. Many were desperately trying to convey a level of sophistication and breeding, as if they went to the theatre every week, instead of once in a blue moon. Secretly, some were pining for a night of dancing and debauchery into the small hours of the morning, as was their wont.

Afterwards, Tudorbury dealers crowded out the bar again, to tank up before renegotiating the cold dark night. About half scurried off for a REAL night on the town, while others remained upon the entry of the cast they had just seen in performance.

These dealers casually endeavoured to give the cast the impression they were great patrons of the Arts. One young dealer, having learnt the knack of doing 'megadeals' only a few weeks previously, started boasting what a brilliant wheeler dealer he was. He fingered his Filofax leisurely as he droned on. The actors and actresses raised their eyebrows politely, and only occasionally smirked.

The dealers were taking time to realise that the cast was just as laid back and down to earth as they were.

The next day, dealers reminisced about the production, and its electronic lighting effects. They could not forget the replica electronic ticker tape. One dealer spoke for the majority when he opined:

' We should have a ticker-tape like that here, quoting prices of the stocks we do, every two seconds. That'd get the dealing room really revved up.'

A colleague shouted:

' BOM down ¼. Chemex down ½. Really those are the two announcements that should appear first on the ticker tape.'

He was referring to recent price changes. The dealers almost collapsed with laughter.

The excitement in licensed dealing as a profession had long since waned. Dealers were constantly searching for a new and stimulating means of maintaining a buzz on the dealing floor.

Help was however at hand. RAI Hamilton was to herald a new direction for Tudorbury Securities as he summoned dealers and staff one afternoon to his office on the second floor. All were ready and waiting when his petite and devoted assistant glided out announcing:

' Ladies first. Gentlemen second.'

Inside the office, staff stood round sipping champagne, as Hamilton smilingly declared:

' This is to mark the second anniversary of Tudorbury Securities. We're here, and we're here to stay. Whilst others have come and gone, we wait for the dust to settle. Meanwhile, we grow and grow.'

His entire staff was captivated as Hamilton explained that the company had survived the scrutiny of the DTI, and that investment bankers were looking to do a deal with Tudorbury. Great things, he insisted, lay ahead.

At this point, a toast was proposed — to Tudorbury. All present raised their long-stemmed crystal glasses and chanted: 'Hear hear.'

Ex-Harvard, ex-Sheridan, ex-Eyas, ex-London & Norwich, ex-DPR, ex-Fox Milton, ex-Empire Futures, ex-Buckingham, ex-Bailey McMahon dealers had crowded out the room. When before had such a colourful array of dealers with chequered pasts been gathered together under one roof?

Hamilton next congratulated the founder dealers, of whom only a few remained. Then a manager proposed a toast to Hamilton, in tones husky with idolatry, after which all present again lifted their long stemmed glasses, and chanted: 'Hear hear.'

Dealers then downed their glasses, and some started planning how they would 'get high' that night. One manager who was very obviously tipsy started chatting up a female clerk. She recoiled from him, slipping amidst the others.

'He's revolting,' she whispered in a dealer's ear.

Many decided to call it a day. Others stayed around, speculating as to what brilliant prospects destiny held in store for Tudorbury. Only a small band of astute share-pushers could interpret the shifting of the tide.

Before the end of September 1988, a Tudorbury manager abruptly departed. A team of experienced dealers had fought for his removal, on grounds that he did not care enough for their interests.

'On your way Smiler,' wisecracked one dealer. A more sympathetic female dealer remarked:

'He looked dapper coming in, and dapper going out.'

Appearing on the dealing floor to announce his manager's departure, Hamilton quipped:

'There seems to have been some question as to who is really running Tudorbury. I always thought it was me.'

Dealers laughed heartily. They felt this manager had merely had his comeuppance, because less than a fortnight previously he had sacked a new dealer for poor sales performance, without in their opinion giving him a proper chance.

One dealer suddenly developed an obsession with the departed manager, and started imitating him with startling accuracy throughout the day. He would pretend sometimes to be this manager reprimanding staff. Once, he called out to a colleague in the ex-manager's posh drawl:

'- - - - - - , your performance has been lamentable.' The dealer visibly jumped. It took him a few seconds to catch on, then he started panting:

'For fuck's sake,' he screamed: 'You almost had me there.'

Particularly when business waned, the dealer continued imitating this manager, making him into a laughing stock. He even pretended to be this poor man organising a lucky dip, which so amused dealers that the charade would last five, ten, even 15 minutes. The dealer's blandness of facial expression was flawlessly accurate, whilst his shaking fingers nimbly reproduced the compulsive and nervous manner in which the manager had smoked his cigarettes, puff by puff.

Meanwhile, the exodus of employees was steady. One clerk was leaving the company, so he said, to secure his future. On his last day a huge signed card was given to him by the dealers. Suddenly, a strippogram that they had secretly summoned appeared. Lo and behold, it was a transvestite! Dealers lounged around the room swigging beer, and watching the fun. Incoming calls were diverted, the switchboard having been informed of events. Clients wanting to sell stock would just have to wait.

The strippogram swaggered onto the dealing floor in a beautiful black wig. He was clad in a tight miniskirt and sheer black stockings. No less authentic underneath, he had on black knickers and a matching brassiere. Although his body was as curvacious as that of Venus herself, he could not help looking what he was, namely a man in drag.

The transvestite proceeded to greet everybody in a high pitched yet somehow manly voice. Then he swivelled to face the embarrassed clerk, trilling out his name seductively. Wriggling his hips, he grandly declared:

' I've been summoned here today to let you know we love you.'

The clerk was frowning. The blood seemed to have drained from his face. Unexpectedly, he took to his heels, darting behind a back

The Tudorbury dealers enjoy a light moment on the dealing floor with a transvestite (third from right).

row of desks. Gritting his teeth, the transvestite gave chase, displaying a most unfeminine vigour. The dealers did all they could to help him in his task.

Frantically, the victim jumped over desks, contorting his body to escape the transvestite's embrace. He dodged about, and dealers heckled him, betting that the transvestite would catch him almost immediately. They might have been spectators at a cock-fight.

The man in woman's clothing finally caught up with him, and embraced him. The clerk was now at a standstill, trembling at what might be to come.

The transvestite read aloud a cheeky verse whilst dealers gulped down their beers and wolf whistled. The atmosphere suggested that the popular singer James Brown was putting in a guest appearance. Dealers needed no armtwisting to join in a sing-song initiated by the transvestite:

'For he's a jolly good fellow, for he's a jolly good fellow . . . '

Meanwhile, the transvestite embarked on a FULL strip. His legs were as smooth as alabaster, while his waist was petite and tapered. Only his crotch gave away his sexual identity. All this was a shocking sight.

He then stretched out his arms in a mock erotic gesture primarily towards the clerk, but encompassing the dealing floor at large. He danced a sprightly little jig. Suddenly confronting the clerk, he reached out and appeared to slobber over him, attempting to plant a kiss.

The clerk hit out feebly trying to slip from his grasp. The transvestite held on for dear worth, hugging him like a bear. When with his face as red as a furnace, the clerk ceased to struggle and the transvestite moved in for the kill.

The clerk looked like a victim thrown to the lions, with the transvestite being the gladiator. The dealers were like the crowds in the Colosseum, roaring for action.

'Rape him, thrash him,' came the cries from the mob.

Why had a transvestite been selected? — Any victim who could not match up to the dealers' macho image of themselves deserved in their opinion no better. Dealers' own sense of masculinity was doubtless given a boost when they were treated to this spectacle.

Just as history repeats itself, so did Tudorbury's share recommendations. Again the Norton Group appeared on the menu, this time at 15p. The shares were available by the bucketful, Hamilton announcing three million were to be cleared. Some dealers hoped that it might prove a winner.

Nonetheless, most found it hard to sell the shares. By way of motivating them, Hamilton introduced a nice little cash incentive. Cash on top of 2% commission would be paid for Norton shares sold. Dealers put out of their minds the fact that the Norton share price had earlier dropped from 38p to 15p. Some determined on browbeating clients who would not necessarily welcome another 'recovery stock'.

A new stack of leads was now ready. Dealers knew the only way to gain access to these was to offer the punters Norton shares. To prepare themselves for this fray, some dealers nipped round to their favourite pub The Two Chairmen, where they downed beer and cocktails. Thus fortified, they felt ready for anything.

The Two Chairmen Pub in Westminster, just around the corner from New Scotland Yard, where Tudorbury dealers take refuge from the dealing floor.

While this next sales campaign was underway, the Norton Group opened the throttle for an acquisition in the United States. Dealers read about this in the newspapers, noting also news of the vendor placing in the shares. Some suspected then the Norton Group's share price might drop even further. How far, no one could say, but Tudorbury clients, buying on the strength of potential short term gain, might not be impressed.

However, recent events affecting the Norton Group could be presented in a way that would impress clients. Consequently, some dealers were feeling a new boldness.

One dealer announced a new term to describe a fall in share prices — 'spanking'. This term nicely conveyed the effect a fall in share prices had on clients, and, more importantly, gave some of the dealers a significant sexual thrill. Dealers would then shout:

'What's the spanking price on Norton shares today?'

Or if the telephone lines lit up to register an incoming call, a dealer would quip:

'Someone's ringing for a spanking.'

Adverse comment on the Norton Group appeared in the Investors Chronicle (14 October 1988) to this effect.

. . . 'Although the terms of the deal appear reasonable, and tax losses may shade the PE ratio down, the original Norton business is still a drag. The shares have little to recommend them and the offer should be declined.'

Naturally, Tudorbury dealers avoided mentioning this to their clients, but they had to say something when the share price dropped further. One dealer kept pleading:

'We got it wrong, sir. We just got it wrong.'

A new punter, who had just picked up some Norton shares, wrote to his dealer, saying:

'We haven't got off to a good start, have we?'

One dealer went so far as to pin to the pillar on the dealing floor a written warning:

'Remember, shares can plummet, as well as go down,' a travesty of the standard type of wealth warning:

'Investments can go down as well as up.'

Tudorbury Securities invited its clients who had picked up Norton shares to participate in the vendor placing. Clients were ringing at this stage, inquiring why the share price had been falling, especially after Tudorbury Securities had so avidly recommended the investment.

One ex-Bailey McMahon dealer rang a potential punter one evening after market hours, and invited him to buy some Norton shares. The punter seemed to find the whole conversation most interesting.

The next morning, the dealer rang the punter at his work, rather than at his home where he had got through to him the previous evening. On the other end of the line a receptionist announced: 'Hello, FIMBRA.'

The dealer immediately hung up. He started savagely patrolling the dealing floor. 'Just my luck,' he groaned. 'My client must be working for FIMBRA.'

This gave many dealers a nasty turn. But a deeper twist of the knife was enacted by the arrival of two punters to see their dealer. Such a practice was not uncommon, and so naturally the dealers were off their guard.

The two punters in question were perhaps delighted to view Tudorbury's dedicatory Royal plaque in the entrance hall, but the pair behaved very suspiciously on the dealing floor. They said to their dealer:

'Our wives are shopping in the City, so we're free for a few hours. We're interested in how you do things here, so fill us in.'

The dealers politely said that Tudorbury Securities acted in the interests of its clients, so they could both feel secure in the quality of the firm's share recommendations.

One of the punters asked questions like these:

'Tell me, are you paid commission only? Do you work on a terminal system (i.e. produce certain results or leave the company)? Do you offer certain shares, and those only? Do you have a personal target?'

The dealer was flummoxed as to how much he should give away, then was alerted that these two punters were in fact the strong arm of the law.

A feeling of unease rippled through the company as they left. Dealers were instructed that these two punters should receive no advice to buy standard Tudorbury recommendations including Swanyard Studios, and the Norton Group. They should only be recommended higher-priced shares.

Dealers were feeling the pinch as the anniversary of the stock market crash was upon them. For various reasons, punters would not come into the market. Some were superstitious, others were more or less broke. Most were still weeping over the heap of ashes which had replaced their profits during the 1987 bull market.

Some dealers, to entice the punter, would say:

'Remember the American Election is coming in a few weeks. We think the market will go up if the Republicans win, but down if it's the Democrats.'

A Tudorbury dealer examines the dealing room notice boards displaying sales figures upon which high commission is paid.

This pearl of wisdom would give the punter a sense of security, conveying that someone cared enough to monitor the economic conditions of the day.

One dealer was delighted when a picture of his own racing car featured along with his name in a popular motor racing magazine. He stormed onto the dealing floor shouting:

'I can't believe it!'

Some dealers were impressed, but alas not all. One dealer commented in the immortal style of Rhett Butler, the protagonist in Gone With The Wind:

'Frankly I couldn't give a damn.'

The dealer who owned the racing car also had a part share with some other dealers in a race horse, currently although not very successfully being groomed for stardom.

A recently introduced daily cash incentive for 'opening' new clients was suddenly abolished. Dealers resented this, and became correspondingly reluctant to open up new clients. Rewards for their work had to be immediate.

One day Hamilton ushered a visitor round the dealing floor. Some dealers viewed him with great suspicion. One dealer mused aloud:

'Who is that?'

'Don't you know,' said his colleague.

'He's a big one. That's the one and only Dan Dane.'

The first dealer dropped his jaw, and an 'Oh' fell from his lips like dry sand on the scorched desert.

'He didn't recognise me,' continued the dealer, 'because I no longer have a beard. But I'll never forget HIM.'

'Back in the Sheridan days,' he continued, 'Dan came to give us the pitch on the benefits of an up and coming company. He brought with him an overhead projector, transparencies, printed handouts, the works.'

The dealer smirked:

'I remember firing hard questions at him. None of us were interested in what he had to say.'

In fact, many Tudorbury dealers had heard about Dan Dane. He was a director of Renaissance, the unlisted American company referred to earlier in the book.

By this stage a single dealer had been appointed by Hamilton specifically to push shares in Renaissance, in return for very high commissions. Eagerly, the dealer had established himself as the 'Renaissance specialist,' and had been known to scream at colleagues who after a certain time attempted to jump on the lucrative Renaissance bandwagon. His usual sales pitch for the stock started with:

'Have you got a little money you'd like to tuck away till Christmas, Sir?'

Some clients came in 'heavy'. With the new year upon us, there has been little sign of price movement, or more seriously of liquidity in the stock.

Renaissance shareholders had been ringing in daily, wondering if the big deal that may have proposed six months earlier had materialised. They really need not have bothered. The Renaissance specialist would say:

'I believe it's finally happening. We don't want to get out of the stock now. I'm meeting one of the directors shortly, and I should have some definite details.'

By this time, Dan Dane had been seen in the Tudorbury building on various occasions. For what specific purpose, the dealers did not know.

If any punter sold his Renaissance shares — against the specialist's vehement recommendation — it almost went without saying that the specialist would have to offload them on another punter.

Frequently, Hamilton was seen on the dealing floor with an entourage of mysterious businessmen in elegant suits. Doubtless if they had spoken, their nationalities would have been revealed. Before their entrance, the dealing manager would shout:

'I want everybody on the phone pitching, or at least to look busy. We're having some important visitors.'

A buzz would then emanate from dealers who spent most of the day idling, and most picked up the telephone receivers, flicking through client lead cards in a methodical fashion. Suddenly it was all systems go.

'What's the Footsie (FT 100 Index) doing? . . . Indication price on BOM please . . . Dollar against Deutschmark . . . Is Wall Street up? . . . (in a very business-like tone of voice). Thank you.'

These and similar remarks were made until the visitors had departed into the lift, safely out of hearing. Suddenly, paper darts would wend their way across the dealing floor like a flight of doves. Some dealers would launch into their afternoon 'skulk'.

During one month, there had been a massive retailing spree on a few of Tudorbury's share recommendations, so much so that on one historic day, the dealing room did a whopping £275,000 worth of business. Late afternoon on that day, champagne on the dealing floor flowed like water from the Niagara Falls. Dealers were pouring their umpteenth drinks into their funnel shaped paper cups as Hamilton exclaimed:

'Never in the history of Tudorbury do I recall this amount of business being done on a single day. This shows that you can do it. We are the best, and you are the best — in the City. This is what it's all about. Well done!'

A feeling of springtime exploded into the atmosphere, like fragrant gas. Only the experienced dealers felt the pending season, a hard cold winter of discontent.

For most, time was standing still. The stock market need not have existed for all they cared. They lived for the glory of the day. 'Carpe Diem,' they might have said, for tomorrow may have belonged not to them.

Divisions within the Tudorbury dealing force were becoming naturally pronounced. The most authoritative faction without a doubt incorporated the tough and seasoned ex-Harvard dealers. Here were the Spartans of the day. There were few indeed who could put one over these warriors of the Securities Industry. Some would say they had experienced the best sales training anywhere, and mostly on the job. Here was the old school of dealers, last guardians of an Ancien Régime that was crumbling about their feet.

As far removed from these as fire from ice was a faction that came from afar. ' Costa Rica,' they muttered vaguely, but the old hands knew by hearsay that they had been at 'The Big M'. This was nothing to do with McDonalds Hamburgers, but was simply Bailey McMahon, the Dublin based pusher of House of Holland and other unlisted stocks.

These were the barbarians, most of whom sold with a ravenous enthusiasm, delivering loud pitches and pulling in money as if by magic, partly from clients that they may have brought in with them, and whom they might spirit away if and when they should quit this latest haven. They were hungry. Some Tudorbury dealers left the business to them. Would time prove them wise?

More silent and more deadly were the kamikaze. With grim smiles on their faces, they had stepped out of the screaming world of futures pushing, stealthily into the warm glow of Tudorbury Securities. From the first day of arrival, they gave their hearts to the business. They were aiming at the meanest clients and pitching bang on target. They would forge on blindly into the securities battlefield, burning all boats in front of, as well as, behind them.

Some of these had been top professionals at DPR and Empire Futures. They may have known little about shares, but who could teach them anything about the hard sell? The kamikaze successfully dealt with Tudorbury's six month dormant client lists.

Despite their diverse origins, these factions could work in harmony. When clients complained, it was, however, the Spartans who coped best.

Once, one of the kamikaze remarked:

' It's still churn 'em and burn 'em, isn't it? '

The Spartans all glared at him:

' We're not selling Futures here,' a spokesman growled: ' Who knows, Tudorbury's next cash incentive may be round the corner. God knows you'll need the same punters then. They're your bread and butter, don't you forget it.'

Amidst all this, Tudorbury Securities was operating under a shroud of mystery. Some thought Michael Lucas, chairman of BOM Holdings, was at the helm. As reported in the *Daily Mail*, he did in fact have a stake in Tudorbury Securities.

The latest switchboard receptionist was complaining of dodgy phone calls. She was a woman who despite preserving her looks had some years on her shoulders. Dealers preferred the young bimbo type who would give them a good time and no hassle.

The Tudorbury Securities merry-go-round whirls on, not so fast now perhaps as it was but still relentless. Some dealers are tiring of the pace, but brakes are being applied by forces outside of themselves.

The City Programme, a popular TV financial show, featured one week an investor who announced his disgust at the telephone sales industry, and warned of its dangers, brazenly inviting the hard sell experts to ring HIM.

The next morning, dealers at Tudorbury Securities were summoned by the dealing manager for a fireside chat. Tudorbury had just completed a mailshot of some 50,000 punters. Everyone was warned not to 'bull into' these people as any could secretly or otherwise represent FIMBRA or the DTI, and not to indulge in the practices criticised in the programme.

The sharedealing industry remains multifaceted, although it is shrouded in a new cloak of respectability, viz the Financial Services Act (1986). As leading stock market guru Robert Beckman has so aptly pointed out, arranging for the securities industry to police itself through the self regulatory authorities is like putting Dracula in charge of the Blood Bank.

Amongst the authorities under whose wing grave wrongs are still actively practised, FIMBRA is prominent. Many had questioned FIMBRA's elevation to SRO status in the first place. Sadly, some of these doubts may have been well founded.

Regulations, according to FIMBRA's only full time investigator Don Collins, stipulate that dealers who join a firm with full FIMBRA membership are subject to stringent rules. Collins claims that these dealers must submit an application form for registration, and are NOT allowed to give investment advice to the public anyway for 90 days until the member firm for which they are working has been contacted in writing by FIMBRA regarding the outcome of the individual's application.

This rule is breached at Tudorbury Securities as a matter of course. Dealers who walk in there, whether from other sharedealing firms, or off the streets, usually start dealing immediately, before they submit their FIMBRA personal registration forms. Sometimes Tudorbury Securities proposes to submit their forms to FIMBRA after the individuals concerned have been there for a few days.

As Tudorbury Securities is responsible for sending in dealers' forms to FIMBRA, the directors are presumably aware of what is going on. In accordance with the definitions of FIMBRA investigator Don Collins, a number of members of the public who have recently dealt with Tudorbury Securities may have been given investment advice by an unregistered dealer.

Information on whether an individual within a FIMBRA authorised firm is permitted to deal is unavailable to the public on the telephone from FIMBRA or SIB respectively, although each body may refer an inquirer to the other body, and officials within these bodies are not always sure what to say on the subject. 'Go and ask the company concerned whether its dealers are permitted to deal', both FIMBRA and SIB have suggested. These bodies are also quick to confirm whether a *company* is fully authorised.

If, however, the client does discover, by some miraculous unofficial means, that an individual should not be dealing, he rightly has grounds for a complaint. On whom should he lay the blame?

It is the directors and the compliance officers of FIMBRA firms who are responsible for explaining to dealers and implementing these FIMBRA regulations, according to Collins. Obviously then, the directors and compliance officer at Tudorbury Securities are not doing this part of their job. Who should be policing a fully authorised FIMBRA firm in this situation? FIMBRA's compliance department, says Collins.

There is evidence that Tudorbury has had contact with this compliance department, as well as with FIMBRA's legal and investigative departments. Why then have Tudorbury Securities been conducting themselves in this way?

Many dealers at Tudorbury believe that they are allowed to give investment advice to the public while waiting for their firm to hear from FIMBRA with regard to the outcome of their personal applications. However, Collins points out that the concept of 'interim authorisation' does not exist for individuals working in a firm with full FIMBRA authorisation such as Tudorbury Securities.

Of course, most dealers get their ideas about regulation and authorisation from the national press which may have given them the impression that 'interim authorisation' while applications are being processed is the norm.

The frequency and openness with which these particular breaches of FIMBRA regulations are enacted tend to suggest that FIMBRA as a policing body is at the very least inadequate.

Collins points to further inadequacies within FIMBRA, possibly in the computer system and staffing arrangements. These, as well as FIMBRA's apparent breakdown of communication between internal departments may have led to Collins' recent claim that FIMBRA had no record of a Tudorbury dealer's personal application.

However, the registration form in question had been datestamped by the FIMBRA office twice, and was possibly lodged in the FIMBRA offices even as Collins was issuing his denials.

On top of all this, the FIMBRA registration form in question had been tampered with. While his registration form was somewhere in transition between Tudorbury Securities and FIMBRA, a written statement which the applicant had never made was sellotaped over the original version of the form, and was wrongly attributed to him.

Don Collins of FIMBRA claimed that the registration form in question had never been treated as an application for registration. However, the applicant had not understood this from FIMBRA, and had been told actively to the contrary by directors of Tudorbury Securities.

Regulations state that if FIMBRA's Council at any time decides to refuse to register any individual as a registered individual, the member and the individual concerned shall be notified in writing of that decision, and shall each be separately entitled to appeal. However, Collins proposes that this regulation applies only to registration forms that have passed through some mysterious initial scanning process which is apparently immune from this regulation, although FIMBRA has no obligation to inform the individual applicant of the existence of this initial scanning process, let alone its conclusions.

Of course, FIMBRA are only one of the SROs.

Interestingly, amongst obstacles to gaining individual authorisation by The Securities Association (TSA) — which incorporates the Stock Exchange itself — disloyalty to the whole system may feature more strongly than wrongdoing, as illustrated in the case of one sharedealer who was actually refused TSA authorisation mainly for talking to the national press. But some dealers who have pushed shares at outfits like Bailey McMahon get TSA approval, not to mention some who were trained at firms like Harvard Securities.

The bucket shops are inseparably part of the City, and indeed the name refers to the old fashioned broker who would throw clients' purchase orders in a bucket, to be processed after the share price had moved to the client's disadvantage.

Regulatory authorities, stockbrokers, and bucket shops join forces in an exclusive club. As in these hard times the City closes ranks to survive, the rotting backbone to its respectable facade is proving even harder to uncover.

Chapter Twelve

WIZARDS AT WORK

The typical dealer feels stifled in ordinary surroundings. It is not his lot to work for a living. Honest toil has no appeal, indeed is alien to every fibre of his being. He craves to ride on the crest of a wave, and once there, hangs on by a battle of wits, untormented by conscience.

Such people all have some deep private mission in life, often taking the form of vengeance. Perhaps they are compensating for an overprotected childhood, or providing for a loved one. Otherwise they might be building an empire to rob the affluent, guided by a sense of social justice that may become perverted by personal greed.

These multifaceted people are rarely rotten to the core. Some believe at least aesthetically in what they are doing. Most find themselves in a different category from criminals.

Many sharedealers have started life shuffling papers, mending plugs, humping bricks round building sites, or sweating over their books in college.

The young dealer will often embark on an informal apprenticeship. Some artful dodger might take the budding cut-throat under his wing.

Woebetide if the apprentice tries to mislead his master. The elder one might metaphorically flay him alive and make sure he never works for a sharedealing outfit again. Should the master choose it, the apprentice's days as a salesman are numbered.

One young dealer picked up sales techniques from a more experienced colleague. Soon he was glibly saying: 'I'm as sure as I could be about this recommendation, Sir. I wouldn't be offering it to you if I wasn't. I want to be dealing with you in a year from now . . .'

Suddenly the young dealer was stashing money away. Then he made the mistake typical in one at his formative stage. He became too greedy and started trying to win over his mentor's clients where he didn't think they would be missed. But the clients had dealt with the master share salesmen over years. They affably related the boy's tactics, quoting his pitches word for word.

The master sinisterly confronted his apprentice: 'What the fuck are you doing nicking my clients?' 'They rang in,' said the apprentice. 'Like hell,' said the other. 'You're not talking to your fucking mother.

I wasn't born yesterday. You nicked my clients. If it happens again, I'll kill you. I'll smash your head into the ground, drag you downstairs, out of the building, and all the way to the Thames where I'll duck you.'

The easy relationship was rapidly restored. Any master less worldly than this one could not have handled that apprentice and could not have commanded his respect. They were like teacher and pupil in a very tough school.

A few female dealers are still exploiting clients' sex-drive. They make love to them down the telephone lines and persuade them to put their money in the direction that their loins urge. How do they manage it?

Their secret lies in a combined assault on the senses. Breathing heavily down the phone. A naughty joke here. A dash of innuendo there. A low seductive chuckle. Above all, exclusive attention.

When at the male client's insistence, the female dealer eventually meets him, she may be startled how ugly he is. He may also be weedy, stooping, deformed. He may limp and leer. Perhaps he is a miserable man destined for an unwanted bachelorhood.

An eternal truth becomes revealed. This sort of client puts money her way for all the wrong reasons. He craves to develop their relationship. This is a substitute for the affair he longs for. He is easy meat.

The ruthless female dealer will squeeze the last £500 out of him. Sex more than anything else in the world, sells shares.

The woman who makes it as a sharedealer must have cast-iron aplomb, and the exploitative spirit in her heart. Most females turn their backs on this way of making a living in disgust. It is too much akin to prostitution.

There comes a time when every sharedealer needs the advice and services of a broker. It is usual for him to force a professional relationship with some slightly dodgy individual, in an equally dodgy firm.

One top dealer would loaf about all day, lamenting the uncertain outcome of his FIMBRA application. When he pitched clients, his voice exuded the brash monotone authority of the burnt-out dealer.

Because of his reputation for hard selling, this dealer was assigned good clients by his dealing manager, and commanded respect everywhere on the floor.

However, his previous firm, although liquidated, would not lie down in its grave. The following harrowing incident seemed, at least temporarily, to make him old before his time.

The dealer, who shall be called Geoff, received a phone call at his current firm from his godfather. His godfather had invested £18,000 in Transworld Energy, through Geoff at another dealer. Geoff's father had told the godfather that his son dealt in stocks and shares, and would help him invest his capital wisely.

The commission paid by his previous firm for deals on Transworld Energy, or TWE as it was known, varied in size according to how many willing punters there were at any given period, but was always considerable.

Now, many months later, Geoff's godfather was shocked to receive official notification that his specially recommended investment had proved more or less worthless.

Naturally, he turned to his godson. Hence he was ringing him up at his present firm. He asked him out to lunch, so they could discuss the Transworld Energy situation, man to man.

Geoff wavered. This was not a lunch he could look forward to. He agreed a provisional date. After putting down the phone, he started to pace the dealing floor. 'That's my godfather,' he explained to some dealers who had eavesdropped on the conversation. 'He's been in TWE. That's not all that's on my mind. Two of my relatives have it as well.'

From the other end of the dealing room, a respected share salesman shouted out: 'You have no scruples.'

All listening laughed uneasily. Some dealers in the business had, in their time, pushed speculative stocks onto friends and relatives. Sometimes this rebounded, letting the cat out of the bag in terms of what the dealer really did for a living. It is nonetheless a fact that Geoff and the other dealers would not technically have known the fate of the stock they were selling. A few dealers, like Geoff, were caught up in circumstances beyond their control.

The financial rewards have always made it worthwhile for less scrupulous dealers to abuse clients' trust in them. Directors of the dealing firms have often enough turned a blind eye.

Some commissions available would enable an astute dealer to stash away up to hundreds of thousands of pounds for a year's work. It was enough to set him up for life.

Many dealers, particularly if intending to stay a while in the bucket shops, kept their professional activities secret from their families.

One young dealer was still living with his parents, who themselves had achieved eminence in demanding professional careers. They knew nothing, however, about the City and High Finance.

This youth became enmeshed in the rise and fall of several notorious share-pushers.

He told his parents little or nothing of his job changes or of his daily business on the dealing floor. They had no idea when he started working for a share pusher outside UK jurisdiction, but assumed he was still working in the City, while living at a friend's house. Likewise, they were ignorant of his periods of unemployment.

This young man, it might be argued, acted wisely in keeping details of professional commitments private. Shares or futures dealing demands a different way of life from most jobs. Dealers have to be alert to attack from every quarter, quick to seize on opportunities, and socially as well as professionally elastic.

For instance, one young man was until recently employed as a sharedealer in Paris. He worked from a fully equipped dealing room in a central high rise office block. At nights, he lodged in a luxury flat, by courtesy of a mega-rich fraudster, now languishing, not for the first time, in jail. The dealer is uneasy when he looks back on his experience. Speaking of his boss, he says:

'He's charming enough to those who cooperate with him, but it wouldn't do to cross him, even now. There are men the world over who will do anything for money.'

The young share salesman's life, let's face it, has never been comparable to the young doctor's or schoolmaster's. The unpredictable demands of his day might alarm his nearest and dearest, unless they are, or have been involved in sharp practice themselves.

Obviously, the father who has made his fortune out of the used car, or scrap metal businesses for instance, may not be surprised if he detects hereditary ruthlessness and cunning in his son as sharedealer. A chip off the old block, he might sometimes chuckle to himself.

The smooth operator may drink heavily and take drugs. He may womanise and party. He may do dodgy deals on the side. He may skip from firm to firm, picking up new clients, even as he discards the old. This is to be expected. It is the smooth operating sharedealer's apprenticeship.

If he is, however, to reach the top, the smooth operator must avoid excess at an early age. Every time he indulges in the wild life, he must secretly restrain himself. He doesn't want to wind up incurring AIDS, a damaged liver, or a permanently broken nose.

One thirty year old dealer would quite openly brag: 'I'm hooked on cocaine and casual sex. I don't expect to live beyond thirty-five. If I reach forty or over, I'm laughing.' Then he would gruffly warn the younger dealers: 'Don't you kids get into the state I'm in. Take care of your bodies.'

The dealer who wants to make the big time must ensure he drinks and socialises with such colleagues as are also destined for the big time. He should avoid keeping company with those who will become has-beens and drop-outs, or who will turn too upright.

The smooth operator who has made it is a type. He seems to have discovered the secret of eternal youth. In his forties, he may look fifteen years younger. His complexion remains fresh. His body probably has a natural tan as he may regularly flit to the Bahamas or other exotic places — maybe for only a few days at a time.

Here he hides from the various authorities or from vindictive clients. He will, furthermore, seize the opportunity to patronise the best restaurants, not to mention the casinos and nightclubs.

Everywhere he may distinguish himself by recklessly throwing around money, so serving staff will defer to him, and other customers will sit up and notice. The smooth operator is a natural exhibitionist.

Nor is he, professionally speaking, wasting time. He will meet kindred spirits in all these best places. Successful smooth operators are attracted to each other like magnets, and lesser mortals with something of the right spirit are more or less impure metals which the magnets catch.

Sometimes too, the dealer might pretend he is making a trip abroad. This is his cover. In reality, he would remain in the UK, perhaps to pull off a shady share deal without being watched.

Some keep fit at expensive clubs. Here not only do they keep their bodies slim, muscular and beautiful, but they again meet the right people. They will often go skiing, or indulge in other expensive sports with a childish glee.

The true professionals, the glittering stars around 40 years old upwards, who have made good their chequered careers, cannot usually avoid getting their names splashed about in the national press.

This publicity they turn to their own advantage. If it repels the majority of people, it attracts suitable prospective business partners.

These types were the bright boys at school who effortlessly bamboozled their teachers. They have stresses, but not the usual ones of family relationships on top of an honest day's toil and trouble.

Such smooth operators instinctively recognise others of their kind. They don't trust a word such people say on their own behalves, but listen to what they say of others behind their backs.

Misleading rumours are often spread about the licensed dealing community. This is called planting a seed.

Those who run bucket shops have been known to twist rumours to suit their own purpose, finding in them the facts they want to hear. They will come up with a reworking of the story that usually contains its measure of truth. Their version will furnish them with ammunition to do what they had intended all along.

A manager of one licensed dealer announced to his salesmen news of a new West End firm: 'They're paying dealers a basic £2,000 a month. It's a good offer,' he said. 'If you want to go there have the courtesy to tell me. And anyone who rings them on our phones during working hours will be sacked.'

He then took aside a female dealer. Downstairs in his executive suite, he screamed at her: 'You rang them today. You've been fucking talking to them. You're sacked!'

She stood her ground: 'I wasn't talking to them at all, and I'm not getting into a shouting match with you about it.'

'I'll check this out,' he said. 'Don't do any more dealing today. Give me a ring here in my office first thing tomorrow morning.'

She rang him the next morning as scheduled, and he oozed charm: 'I'm so sorry. I was misinformed. Wait till I catch the bastard who spread around the rumour about you. You've got your job back, if you want it . . . '

She returned to work reeling. Had this been a test of her loyalty? Mind you, she *had* made the call.

One frightening characteristic that, with certain notable exceptions, bucket shop dealers have in common is a general lack of real interest in and knowledge of the markets. Many are relative newcomers to the game.

The apprentice dealer may be highly successful at his job, and yet he too is likely to lack not just professional knowledge, but also interest in acquiring it. All too often his heart and soul are otherwise committed.

Many in career terms keep a second string to their bow. For instance, one stalwart, finding opposition to his staying 'in the game', returned to his first career, the service industry. He could by this stage afford the drop in income.

One ex-dealer indulged his penchant for dealing in property. This seemed an easy method of obtaining income without working for it. Some would say it was not unlike sharedealing. After selling shares for a small spell, he had accumulated a huge reserve of capital that was now proving useful.

If dealers can make clients money without they themselves losing out, most will do so.

Thus when the profit figures of Blacks Leisure, a quoted stock, turned out to be as good as expected, dealers hurriedly took their clients out at a small profit before all the 'mega clients' or 'real dealing men' came out, which might have depressed the share price.

Likewise, some hurried to get clients out of Helical Bar, after the shares had shot up from £2.78 to over £3.00 in the space of four days. Naturally, where possible, they made sure that they had got out of Helical Bar themselves first.

Here is a cause celebre. Money has been made, in the first place for themselves, in the second place for their clients. Time to let their hair down . . .

Dealers from countries such as Africa, Australia, Denmark, and the United States, bring their ethnic techniques into European firms. The dealing room flares into a cosmopolitan selling machine. It is a fireball blend that can make or break the firm in question. Sadly, it can also make or break its clients.

One young American dealer became a skilful operator, hard selling both shares and futures from a succession of London firms.

He started keeping work telephone numbers from family and friends. In case of emergency, the dealer instructed his relatives to send a telex or a telegram. All the secrecy was because he was now seeing the firms where he worked in their true light.

'Dodgy,' the dealer said to himself. 'This is really dodgy. My colleagues back in the States would be appalled if they knew what I was doing. But I'm having too much fun to give all this up. I'm becoming a *character*!'

This is precisely what the young dealer is. The bucket shop school, for instance, is in most dealers' view more *character*-building, more truly educational than University, than other careers, than travel, anything . . .

The dealer, having become a character, goes on to ride the hire 'em and fire 'em roller coaster of the various firms. He wears the mask of his character, and beneath it lurks a circus of uncontrolled personalities who have made him the dealer that he is.

Meanwhile, his ghost lives after him within the firms he has left, a model whose image and echoes fresh young recruits can adapt as they think fit. Thus is sustained a tradition.

Newcomers to bucket shops who prove successful are at an impressionable stage of their lives. Most often they are coming from a dead-end job, and are just desperate for money.

Otherwise, they might be fresh out of full-time education, and knowing nothing much of the world.

They might even be older men, trying to recapture their lost youth — in which case it is probably too late for them to develop into fully blown high pressure salesmen. That is a life's work.

The men who boss these youngsters, has-beens and fortune-seekers are in most cases building no monuments, creating no edifice that will sustain and enhance our community.

Their natural selfishness sometimes manifests itself as bounty, but no philanthropy melts their steel hearts. If they donate to charity, it is for tax purposes or to appease the right persons. Office parties are to instill gratitude in dealers, as a way of getting more business out of them.

Nor will they choose any but a few to follow in their footsteps. The dealing room at the now liquidated Walter Jacob & Co Ltd was typical of what was reserved for the hoi polloi.

Dealers here sat in tiny cubicles, which conveniently isolated them. They lacked proper facilities such as dealing screens. At one stage, they just rang clients, reading aloud written pitches for the highly speculative 'Magnacard' shares, and bellowing down the telephone lines: 'Magnacard! Magnacard! . . . !

Walter Jacob developed a controversial name in the industry, and after it had gone under, a few ex-dealers had the utmost difficulty in getting re-established to their satisfaction.

The sort of firm which turns dealers into telephone selling automatons may not fully enhance their development, but it may enable them to keep a useful distance from their clients.

In contrast, one dealer at Eyas Securities arguably made the mistake of getting to know his clients too well. He had the knack of gaining their trust, then persuading them to part with huge sums of money. Not yet out of his twenties, but looking and sounding older, this share salesman put his upper class accent to profitable use.

Over a period, he sold some £200,000 worth of shares in OTC traded Crane Holdings to a former client who then became famous throughout Eyas.

When the farmer came into Eyas Securities' offices to present his first cheque, dealers felt he was posing, and secretly laughed at him.

What a lot of money he was throwing about, they thought. One dealer even suggested behind his back that he might as well get the cash out of his building society in bank notes, and throw it into the Thames.

The farmer's dealer regularly topped up his holding with another dose of Crane shares. What a nasty medicine it was to prove.

Eyas dealers conspired to maintain a facade. When the farmer rang in, at regular intervals, to ask the price of Crane shares, no one was to tell him what it currently was, but was instead to quote the price he the client had last paid for the shares.

In this way the client would not feel that he was losing money. Most dealers cooperated in this manoeuvre. Most dreaded that he might insist on selling his Crane shares which could lead to a massive decline in the share price.

When Eyas Securities crashed, and the client discovered his massive loss on Crane Holdings, he felt humiliated and crushed. Never did he find out the real manner in which he had been treated.

The client's large holding of Crane shares had given a staggering commission of 4p a share to his dealer. The client naturally knew nothing of this.

From this one trade, the dealer had been able to pay back money borrowed from his bank for his Porsche, and to contribute towards the purchase of his expensive West End flat.

While working as a sharedealer, he had been enjoying an extravagant lifestyle, sometimes spending substantial sums on a night's entertainment for himself and a girl, as well as offering financial support to his steady girlfriend, and her children.

Furthermore, he had been known to make trips to the Continent, where he might meet up with old friends.

With the recent demise of Eyas Securities, the young man has allegedly left the country.

In no other work environment will the young and talented find such scope to indulge themselves or to burn out. Once they have tasted the fruits of sin, no matter what the regulatory environment dictates, there will be no looking back.

Chapter Thirteen

CAN THE LEOPARD CHANGE ITS SPOTS?

The veteran dealers of bucket shops are fighting a winning battle. They know they must adapt or die. They are learning to use their techniques more secretively, and from firms which do not live in terror of the national press. Thus, they are looking wisely to their futures.

Some Stock Exchange member firms have until recently delighted in turning down applications from share salesmen of licensed dealers.

'I'm afraid we have no vacancies,' they might say. One gem that a dealer encountered was: 'There seems little point in taking you on. When the market's down there's nothing for anybody to do. On the other hand, when the market's up, we've got more business than we can cope with coming in.'

Indolence, high living, and lack of immediate financial necessity have turned some dealers, still not thirty years old, into has-beens.

One dealer of the author's acquaintance saw himself as the best salesman at Tudorbury Securities. This was because he had done one good month there, after achieving good sales figures at Harvard Securities, his previous work place.

He begged two brokers at AJ Bekhor, who had been his colleagues at Harvard, to help him in there himself but they stuffily refused to cooperate.

The dealer sulked, then set about trying to do something for himself.

Another Tudorbury dealer pestered a colleague who had worked on the floor of the Chicago Exchange: 'Can you get me a job in the States?' he demanded. 'Do you think I have enough experience? Do you think I'd get on well there? I'm thirty years old and I want a future . . . '

'Maturity is an advantage in the States,' pointed out his colleague.

'Sounds better and better,' said the dealer.

One ex-bucket shop dealer was sacked from a well known City stockbroker after its chairman said to him: 'One of your clients owes us £8000. He's a bankrupt.'

The dealer quaked: 'He told me he had a £100,000 portfolio.'

'Don't you know, clients lie,' snapped his boss. 'Just like you used to lie in your previous work.' If this was the way he felt, why had he taken him on in the first place?

The selling of speculative stocks and all that this involves is in sharedealers' blood. This had constituted their formative training in the business and now they are being told to put the client first. Are their get rich quick days gone for ever?

Some are dropping out. Others change tactics, but inside themselves they die.

One ex-Harvard Securities whizz-kid, who graduated into a position as a sober broker with a well known firm said: 'It's not so very different here. We still have to squeeze money out of clients.'

Another ex-Harvard Securities dealer who had become a broker commented: 'I had to play it low-key at first. Now I sometimes punt out the stock. It's just like the old days at Harvard.'

One ex-Harvard dealer went to a stockbroker where he discovered, to his horror, that a director there had got some of his best share tips from Afcor Investments Ltd.

One stockbroker was, in his own words: 'Still a licensed dealer at heart.' He claims that to this end, he had a secret meeting with a Harvard manager, and asked if he could go back to Harvard, his previous work place.

'No way!' exclaimed the manager. 'Mind you, I'm not gloating. I know it's a tough world out there.'

One group of ex-Harvard brokers regularly punt out stocks at their Stock Exchange member firm. Their managers are well pleased with the levels of business they achieve, rewarding them with high commission payments.

Just as dodgy sales methods linger, so do dodgy connections. Some stockbrokers, who maybe ought not to be stockbrokers, do naughty little jobs on the side.

One dealer of the author's acquaintance was writing fortnightly newsletters for a continental share-pushing network (1988). His method was to re-work material from established magazines such as *What Investment* and the *Investors' Chronicle*. He was offered payment of £300 a throw, and was guaranteed anonymity.

His contact, a dealer working in Paris, flew to London and picked up his work, promising to pay him cash in French francs.

Shortly afterwards, the dealer received a phone call from his contact's boss in Paris: 'Yes, we liked your newsletter. It makes a change to get one that is readable.

'We want you to write these regularly. Pad out the text a bit more, or in print it looks like nothing. Be bullish too. The market is always going up . . . Which companies have you worked for?

'The usual,' said the dealer. 'I started at Harvard.'

The dealer gave him the number of his secret Swiss bank account, so further payments could be made, and he jotted down specifications for the next newsletter. He lastly gave him his fax number, so proofs of his work could be speedily transferred to him.

On that very day, the dealer had heard that his application with The Securities Association (TSA) had been successful.

The sharedealer effectively started living a double life. Respectable stockbroker by day, he became a dodgy newsletter writer by night. How long would he keep it up?

In the post A-Day commodities business, an enterprising individual was gathering his evidence. He was an executive of the now defunct DPR Futures.

He visited on appointment the so-called 'respectable' futures dealers where affable young account executives interviewed him on luxurious premises.

The firms, unlike his own DPR, were fully sanctioned by the Association of Futures Brokers and Dealers (AFBD).

Posing as a client, he asked all the typical questions. A tape-recorder, tucked away in his briefcase, recorded their eager sales pitches.

He gravely presented the fruits of his research to the regulatory authorities. Member firms, it seemed, might be using hard sell tactics. DPR, he claimed, wasn't necessarily the only one.

Sadly he did not save DPR from being wound up, with its assets frozen. The evil day had, however, been delayed for a long time.

Many DPR salesmen were not out of work for work for long. Bucket shop practitioners are survivors. The City firms that openly spurn them would secretly often like to have them.

Licensed dealers are the whipping boys of the City Establishment. Stockbrokers sanctimoniously magnify their defects, to make their own firms' virtues shine the whiter.

Hence the problem that ex-London & Norwich dealers encountered when trying to find work.

The long periods of unemployment, the problems over references, and the loss of face that the ex-London & Norwich dealers had suffered before getting re-established, led some to regret what they had become involved in.

Some succeeded only by insisting how they now wanted to disassociate themselves from that firm.

In reality, many had found their time at Harvard and at London & Norwich had been most enjoyable and lucrative. For a brief period they were paying the price of associating with controversial firms. Most reckoned, though, that soon all would be forgotten.

Two ex-London & Norwich dealers had started work at an options dealer. Allegedly at the intervention of a licensed dealer, one of these was sacked. Another ex-London & Norwich dealer became an insurance salesman for a major financial services group. An ex-London & Norwich dealer who had earned a great deal from placing Silverton shares was allegedly in the South of France, chartering a yacht he had bought.

Perhaps least fortunate of all was Neil Miller, for whom less doors in sharedealing seemed open now than ever before. He could console himself that he had earned a substantial sum from the sale of Silverton shares, although he was later to claim that he had had to meet some of London & Norwich's substantial expenses.

He had himself paid perhaps too high a price, in aggravating not just the investing public, but also some of his former staff who had acted on his orders. Some still resented how he had claimed from the start that London & Norwich was a Stock Exchange member firm.

It almost seemed as if Miller had to carry the can for the entire fiasco now that Pattinson Hayton had disappeared.

Some dealers in the surviving bucket shops are living on their nerves. A few in continental firms particularly still work under false names. When the chips are down, they don't wish to be associated with what they have been doing. They are likely to choose pseudonyms with the stamp of British reliability. They occasionally give themselves equivocal Christian names, such as 'Lord.'

Feeling restricted by the new legislation, some of the dealers at Tudorbury Securities started looking for victims within their group. They now wished to be seen as moral, and any scapegoats they could muster, would be landed with responsibility for the old sales methods.

They first picked on a quiet-spoken dealer in his early twenties, who for the purpose of this book shall be called Michael. His only crime was churning, at which his confrères were all old hands anyway.

One morning Michael earned himself a cash bonus of around £40, but due to a dental appointment, he would not be around the end of the day to collect it, so was relying on his colleagues to do so on his behalf. Michael would meet up with them after work in the pub.

When Michael came into the pub that night, the dealers were all smiling at him as they sipped the froth off their beers. 'Thank you for buying us all drinks,' they taunted. Michael's face reddened. So that was where his £40 had gone. Laughter rippled through the circle of dealers like a tonic, and one thrust at him a handful of coins — his change. Clenching his teeth, he turned and walked out of the pub in a rage, then flung his change across the road. The coins cracked into the windscreen of a slow moving car.

Michael did not come into work for the next two days. He had become the laughing stock of the dealing room, and dealers talked incessantly about the incident.

When he returned he gradually learned to churn less obviously and the dealers turned their attentions to another offender.

One morning, the young dealer now under their scrutiny told the switchboard girl to divert to him all calls for a dealer that had just been sacked. When one such client was put through to him, he enquired what stocks he was already holding. The client quoted several Alpha stocks.

'These are a lot of rubbish,' said the dealer. 'Come out of them and into BOM Holdings, Swanyard Studios, and Barbican.'

Against his better judgement, the client assented, only later to discover that one of the Alpha stocks was being bid for so the price had afterwards shot up.

This dealer further advised another new client to come out of the Norton Group to release funds. The client agreed, subject to a minimum price of eighteen pence. The dealer put through the sale at sixteen pence.

The client complained, and so the price was altered to eighteen pence. Tudorbury Securities bore the loss.

Both these clients sent in letters complaining that he had churned them. Due to the new moral tone now prevailing on the dealing floor, dealers made this trainee for a brief period wish he had never been born.

A dealer proffered a word of unofficial advice: 'If you're going to churn, put the ball in the client's court. Make him think that he's made the decision to come out of Alpha stocks himself. Ask him: "Are there any stocks you're not happy with?" It usually works . . . '

On one occasion, a manager at Tudorbury Securities bade dealers not to say 'Trust me' to clients. That very day, he himself did £50,000 worth of business, earning £1,000 commission plus cash bonuses for himself. He, of course, was heard saying 'Trust me' on the telephone.

The dealers who had overheard this nudged each other and sniggered. An ex-Sheridan veteran sang out: 'Compliance goes out of the window.'

The manager glared: 'When you do £50,000 worth of business a day, you make your own rules.'

For a moment he had thrown discretion to the winds, and had spoken from the heart.

The dealers knew they now had to occasionally prove their word was worth something if they were to survive, and obtain their much coveted licences to deal.

One morning a Tudorbury manager rushed onto the dealing floor.

He urged that all dealers should take clients out of a stock called Pavion International: 'The share price has climbed only because there was a bid for the company. The deal is now off. The stock is about to crash. There's nothing in Pavion, take my word for it. Put the clients' money into another stock. York Trust, anything . . . '

His whole manner was both imperious and desperate, like that of a general urging on his men in battle. Some of the more experienced dealers felt uncomfortable. Why was he so anxious to avoid showing the clients a loss?

One dealer quickly rang her broker at Collins Coombs. 'Find out what's happening with Pavion,' she said.

He rang her back quickly. Something was up, he confirmed. Pavion's future was looking rosy. There was no bid for the company, but there had been a buyer in a great number of call options on the stock. That was why the price had started moving.

At this point, mid-morning, the share price of Pavion was 9-10. Wonder of wonders, it was back to the level at which dealers had originally placed it. Clients were breaking even!

Any clients who found out the latest prices were delighted. And now, dealers were being pressed to sell them out. They began to reason, 'This is the old .... hanky panky. These days, we can't afford to stand for it.'

Strangely, one young dealer was of a different opinion. Actually, he had no opinion at all. He wanted nothing more than an excuse to churn and make money.

He briskly set about the tedious task of speaking with his clients who had bought shares in Pavion. 'We're coming out of Pavion now,' he told them. 'You're only losing about a penny. Don't worry. The price is dropping now and frankly, I'm nervous about it. We're reinvesting the capital in York Trust. I'm not asking you to put in a penny of fresh capital. In fact we're sending you a small difference. Take your wife out to dinner on it. Then me out to lunch. Your shares in York Trust should skyrocket.'

A dealer later murmured in his ear, 'RAI Hamilton will be pleased with you.'

The manager kept returning to the dealing floor, to press dealers to get *all* clients out of *all* Pavion shares immediately.

They became infuriated now. 'I bet you Pavion's price will have shot up by the end of the day,' shouted one veteran. The dealing floor chortled uneasily, almost to a man.

By mid-afternoon Pavion's share price was still climbing. Pavion's price was now 10½-11½, up 1½p, or 15% on the day.

Dealers were delighted that that their own instincts about the stock had been vindicated. They felt noble because they were for once looking after their clients' interests. From that moment on they determined never again to be browbeaten into not doing their best for clients.

A manager, still advising clients to come out of their Pavion, sidled up to the young dealer aforementioned who started panting at his feet like a dog. 'I'll make you a deal,' he said quietly. 'Sell your clients out at 10½p net price . . . ' Almost before the words were out of his mouth, the zealot said, 'Consider it done.'

Shortly thereafter the price of Pavion climbed another penny on the day, and the shares closed at 11½-12½p.

What may be confusing to you, the reader, is why the company was so anxious to take clients out of the stock.

It was known that Tudorbury Securities took a Principal Interest in its stock recommendations, that is, picked up lines of stock for themselves.

The Pavion shares which clients were sold out of at 9p were worth an additional 2½p to the company at the end of the day.

All this may sound technical, but the bottom line was profit for the company and not for the clients. The dealers were fully aware of this, and their siding for once with the client was a sign of genuine change. For how long would it last?

Even at this stage, dealers in various firms felt no compunction about hard selling their clients, if they themselves and not their managers chose to do so. They were guided not by morals but by the wish for independence.

Clients and dealers alike remain locked in an eternal haggle that brings out their intrigue and avarice.

On one occasion, a police detective said to a sharedealer something to the effect: 'Why don't you try working for a living?'

The detective knew right, and the detective knew wrong. How can sharedealing be called working for a living? A few quick phone calls, raking in others' hard earned cash. And yet . . .

The dealer is playing at God, and is successful because so many need a God there, in the flesh, who can suggest to them a little something for nothing, the crock of gold at the end of the rainbow.

Some clients deliberately lose money in the market, so the pathology of gambling suggests, in order to punish themselves for real or imagined offences committed in obtaining it in the first place. Thus, they purge their guilty souls.

The sociologist might argue that all evaluation of worth is subjective, that the most speculative of investments have emotional value to the punters. There is obvious truth in this.

Many, victimised by their own prejudice, choose to invest in companies that sound exciting, regardless of how good an investment they are.

The pundits of salesmanship will point out that it is the person and not the goods which a client buys. The good dealer is a person of exceptional charisma, even if his stock may not turn out so well.

The good dealer bears about him an aura that seems to say 'Yes' to life. That is why punters will buy from him again and again, yet not seem to learn from their mistakes. They are prey not just to their own greed, but, more insidiously to a 'simpatico' personality.

The client and his dealer, like the proverbial donkey and his master, are two sides of the same coin.

Their relationship, like the sexual act, has its heights and its sickening frustrations, with long hours of oblivion in between.

Ex-dealers of defunct bucket shops such as Sheridan Securities are still being hunted by old clients.

They crave to be told that their crashed dreams have come true, that they have made their fortunes after all. They cling to the ecstasy of hopes that should have died.

One ex-Sheridan client asked a dealer as to the whereabouts of the ex-Sheridan salesman who had lost him thousands. The dealer pretended he had never heard of him. In fact the guilty party was at that moment pitching a client from the desk behind him.

The clients have no simple way of discovering whether individual dealers have been judged suitable by an SRO. Those who are considered unsuitable can continue working while tackling the lengthy procedure of appeal. The new legislation protects them.

The City proper likes to be seen to detach itself from smooth operators, but is inextricably linked in the same racket. Licensed dealers often pick up stock in bulk from stockbrokers who need to offload it.

The punter who spends £3,000 a time with a licensed dealer is made to think he is investing. Likewise, the punter who spends £3,000 a time with a stockbroker. But both must wait longer for their profits than the professionals who buy in bulk shares in the same company for the purpose of manipulating the market.

Any Insider Trading that may take place in licensed dealers is far more widespread in the City proper. Likewise, the City's so-called respectable money-men promulgate rumours to cause desired fluctuation in share prices. Phantoms still make hundreds of anonymous calls to announce that shares will go up or down, while they take, in anticipation, huge stockholdings themselves.

The reputable firms do, in a less obvious way, only what the bucket shops do.

The dealers pushing stocks at inflated prices from the continental bucket shops, for instance, are involved in a cruder version of what is going on in the City. They are smooth operators, but no more so than the real City types. The goal of profit is universal, the means not inquired into too deeply anywhere.

Only the buccaneers are more open about what they are doing. They make lots of money, and retire early in disgrace. Their counterparts in the City proper make lots of money, and retire early in honour.

Although the price manipulation of speculative stocks in the bucket shops is nauseating, there are similar practices involving larger sums of money, in the real Square Mile.

It also had to be said that the cleverest frauds of all are often perpetrated in the City proper. The fringe City scoops up mere crumbs from the rich man's table.

The popular image of the City as a virtuous and gentlemanly place where young men work hard to make Britain prosperous is a fallacy. The stock market, despite its plausible reassurances to the small investor, is a casino, or as financial analyst Bob Beckman says 'The biggest floating crap game in the world.'

The City broker is no more honest than the sharp practitioner, although he will seem so as he is better protected by tradition. As the story goes, Lucky Luciano, when paying a visit late in life to the New York Stock Exchange said, 'Gee all these years, I've been in the wrong profession.'

Licensed dealers who hide behind the veneer of City respectability, are doing the same as their counterparts in the Square Mile. When will the public stop dreaming that the friendly voice on the end of the telephone really wants to make them money?

When will they realise that the portly and charming man they meet in a posh City restaurant is not always the pillar of respectability that he appears, that there is no such thing as a truly impartial adviser?

The public is getting there, but it is taking its time.

Dealers who leave bucket shops for firms in the Square Mile proper will be in a sense coming into their own. This is the second phase of their professional lives, and the more discreet one.

Like other City people, they will keep up the image of propriety and respectability. It is not in their interest to let on how simple their work is, how highly paid in proportion to the effort they actually put in.

All over the world there are sharp salesmen, street beggars and pickpockets. These have the flair to sell shares and futures, if they would only pack their bags, and shift over to the City of London.

There is nothing wrong with making a profit if you offer something for your money. But the salesman of shares and futures may be offering just tawdry dreams.

For you the reader, the author has this authoritative advice. Never buy dreams unless you have some understanding as to their likelihood of turning into reality. Never take a friendly stranger's word for it!

The sales techniques exposed in this book are going on every minute of the day, inside, as well as around the City of London, and in a sometimes less sophisticated way in commercial transactions throughout the world. People are parting with millions of pounds for concepts and dreams they do not understand. They are at the mercy of professionals who manipulate words to send hands towards cheque books. The world becomes not what people need but what these clever ones create, for their own gain.

As stockbroker and financial journalist Donald Cobbett advises after a lifetime of observing the City 'Keep the cheque book well to the back of the bureau.'

A sentiment with which your author wholeheartedly agrees.

Chapter Fourteen

DUST TO DUST

The Harvard Complaints Committee had been battling for three years, against the odds. What testimony was there for its allegations of wrongdoing? Few dealers would come forward to help its inquiries, since by so doing, they might implicate themselves.

Meanwhile, Dale Campbell-Savours, Labour MP for Workington, was making great strides towards preventing Harvard Securities from obtaining authorisation by bringing up valid points in the House of Commons.

Francis Maude, Undersecretary for Trade and Consumer Affairs, interrupted his holiday (September 1988) to hear two Harvard dealers speak about their firm in the escort of Dale Campbell-Savours.

If the Government did not act, it might be seen to be upstaged by a *Labour* MP. This could be politically disastrous.

The trickle of disillusioned Harvard investors writing to Mr Campbell-Savours at the House of Commons was now becoming a flood.

At 5.00 p.m. on 29th September 1988, Harvard Securities ceased trading. Dealers were given a send-off party, and offered excellent references. In its last appearance on stage, Harvard Securities was showing itself in the colours of greatness.

120 Harvard staff were made redundant. The news almost immediately filtered on the Tudorbury Securities dealing floor late on that historic Thursday before the close of business. 'It's a wind-up' dealers chanted. But no, their dealing manager insisted. Harvard was no longer trading and that was that.

Unease rippled through the ranks of securities dealers everywhere, tempered with a weird rejoicing. The old Harvard conundrum had never been so apparent. Ex-Harvard dealers have craved for their old firm to close down, ostensibly out of moral indignation, but secretly from jealousy. Almost all would have given much to be back on the phones in the UK's most incredible dealing floor, but were barred from it. No Harvard dealer who had resigned was ever allowed to return there. This is why some have connived in the destruction of the most extraordinary securities dealing house in the world. Perhaps they are satisfied now.

All Thursday night and the Friday following, telephone lines were buzzing as City professionals everywhere marvelled at Harvard's collapse. Tom Wilmot had pulled a last rabbit out of the hat, and it didn't seem quite real.

On the evening of Friday 30th September 1988, dealers from various securities houses gathered for a party whose furtive purpose was to celebrate Harvard's collapse. And yet, uncannily, the laughter turned to mourning.

On Saturday, 1st October, the national press had a field-day. Harvard's OTC price-listing bravely made its usual appearance in the *Sunday Telegraph*. The quoted wealth-warning, so often disregarded, proved now the OTC's death-rattle.

Although Tudorbury Securities announced internally that it did not want ex-Harvard dealers, the City was opening its arms to them.

Maybe some responded to this advertisement Gow Securities placed in London's Evening *Standard* on 3rd October1988:

'City based firm requires motivated professionals to join expanding company. Very attractive commission package and full support provided.'

In the same paper appeared an alternative opportunity:

'SUCCESSFUL EX-HARVARD EMPLOYEE seeks like-minded people to join him in a thriving and expanding area of the Financial Services Industry.'

A few faithfuls were meanwhile manning Harvard's telephones. Clients would later be able to deal in Harvard's OTC shares on a matched bargain basis.

'I'm putting all my regular portfolio clients into this one, and I would suggest you come in too,' was a classic line a Harvard manager had taught trainees some time back, and he had added: 'Do as I tell you, and you'll make money.'

So many lavish predictions of Harvard dealers had turned to dust. It was gold dust to them, but chokingly solid dust in many ex-Harvard clients' memories, now and for eternity . . .

Dale Campbell-Savours has demanded of the regulatory authorities that Harvard's application still be processed, 'So that those persons who are connected with the company today are identified with any final decision made by the SIB.'

Harvard plans to stick around, in the form of an industrial holding company. And maybe, as Tom Wilmot has put it, 'Harvard will rise again.'

Compulsively, the author still crosses Blackfriars Bridge, and lingers outside the legendary Harvard House.

The building looks smarter now than it had in his time, but remains instantly recognisable. There is the huge flat roof, circled with railings: 'Airship Industries' take-off ground,' the dealers would pretend it was.

Outside 95 Southwark Street it is quiet, so quiet. Ordinary young men walk by without a glance. The author is reminded of the apocryphal dealing room wisecrack: 'I was sheltering in Harvard House from the rain, and they forced me to come in and sell shares over the telephone.'

Harvard is not for going back to, but there is nowhere else to go. Other securities dealing firms have waxed and waned, mere pale imitations of the real thing. There is and only ever was one Harvard.

To Harvard and all the City, the author bids a fond farewell, and it is not without some sadness, for he knows that after having here told it like it is, he may be barred from ever working in the City again.

He knows that the regulatory authorities, who have made life extremely difficult for him ever since he spoke out in the *News of the World* will continue to protect their kind, in or out of Stock Exchange member firms.

We are at the end of an era but the story does not end here. It is February 1989 now, and every so often a national newspaper journalist rings up the author and asks: 'What's John Solleigh doing? Where are the old Sheridan dealers? What's happening these days at Tudorbury? What are the old Harvard boys doing?'

The author has no specific answers, but like the journalists, like the dealers, like the investing public, he knows that somewhere, somehow, the cycle of events portrayed will repeat itself.

GLOSSARY

Account Period A two, occasionally three week trading period on the Stock Exchange calendar.

AE Account Executive (futures).

Account Trading Also known as buying on the account. This consists of buying and selling the same shares, often in huge quantities, within the Stock Exchange account period, ie usually two weeks. A perk is that stamp duty is waived. Account Trading is nonetheless a gamble that most clients lose on, although dealers have encouraged this practice for commission purposes.

Alpha, Beta, Gamma, Delta Grading according to size and capitalisation of stocks traded on the London Stock Exchange. Alpha is the largest category, and Delta is the smallest.

Business Expansion Scheme (BES) A Government sponsored scheme for claiming tax relief by investing in specified high risk companies. Only really of interest to the high tax ratepayer, who is also a bit of a gambler.

Bid Only The dealer will buy the shares in question from a client, but will not sell them to him.

"Big Bang" A revolution in the City of London (October 1986). Electronic networks replaced trading on the Stock Exchange floor. Stockbrokers' minimum commissions were abolished, as was the distinction between jobbers and brokers. The subsequent, more competitive market place has seemed increasingly biased towards institutions, at the expense of the private client.

Blue Button The long-suffering junior employee on the floor of the Stock Exchange, who was destined to rise above his humble station. Some licensed dealers have made feeble attempts to include the Blue Buttons, but the hierarchical implications normally preclude this.

"Boiler Room Operation" An outfit whose dealers singlemindedly hard sell securities. They will usually be paid extortionate commissions, and their clients will usually lose much, if not all of monies invested.

Bucket Shop A firm that sells little known or unquoted securities in companies that may or may not exist. The bucket shop is finding survival hard now in the United Kingdom but still flourishes on the Continent. Some financial journalists and stockbrokers categorise all licensed dealers as bucket shops.

Chartists Self-styled analysts who claim they can predict movements of share prices by reference to graphs plotting past market trends. The Chartists have some credibility, although the market place is not always governed by logic.

Chinese Walls An artificial barrier between two departments within a firm, to prevent leading of information in situations of conflicting interests. 'Chinese Walls' have been erected in many firms, following Big Bang. In some cases, they have proved ineffectual, or have been used as an excuse for sharp practice.

Churning Buying and selling of stock, purely to generate commission for the dealer. Churning is officially forbidden, but in some firms has been tacitly encouraged.

The City (of London) The square mile in London that is one of the financial centres of the world. Licensed dealers are psychologically, often physically excluded. Many delude themselves otherwise.

To Close a Sale To obtain a definite buy order.

Cold-Calling Selling or trying to sell investments on the phone to people who are not officially clients. This can be a grey area. For example, do client referrals slip through the net?

Convertible Preference Shares Shares offering priority claims should the company in question collapse. These are convertible into ordinary shares at a definite later date, at a price usually at a discount to the current market price.

Corporate Finance The department within a licensed dealer that arranges flotations (q.v.) of companies.

Debentures Financial instruments similar to shares, only secured and with a fixed annual yield.

Delta See Alpha.

Dividend A company's small payout to its ordinary shareholders, usually made twice a year. Most investors with licensed dealers are more interested in short-term capital growth than in shares yielding a dividend.

Equities A technical term for shares.

Extel Cards Published information sheets on Public companies. The presentation is uninspiring. Many dealers understand the accounting information contained therein no better than their clients, although will naturally not let on.

Financial Intermediaries, Managers & Brokers Regulatory Association (FIMBRA) The much criticised, self-regulatory organisation (SRO) for most licensed dealers.

The Financial Services Act (1986) The heavily criticised new legislation, that was phased in during 1988. Any who survive are now subject to stringent new regulations of business conduct, in particular, to know the client, and not to cold-call.

Flotation A company's entry onto a recognised market, so that its shares can be bought and sold.

Futures Financial instruments for speculating on 'future' prices of commodities such as wheat, cocoa, cattle, and metals such as gold, copper etc.

Government Privatisation Issues When the Government issues shares in a Government owned company, usually but not always for the first time (i.e. new issues). Investors frequently gain an instant profit as in British Telecom, British Gas, British Airways, TSB. The issue can, however, flop as did British Petroleum.

The Index (FT-30, FT-100) The FT (Financial Times) 100 (or "Footsie") index or otherwise FT 30 index. These indices rise or fall according to the performance of selected large stocks listed on the London Stock Exchange.

Insider Dealing Trading stocks and shares with the unfair advantage of inside information. This is illegal, and penalties are getting increasingly severe. Nonetheless, insider trading still flourishes.

Leads Names, addresses, and most importantly phone numbers of potential clients. These are often stored on index cards.

Registered Representatives' and Traders' Examination An examination whose questions are compiled by Stock Exchange officials, that is becoming obligatory for licensed dealers and stockbrokers alike. The syllabus is highly technical. Due to the high 75% pass mark, and the difficulties involved in cheating, many intelligent dealers are failing the exam. This doesn't remotely affect their level of business, but may eventually bar them from trading.

Liquid When cash is available. A liquid portfolio (q.v.) is one consisting of shares that may be sold at a reasonable price, and without undue difficulty.

Listed Fully quoted on the Stock Exchange. This is to be distinguished from the USM (q.v.) or Third Market (q.v.).

Loader An experienced dealer in Continental bucket shops who strips punters of all the money he can, after another has traded them once.

Market-Maker A company or individual that makes a market in shares i.e. sets buying and selling prices. Pre-Big Bang, this was the jobbers' task.

NASDAQ National Association of Securities Dealers Automated Quotation. A highly efficient electronic system for trading shares in the United States.

Offer Only The dealer will sell the shares in question to a client, but will not buy them from him.

Options Instruments offering the right and not an obligation to buy or sell stock at specified prices within a specified period. Appealing for gamblers who have the means and inclination to keep an eagle eye on market fluctuations.

Over-the-Counter (OTC) A market for trading shares in young companies outside the London Stock Exchange. This is a high risk market, suitable only for experienced investors, although the inexperienced are all too often lured into its treacherous waters.

P/E Ratio Price Earnings Ratio. This is the relationship between share price and earnings per share. Broadly speaking, the higher the figure is, the more rapid growth do investors expect of the company concerned.

Penny Shares Shares priced under 60p. A large amount of buying or selling can make the price fluctuate violently. Spreads (q.v.) tend to be dangerously wide (around 25%). Many clients of licensed dealers are hooked on this type of speculation.

PEP — Personal Equity Plan PEP offers the public tax relief through share investment, and was introduced by the Thatcher Government in 1986, to encourage wider share ownership. PEP has largely flopped, probably because it has too little to offer the basic rate tax payer, particularly in the short-term.

Pink Sheets An American quotation service for small highly speculative companies whose shares may be traded very infrequently.

Pitch A photocopied spiel about a company whose shares are for sale. The dealer regurgitates the substance of this to his clients, often word for word prior to asking for his order.

Portfolio The mix of shares a client has. He who has invested with a licensed dealer may have far too much OTC stock (q.v.) which might be hard to sell, and slow to increase in value. This is called an unbalanced portfolio.

Punter A gambler masquerading as an investor. The inside word for client.

Ramping When a dealer/stockbroker or company sells a particular stock to clients in order to artificially raise the share price usually for a brief period.

Rights Issue An issue of new shares to shareholders in proportion to their existing holdings.

SAE Senior Account Executive (futures).

SEAQ Stock Exchange Automated Quotations. Electronic quotation system implemented with Big Bang (October 1986). Screens show real time and up to date prices of stocks. There are alternatives, such as Reuters, Prestel or Quotron (United States).

Settlement Day When clients and firms alike settle outstanding monies for the preceding account period (q.v.). Settlement Day is usually on a Monday, ten days following the last Friday of the account.

Share Certificates Buyers of shares should normally receive certificates a few weeks after the purchase, as evidence of ownership, unless they are held under a nominee name. Long delays are frequent with licensed dealers, and this has been a major cause of complaint.

Shell Situation A clapped out company that has known better times, now in action as a vehicle for taking over other companies.

Spread The difference between the buying and selling price of a particular stock. Licensed dealers often set an outrageously wide spread, to increase their own profits.

Stag To buy and sell a subscribed share, usually a new issue, within the first week of trading, with the aim of generating instant profit.

Take over When one company buys another. Shareholders become involved, and the target company's share price often shoots up.

Third Market An embryo market for up and coming small companies, which was introduced by the London Stock Exchange, implemented in January 1987 as a respectable alternative to the OTC market.

Tipsheets Often expensive, heavily advertised newsletters, sent out to private subscribers, recommending investment in selected, often little known companies. Tipsheets are sometimes written in a sensational style, and their quality varies widely, as indeed does their circulation. The better ones, such as *Fleet Street Letter* and *Stock Market Confidential,* do have power to move markets.

USM — Unlisted Securities Market A secondary market for companies that have not attained a full listing. The USM has grown in power and influence over the last six years.

Warrants An offer by a particular company to an existing shareholder providing the right to buy its ordinary shares at a specified time and price.

BIBLIOGRAPHY

Beckman, Robert, *Into The Upwave*. Milestone Publications 1988.
Blundell, Nigel, *The World's Greatest Crooks & Conmen and Other Mischievous Malefactors*. Octopus Books, 1984.
Bosworth Davies, Rowan, *Too Good to Be True — How to Survive in The Casino Economy*. Bodley Head, 1987.
Cobbett, Donald, *Before the Big Bang*. Milestone Publications, 1986.
Dickens, Charles, *Martin Chuzzlewit*.
Freudenberg, Herbert J, *Burn Out. The High Cost of High Achievement*. Arrow Books, 1985.
Lamb, Charles, *The Essays of Elia — The South Sea House*.
Levene, Tony, *The Shares Game*. Pan, 1987.
Levi, Dr Michael, *The Phantom Capitalists*.
McCormack, Mark, *What They Don't Teach you at Harvard Business School*. Collins, 1984.
Robinson, Jeffrey, *Minus Millionaires. Or, How to Blow a Fortune*. Unwin Hyman, 1987.
Walters, Michael, *How to Make a Killing in the Share Jungle*. Sidgwick & Jackson, 1986.
Waugh, Evelyn, *Scoop*.
Wilmot, Tom, *Inside the Over The Counter Market*. Woodhead Faulkner Ltd, 1985.

OTHER PUBLICATIONS

Chapter 1
Market Maker February 1984.
The Observer 14 December 1986.
The Sunday Times 24 April 1987.
The Daily Telegraph 12 August 1987.
The Independent 8 January 1988.

Chapter 3
The Daily Telegraph 1 September 1985.
The New Statesman 19 February 1988.
Private Eye (Article: "Men of Letters") 29 April 1988.

Chapter 4
The Daily Mail various issues.
The Times 9 February 1985.
The Sunday Times 31 August 1986.
The Sunday Times 29 June 1987.
Canadian Business September 1986.
Family Wealth (Article: "You're OK with us, we're a British Company", Tony Hetherington) June 1988.

Chapter 5
The London Evening Standard 2 September 1987.
Investors Chronicle — The Good Broker Guide : London 19 June 1987.
The International Herald Tribune (Article: "Plunging into Pink Sheets", Cynthia Catterson) 13 June 1988.
Time Out 26 August 1987.

Chapter 6
The Daily Telegraph 24 May 1979.
The Sunday Times 4 October 1981.
The Daily Mail 27 March 1986.
The Daily Mail 18 February 1987.
The London Evening Standard 31 January 1987.
The London Evening Standard 9 May 1987.
BUSINESS (Article by Arthur Johnson) September 1987.
Financial Services — A Guide to the New Regulatory System, SIB Ltd, 1987.
Harvard Securities Training Manual (1986-1987).

Chapter 8
Market Watch (Bailey McMahon Newsletter).

Chapter 9
The Investors Chronicle 5 February 1988.

Chapter 10
The Financial Times (Article: "Rules Come to the Frontier", Heather Farnbrough) 23 April 1988.
The Daily Mail 31 May 1988.
The Independent 4 June 1988.
The Daily Telegraph 25 May 1988.
The Daily Telegraph 24 June 1988.

Chapter 11
The Daily Mail 20 June 1988.

Chapter 12
The Observer 26 June 1988.